DEMOCRACY IN A
GLOBAL WORLD

Philosophy and the Global Context

Series Editor: Michael Krausz, Bryn Mawr College

This series addresses a range of emerging global concerns. It situates philosophical efforts in their global and cultural contexts, and it offers works from thinkers whose cultures are challenged by globalizing movements. Comparative and intercultural studies address such social and political issues as the environment, poverty, consumerism, civil society, tolerance, colonialism, global ethics, and community in cyberspace. They also address related methodological issues of translation and cross-cultural understanding.

Intellectual Property: Moral, Legal, and International Dilemmas (1997) by Adam D. Moore
Ethics of Consumption: The Good Life, Justice, and Global Stewardship (1998) edited by David A. Crocker and Toby Linden
Alternative Visions: Paths in the Global Village (1998) by Fred Dallmayr
Philosophical Reflections on the Changes in Eastern Europe (1998) by William L. McBride
Intercultural Philosophy (2000) by Ram Adhar Mall
Philosophical Questions: East and West (2000) edited by Bina Gupta and J. N. Mohanty
Formal Transgression: John Stuart Mill's Philosophy of International Affairs (2000) by Eddy M. Souffrant
Limits of Rightness (2000) by Michael Krausz
The Human World in the Physical Universe: Consciousness, Free Will, and Evolution (2001) by Nicholas Maxwell
Tolerance: Between Forbearance and Acceptance (2001) by Hans Oberdiek
Persons and Valuable Worlds: A Global Philosophy (2002) by Eliot Deutsch
Yesterday's Self: Nostalgia and the Immigrant Identity (2002) by Andreea Deciu Ritivoi
Ethical Questions: East and West (2002) edited by Bina Gupta
Universal Human Rights: Moral Order in a Divided World (2005) edited by David A. Reidy and Mortimer N. S. Sellers
The Resurgence of Anti-Semitism: Jews, Israel, and Liberal Opinion (2006) by Bernard Harrison

DEMOCRACY IN A GLOBAL WORLD

Human Rights and Political Participation in the 21st Century

Deen K. Chatterjee

ROWMAN & LITTLEFIELD PUBLISHERS, INC.

Lanham • Boulder • New York • Toronto • Plymouth, UK

ROWMAN & LITTLEFIELD PUBLISHERS, INC.

Published in the United States of America
by Rowman & Littlefield Publishers, Inc.
A wholly owned subsidiary of The Rowman & Littlefield Publishing Group, Inc.
4501 Forbes Boulevard, Suite 200, Lanham, Maryland 20706
www.rowmanlittlefield.com

Estover Road
Plymouth PL6 7PY
United Kingdom

British Library Cataloguing in Publication Information Available

Library of Congress Cataloging-in-Publication Data

Democracy in a global world : human rights and political participation in the 21st
century / [edited by] Deen K. Chatterjee.
    p. cm. — (Philosophy and the global context)
    Includes index.
    ISBN-13: 978-0-7425-1451-5 (cloth : alk. paper)
    ISBN-10: 0-7425-1451-X (cloth : alk. paper)
    ISBN-13: 978-0-7425-1452-2 (pbk. : alk. paper)
    ISBN-10: 0-7425-1452-8 (pbk. : alk. paper)
    1. Human rights. 2. Democracy. 3. Political participation. I. Chatterjee, Deen K.
JC571.D356 2007
    323—dc22   2007003819

⊗™ The paper used in this publication meets the minimum requirements of American
National Standard for Information Sciences—Permanence of Paper for Printed Library
Materials, ANSI/NISO Z39.48-1992.

Latika Chattopadhyaya
author and philosopher
embodiment of reason, love, and patience
my mother

Contents

Part Four: Global Public and the New World Order

Introduction

Deen K. Chatterjee

THIS BOOK EXAMINES THE EFFECTS OF GLOBALIZATION on democratic principles and practices from a variety of philosophical points of view. As globalization has affected all aspects of modern living, including all social and political norms, institutions, and arrangements, its impact on democracy has been especially pronounced. Along with the worldwide trend toward democratization in the past few decades, today's rapid globalization has generated new challenges for democracies everywhere. The democratic recognition of a broader range of human needs has assumed a global dimension, setting a gradual trend for international recognition of justice and human rights. The surge of pluralistically oriented social and political movements within both democratic and nondemocratic countries is another result of globalization. Though these two global and domestic trends manifest differently, they share the common democratic ideals of autonomy, equality, and political participation, as well as the spur of globalization. Now that the democratic ideals have been seeded widely and the world is coming closer together as a consequence of globalization, scholars debate the implications of globalization for democracy.[1]

Modern democratic ideals, among all political ideologies, are widely regarded as the most viable norms for legitimizing political institutions. This is because, among other things, contemporary formulations of democratic theory offer a mechanism for transparency, public discourse, and participation in the political process that strives to ensure truth and accountability in the public arena and safeguard human rights.[2] Initially, the gradual emergence of the global human rights culture in the past fifty years led to a certain level of international recognition for justice when norms of just-war are violated or when there is an egregious violation of negative human rights.[3] But the configuration of democratic norms and globalizing trends has eventually yielded another set of rights—the rights of subsistence and welfare. These "second-generation" rights are now being recognized as important components of international justice, though their violation does not evoke the sort of immediate and urgent response by the international community as the ones with regard to crimes of war and crimes against humanity. However, there are signs that this may be changing. Global leaders are becoming increasingly vocal in calling for and promoting international collaboration so that measures to combat poverty-related deprivations would be no less urgent than the global responses to violations of negative rights.[4]

The global recognition of endemic poverty and systemic inequity as serious human rights concerns has put pressure on individual countries for internal democratic reforms and made vivid the need for more just and effective international institutional directives. The demands of the developing countries in various world summits for democratic reform of the international global order are getting progressively vocal.[5] Likewise, global socioeconomic issues are increasingly dominating the agenda of the rich countries in their G-8 meetings. The pervasive state-failure to respond to its citizens' broader human needs is now being recognized as linked to the inequity in the global order itself. The unregulated global market is cited as a prime reason for this.[6]

The emergence of a highly aggressive global market and the steady rise of powerful nongovernmental forces seemingly writing their own rules have posed a serious challenge to the safeguarding of the public interest, even while globalization has contributed to the international recognition of a broader range of human rights and a redefinition of the sphere of the public. A broader accommodation of human needs is becoming increasingly difficult even within the rich democracies, given the nature of the global market, but it is especially problematic with regard to the concerns of the developing societies. The global culture of excessive consumerism is responsible for the depletion of resources and environmental problems that are exacerbated in the poor countries, along with being a threat to their cultural identity and national sovereignty.[7] The gap between the rich and the poor is steadily widening both within and among the countries, making the prospect of democratic accommodation on a global basis increasingly challenging.

Accordingly, the so-called global democracy deficit is not only about individual countries failing to meet the requirements of democracy, but about the lack of an equitable and participatory institutional mechanism in the global order that would effectively respond to the market's failure to check the excesses of the powerful. Democracy's global reach cannot be made viable unless democracy is able to put a human face to the global market and provide effective strategies for just global development, poverty reduction, and human flourishing. Economic globalization without strict guidelines and strong enforcement mechanisms for justice and equity is bound to be detrimental to the poor.[8] If an unregulated global market is subverting some of the most important democratic norms, then one may wonder whether free market and democracy always go together or whether they are clashing ideals in a globalized world.[9]

Globalization's impact in the redefinition and internationalization of the public sphere has been evident on several other fronts besides the market, although many of them could be linked to it. In today's interconnected world in which effects of technology, national policies, global institutions, and even individual actions often have global outreach, the result is a gradual deaggregation of sovereign jurisdiction whereby a diverse constellation of groups is formed not on the basis of peoples or national boundaries, but on specific issues or decisions at stake, resulting in overlapping spheres of participation.[10] This may well be the beginning of a new era of sovereignty, removed from its exclusive domain of national jurisdiction to an open-ended global arena. Thus, although the globalization process has heightened tension and accentuated the gap between rich and poor, thereby seemingly making the prospect for a global public all the more difficult, it also may offer the opportunity for the world to come closer together through numerous channels of communication and cross-border constellations of participation. If democracy is reinforced by civic and public dialogue either directly or through public representatives, and if the viability of human rights depends to a large extent on whether they can withstand unobstructed public scrutiny, then the worldwide reach of public deliberation in the era of globalization should be a mitigating force toward the global democracy deficit and random suppression of human rights.[11] Also, if the claim is in fact overblown that there are incommensurable differences across cultures on such issues as human rights, then any undue restriction of rights in the name of local culture would be difficult to sustain in a globally vigilant and interconnected world.[12] Thus, the dynamic of global interdependence has opened up fresh horizons for democracy and human rights. On the other hand, globalization has brought forth new challenges to democratic norms and political participation. For instance, the global trend of overlapping spheres of participation among dispersed constellations would require a reevaluation of the normative status of national boundaries, with implications for the standard idea of democracy based on state sovereignty.

The two chapters in Part I discuss various normative and institutional links between globalization and democratization, focusing on a critical assessment of globalization's potential for global public good and democracy's role in it. Keeping in view the role of rights at the normative foundations of justice and democracy, the chapters explore some of the central problems and challenges of human rights and justice as democracy responds to globalization. In chapter 1, David Crocker claims that globalization can be ethically justified if it promotes human development through democratic arrangements in their respective variations and applications locally, nationally, and globally. For Crocker, an ethical understanding of human development should not be primarily in terms of economic growth but judged as human well-being that requires among its conditions the overcoming of social, political, and economic deprivation—a theme echoed in some subsequent chapters in this book and forcefully articulated by Martha Nussbaum in chapter 4.[13] Accordingly, development ethics—the "boundary-crossing ethical inquiry" of development policies and practices of domestic and international institutional arrangements related to human well-being—can be an effective guide to ethically assessing both globalization and democratization. Development ethics should promote strategies for human progress that are based on certain universal norms and principles applicable to all societies, while at the same time being context sensitive beyond a certain "threshold" level for accommodating societal and cultural differences. This approach toward contextualization without being relativistic is again a theme taken up in the subsequent chapters by authors exploring the cross-cultural viability and applicability of human rights and other democratic norms.

Crocker points out that the theory and practice of deliberative democracy go well with the approaches of development ethics. Democratic consensus through public deliberation provides a good mix of agency and reciprocity that successfully embodies the ideals of autonomy and agency-centered development conducive to human well-being. These are also the ideals that Crocker believes should be taken as criteria for the moral appraisal of globalization. Toward that end, Crocker finds it helpful to use the ideas of two noted economists, Amartya Sen and Joseph Stiglitz, in exploring how globalization can be an agent of justice. The respective paradigms for development put forth by these two theorists—for Sen, the agent-oriented "capability" perspective, and for Stiglitz, "development as transformation"—show how democracy can play a pivotal role in fostering just development via the myriad forces of globalization at the national level and through the reforming of global institutions. As Crocker explicates these ideas, he discusses the most relevant theories and forms of globalization and elucidates three leading theories of democratizing the globalization process to assess what kind of globalization would be most conducive to human well-being and how best to achieve it. Most of these ideas are taken up in subsequent chapters for thematic elaboration.

The idea of democracy itself is a broad and contested notion in a divided world, raising questions as to which of its various forms and understandings may be relevant in what cultural and sociopolitical contexts. If the idea of democracy, broadly speaking, is autonomous self-government, not government dictated or imposed by outside forces, then democratic arrangements can vary depending on how they are contextualized in diverse cultural and political settings. In chapter 2, Carol Gould echoes this idea by asserting that democracy should be understood and endorsed at various levels of generality and specificity. Although autonomy and self-determination have the best potential in local communities, local governance often may not exemplify democratic decision making. Accordingly, along with attempts to empower communities with participatory governance, Gould suggests new ways of conceiving communities that, in today's new forms of global interconnectedness, are rapidly turning into cross-border localities. The significance of democratic autonomy in such communities has yet to emerge clearly, but the concept of self-determination that may mean freedom from outside imposition can perhaps be expressed in the old idea of solidarity now understood in the nuanced modalities of cross-border interactions among members.

Like the concept of democracy, Gould asserts that the idea of human rights too should be context sensitive so that it can be applicable in any cross-cultural and transnational milieu, but for Gould there should be more flexibility of culture-specific applicability of democratic norms than of human rights. With human rights, the options should be more limited because of the need for appropriate global enforcement of rights. But in either case, to avoid the possibility of relativistic vacuity, Gould suggests a democratic framework based on promoting equal rights of meeting certain basic needs that would make possible individual and collective self-transformative activities leading to human flourishing. This is what Gould calls "concrete universality" with regard to the concepts of democracy and human rights that provides for certain cross-cultural, universal norms, but is also grounded in the individual and collective activities that make possible the actualization of the human capacity for change and self-change. According to Gould, this calls for a democratic arrangement that recognizes equality of certain basic rights, which would ensure political noninterference as well as meet certain basic social and economic needs. In chapter 4, Martha Nussbaum provides a powerful statement of a similar idea in her capabilities approach. For Gould, democratic participation in the tradition of deliberative democracy that provides empathy and solidarity is a viable arrangement for her ideas, but she acknowledges that given the global nature of multilateral institutions, it is not clear yet how such an arrangement of democratic input and accountability may work out in theory and in practice.

The gradual redefinition of national sovereignty due to the forces of an aggressive global economy, the changing global ecology, and the emergence of a human rights culture have increasingly called into question the moral relevance of national boundaries.[14] In addition, the global nature of today's politics, commerce, and institutions is all too evident, along with the many existing measures in the current international system that are designed to enforce order and human rights. Accordingly, if democratic theories should reflect this new international reality of shifting borders and boundaries, then they should pay serious attention to the cosmopolitan ideal of universal human rights. However, as the contested issues of identity and diversity have become the focus of heightened debate in the current context of emerging identity politics and evolving new democracies, theories of rights that provide for a cosmopolitan framework strive to make room for local variations consistent with alternative versions of democratic decision making. In view of the standard critique of abstract cosmopolitanism—that its message of universal egalitarianism is unrealistic and utopian in a fragmented world—this "situated" version of cosmopolitanism looks more credible. In fact, some rights-based cosmopolitan theorists have done promising work to find a middle ground between abstract universalism and cultural specificity to validate the contextuality of the egalitarian human rights ideal within a democratic setting. Appealing to realities of current global practice, they emphasize the actual vitality of cross-cultural discourse concerning human rights and the heterogeneity of religious and cultural communities that tend to be treated as uniformly committed to restrictive views.[15] This is an approach whereby abstract cosmopolitanism committed to universal egalitarianism becomes situated and negotiable by adopting some version of deliberative democracy.

Critiques of deliberative democracy contend that construing deliberation as an egalitarian forum for representation does not work because it is based on an idealized view of reality that fails to take note of the asymmetry of power and knowledge.[16] Regardless, a new genre of scholars addresses the issue of egalitarian representation in a pluralistic world through the lens of deliberative democracy. Some of them take liberalism to task by showing the limitations of what they call the *a priori* liberal approaches to the problem, manifested in a prepolitical commitment to certain nonnegotiable rights. They argue that the issue of democratic representation in a pluralistic world is essentially a political one requiring a strategic response, not a liberal normative resolution, because the conflict, regardless of its appearance, is not a clash of liberalism versus illiberalism. For them, an *a priori* normative framing at the foundational level tilts the discourse in favor of liberalism, resulting in the marginalization and alienation of minority groups (and individuals) that differ from the mainstream liberal ideology. So they offer a resolution to the liberal cosmopolitan dilemma of respecting individual rights and cultural pluralism by reframing the conflict through the lens of deliberative democracy.[17]

This debate relates to what has been dubbed "The Paradox of Democratic Legitimacy," involving a conflict between liberalism and democracy that cannot be resolved through mandates or directives from the top down, but can be assuaged through public deliberation and negotiations at the grassroots level.[18] The egalitarian commitment to justice and human rights and the democratic ideal of legitimacy through self-rule and autonomy are often manifested in the tension between individual rights and group rights. Although there is more room in negotiating the boundaries of democracy than in interpreting the limits of rights, both concerns are in a continual state of flux and readjustment due to the shifting nature of the forces of globalization. To work out the right balance in theory is not easy. For instance, Rawls's liberalism in his law of peoples is critiqued by cosmopolitans for being much too negotiable and not sufficiently substantive, whereas various democratic theorists critique Rawls for not working at the grassroots level due to his liberal precommitments.

The two chapters in Part II of this book emphasize the importance of universal human rights that is consistent with various forms of democratic decision making. As important as the values of international tolerance and autonomy of nation-states may be, they should not override the dictates of certain fundamental rights. To work out the nuanced balance between respect for cultural diversity and the autonomy of peoples on the one hand and the inviolability of certain core rights on the other is not easy—it requires a careful analysis of the rights, specific cultural practices, key constitutional provisions in various democracies, and the international treaties and obligations that bind nations together. Above all, it calls for certain conceptual tools that can reframe the debate to accommodate demands of justice and human rights with tolerance for cultural and national autonomy. In chapter 3, James Nickel and David Reidy defend what they call "moderate prescriptive relativism" to negotiate a middle path between mandates of rights and weight of culture and self-determination, whereas in chapter 4 Martha Nussbaum proposes the "capabilities approach" as a better starting point for understanding fundamental constitutional entitlements than rights-based approaches have proven to be. This she considers a promising approach for the task of exploring issues of social justice in a modern constitutional democracy as well as for respecting cultural pluralism. Implied in both chapters is the claim that endorsing cultural differences does not mean that cultural relativism is true.

Nickel and Reidy state that respect for national self-determination and tolerance for cultural diversity are compatible with respect for universal human rights. This is modest prescriptive relativism that favors international tolerance within limits to honor the right of self-determination of nations. Although sometimes a nation's policies may go against some rights of its citizens, if the violation does not involve the very core of fundamental human rights in a sustained and egregious way, then those policies may still be tolerated out of respect for autonomy, though they need not be approved and can be targeted for international criticism (which may eventually bring changes in those policies). Just as there are moral limits to tolerance toward cultural practices, likewise there are moral limits to tolerance toward autonomy of states depending on how they honor basic human rights of their own members. Rights and transgressions to be included in such a list that would trump the self-determination principle and thus pose a limit to international tolerance are not easy to spell out and may range from the more obvious ones (like genocide and crimes against humanity) to most of the "second-generation" economic and social rights. The extent to which any of these rights may be considered fundamental enough to pose a limit to tolerance should be judged against the backdrop of a variety of considerations that a state may be reasonably entitled to engage in, up to the limits of the most basic core in each item on the list. For instance, it is possible for a state to allow considerable freedom in the arena of social and political liberties without embracing standard democratic institutions, although such arrangements could make the exercise of political freedom easier by providing it an institutional platform. As noted earlier, democratic norms can have a wider range of interpretative latitude and country-specific implementation based on cultural, social, historical, and other considerations than what should be allowed for core human rights. Given the fact that failed or inept states have a systemic problem of effectively responding to the concerns of economic and social rights, and that often the pervasive state failure to cater to its citizens' basic needs is linked to the inequity in the international order itself, it is evident that the degree of international tolerance should be much greater in cases of violation or nonenforcement of welfare rights, even when endemic, than when there is violation of rights involving crimes against humanity.

Nussbaum claims that her capabilities approach offers great potential in deciding on the fundamental constitutional entitlements for citizens in a just democratic state—entitlements that can be put together in constitutional guarantees. It starts with the broad idea of human dignity—an idea that is foremost in many modern liberal democratic constitutions—and then goes on to include a list of ten capabilities as key ingredients of a rich plurality of life activities that constitutes a life with dignity. A just society must secure for all its citizens each of the ten capabilities up to a threshold level as constitutionally guaranteed basic entitlements. Both Nussbaum's list of fundamental entitlements and the list of basic rights that Nickel and Reidy enumerate cover the same domain of liberties that features prominently in the discourse on human rights in international politics. Also, both chapters view their respective lists as essential requirements of justice—not just aspirational but, for

Nickel and Reidy, "a morality of minimum requirements" and for Nussbaum "fully justiciable," in the sense that the denial of any one of the capabilities on the list is a matter of urgent concern and subject to appropriate judicial review.

For Nussbaum, seeing rights as capabilities has some helpful advantages in that it indicates that all human rights have broader economic and social dimensions because the capabilities approach emphasizes the actual ability to do or to be. The rights talk in itself does not clarify what is needed to make those rights a reality unless they are understood as securing effective measures to make people capable of appropriate functioning in those areas involving needed material and institutional support. It is thus not helpful to rely on the usual distinction between political and civil rights on the one hand ("first-generation rights") and economic and social rights on the other ("second-generation rights"). Because capabilities are integrated together for maximal human functioning, the capabilities perspective can reframe the debate in more substantive terms. For similar reasons, the capabilities approach does not accept the narrow notion of "negative rights" per se. Another advantage of the capabilities language over rights talk is that because functioning of the central human capabilities is culturally neutral and sufficiently universal, cross-cultural agreement on basic entitlements is easier to obtain than when the politically and culturally loaded concept of rights is used.

Just as Nickel and Reidy state that the broad language of human rights justifiably leaves room for latitude in local interpretation and implementation beyond a certain threshold level, Nussbaum likewise asserts that the threshold levels of the fundamental capabilities are set in different constitutional traditions according to their own history and current possibilities. Nussbaum cites examples from the U.S., Indian, and German constitutional traditions to illustrate her point. In general, she claims that the spirit of the Indian Constitution comes closer to her capabilities approach than the language of the U.S. Constitution, although the Indian Constitution does not specifically use the term "capabilities."

Economist Amartya Sen is the original architect of the capabilities approach that was later endorsed and expanded by Nussbaum. Sen states that since human rights are seen as rights to certain specific freedoms, and since capabilities are certain types of freedom, they both go well together, although operating in different domains.[19] Nussbaum too, while being in favor of some combination of the capabilities analysis with the rights language, acknowledges that the capabilities approach is one species of a human rights approach. Nonetheless, both she and Sen agree that to reframe some rights by incorporating the capabilities agenda gives the discourse the latitude it needs without making it too thin or abstract. Especially when people are situated differently and have different levels of needs and expectations, certain rights claims can be better understood as claims regarding an equal level of capabilities to function than simply, for example, the equal rights to resources, which may turn out to be unequal in real terms. For similar reasons, both Sen and Nussbaum claim that Rawlsian primary goods should be understood in terms of central human capabilities. Nussbaum goes on to argue that this view provides a better account of the need, dependency, and vulnerability of many real people than the account of needs conveyed by the notion of primary goods of imaginary contracting parties in the Rawlsian original position. Accordingly, although Nussbaum's position is close to Rawls's in many ways, she claims that her capabilities approach can overcome certain deficiencies in the Rawlsian notion of social justice. Sen, on the other hand, claims that because capabilities are certain indicators of individual functioning and opportunities only, they cannot adequately account for the fairness or equity of the process involved in justice. Accordingly, for Sen, the bigger arena of justice where priority of liberty and procedural equity matter is outside the reach of the capabilities approach.[20]

Nussbaum is more optimistic about the justice implications of her capabilities approach, and this is where she challenges Sen over the issue of endorsing a list of basic capabilities as essential requirements of social justice. Sen is reluctant to endorse a predetermined set of basic capabilities that is not context specific because the capabilities approach allows significant latitude in interpretation and implementation. Underlying this difficulty on his part is his insistence on the need for public reasoning for the validation of rights as capabilities. Given the importance of unobstructed public reasoning in a democracy and the open-ended nature of capabilities, Sen would not like to see a fixed list of capabilities unduly influence the tone and direction of civic discourse that is vital for the evolving social judgment and policy assessments in a democracy. The discourse should be open and have as broad a reach as possible, both for objectivity and fairness. For Sen, public discourse is vital for democracy. Capabilities themselves depend on it, emerging from and being shaped by it, so any theoretical list should not be allowed to preset the tone of the debate.[21]

Unlike Sen, Nussbaum is more insistent on listing a core group of capabilities as valid and applicable through all cultures. Instead of regarding such a list as "a denial of the reach of democracy" (Sen, 2005, 158; see note 19), she believes that her list should be a challenge to all democratic regimes to take rights talk seriously.[22] As she puts it, rights and entitlements are too important to be left to the whims of individual decisions of groups or cultures. In fact, Nussbaum thinks that there is considerable tension between Sen's insistence on a strong priority of certain capabilities as fundamental entitlements of all people everywhere, along with his generic endorsement of capabilities as freedom, without saying which freedoms are important and which ones lack merit, which are socially desirable and which not (as she aims to do in her chapter). Nussbaum acknowledges that public reasoning is crucial in understanding and implementing the range of capabilities in different cultures, and she leaves room for that discourse in her list, which is thick but left open-ended regarding the viability of specific functionings. She nonetheless is left wondering how Sen can avoid evaluating human freedoms and not endorsing a core list of capabilities if he were to embark on a coherent social and political conception of justice. If a constitutional democracy tries to pursue a reasonably just political order, its constitution has to specify, as a minimum requirement of justice, certain freedoms or capabilities as basic entitlements for its citizens.

The democratic implications of global interdependence, made possible by today's rapid globalization, have generated calls for an overhauling of global governance to make it more democratically representative and effective. Scholars argue that global governance should be restructured to make it more accountable to public interests and more responsive to human needs. Toward that end, they suggest a reconfiguration of international institutions and a measured dispersion of national sovereignty, both for the sake of fair political representation and to accommodate the increasingly critical global reality of overlapping jurisdictions of participation. In general, the challenge to work out a cosmopolitan vision of democracy and justice rests not only in suggesting specific institutional reforms but, more fundamentally, on reconceiving the cosmopolitan reach of international law. The idea is to move away from the prevailing statist model of sovereign equality in international law in favor of a justice-based human rights paradigm that is taken to be the normative foundation for an international legal system. The trend thus is to advocate a more democratically responsive international order that, while downplaying the primacy of state sovereignty, at the same time ensures that states too must satisfy a minimal democracy requirement to be recognized as legitimate under international law. Various nuances of this idea have been suggested by scholars in literature under the broad rubric of cosmopolitan democracy.[23]

In contrast to this trend, Andrew Oldenquist in chapter 5 argues that nationalism and group loyalty need not be antithetical to democratic norms and to a democratic global order. Nationalism, ranging all the way from national consciousness found in all nation-states to ethnic separatist nationalism and assimilative nationalism of voluntary units of similar peoples, is not necessarily xenophobic. Oldenquist goes on to say that nationalism can coexist with the guiding universal moral principles of a civil-constitutional state *and* be open to the trends of globalization. In essence, nationalism typifies the yearning for self-determination and a desire to be ruled by one's own, but because

of its tribal connotation, nationalism is typically misunderstood and blamed
for divisiveness and intolerance, leading to its denigration, which Oldenquist
finds unfortunate. According to him, different shades of nationalism may have
different, even opposite, goals, although they all contain certain tribal ideas of
group loyalty, even if only metaphorically. Today's separatist nationalism, for
instance, can be traced back to thousands of years of clan and tribal loyalty as
manifested in the pursuit of land and independence by ethnic groups for
themselves, whereas unifying nationalism is a relatively recent phenomenon
that exhibits a desire to go beyond one's ethnic identity for a broader unifying
identity and loyalty. Likewise, nationalism as national identity that citizens in
a nation-state exhibit toward their own country is the politicized national loyalty of patriotism, which is a form of group loyalty that is as old as clans and
tribes; but unlike the two other forms of nationalism, it is neither a desire to
unify nor one to secede.

Patriotic nationalism can degenerate into xenophobia; unifying nationalism, if not voluntary, can turn into imperialism; and separatist nationalism
may exhibit ethnic intolerance—but at their core, they all are based on the
tribal idea of group loyalty that need not be incompatible with the movement
toward globalization or the egalitarian democratic values. The ideal of political globalization based on egalitarian norms is not yet a reality because it does
not correspond to people's desire to be ruled by themselves in their small
units, but if and when people's felt identities and their objects of loyalty expand to coincide with the global domain, a democratic political globalization
can emerge. According to Oldenquist, the assumption that peace or democracy requires the suppression of nationalism, based on the faulty idea that nationalism invariably leads to fanaticism, may cause more harm than good. In
fact, although nationalism and democracy are independent concepts, it is the
drive toward nationalism that has led to the breakup of colonial empires and
resulted in the surge of births of new democracies in the past few decades.
Claims of nationalism may sometimes compete with wider objects of loyalty
such as humanity, but nested multiple loyalties is a challenge that people negotiate all the time. This is the challenge that Kok-Chor Tan tries to articulate
in the chapter that follows Oldenquist's.[24]

In chapter 6, Kok-Chor Tan proposes to reconcile the reality of globalization with the nationalist thesis that the nation is the primary locus of democratic politics. Unless the democratic reach extends beyond national borders
in a global world of overlapping jurisdictions of participation, democratic
decision making would not be accessible to the affected parties, thus raising
questions regarding the viability of democracy in the age of globalization.
However, Tan does not conclude that to make democracy compatible with
globalization one needs to downplay the primacy of state sovereignty, as the

project of cosmopolitan democracy demands. Citing David Miller's and Will Kymlicka's observations that seem to support Oldenquist's idea that democratic politics is most likely to flourish within the smaller unit of a nation-state than on the bigger domain of the world at large, Tan is challenged to respond to the so-called democratic deficit in the global order. Virtues of nationalism such as group loyalties, fellow-feelings, shared histories, or common sympathies should be retained, Tan argues, to make democracy feasible on a national level, but such local structures should be supplemented by a democracy of democracies at the international level. Tan proposes the idea of an "inter-national" democracy composed of a democracy of national democracies that, for him, is a more realistic way of achieving global democracy than the cosmopolitan democratic ideal of a cross-national political and legal system in which individuals have direct access to some variety of democratic governance.

There is no reason why the citizens of a democratic nation cannot extend the democratic norms of justice and egalitarianism beyond their national borders. In fact, if democratic citizenship is based on the idea of a shared allegiance to certain common ideals, then nationalism is indeed compatible with concern for justice for all human beings. As Tan observes, even if the nationalist thesis is true that the deliberative site of democracy can be best construed within nation-states, the ideal of justice requires a certain cosmopolitanism that can be reinforced by the inculcated values of democratic egalitarianism and democratic humanism. Thus, democracy within nations can have a beneficial influence toward achieving democracy between and among nations. Democratic citizenship in a global world requires confronting the challenges of competing loyalties between nationalist claims and one's obligation to humanity.[25] Accordingly, if nations are not democratically represented at important global institutions, as Crocker points out forcefully in the first chapter (citing Stiglitz), or if some nations are unable to meet their citizens' basic human rights needs or become guilty of egregious violations of rights of their own citizens, then it is the collective responsibility of nations to work toward a more equitable international order, including reforming existing institutions, responding to the plight of the failed or inept states, and taking corrective measures to prevent the undermining of democratic accountability.

All this has vast implications for international law. In spite of the global nature of today's politics, commerce, and institutions, and the many existing measures in the current international system that are designed to enforce order and human rights, international law has yet to work out the moral and legal implications of the fluid dynamics of the new global reality. Nor is the existing legal system equipped to respond to the challenges of cosmopolitan justice that underscore the importance of international solidarity. Positivism and state sovereignty still being the operating norms in international law, the challenge is great to work out the democratic foundations for a legal framework for governing the newly emerging international society. If globalization has opened up the planetary dimensions of democracy, then the lack of an equitable international legal paradigm in the face of rapid internationalism also makes vivid the problem of democratic global governance. This is a serious challenge to both cosmopolitan democracy and "inter-national" democracy, regardless of their respective viability.

Some scholars point out that international law is not a neutral apparatus in which the lack of equity is a contingent factor in the system. They argue that discrimination and exploitation are entrenched within and constitutive of the very basis of international law due to the fact that the formation and evolution of international law have had a built-in "civilizing mission" for governing non-European people. The same trend of domination is said to persist today as globalization replaces colonialism by switching from the old motif of racial and cultural superiority to the current focus on international economic and human rights mandates based on Western terms.[26] A similar point has been echoed with regard to liberalism itself: in spite of its purported liberating mission of autonomy and self-determination—quintessential democratic values—the liberal tradition has provided the rationale for imperialism rooted in the liberal assumptions about reason and historical progress.[27]

Today, with the continuing U.S. military involvement in Afghanistan and Iraq in the name of spreading democracy and self-governance, the specter of an imperial democracy is looming large. Although the United States denies any imperial ambitions, she has been characterized as "unmistakably an empire"—based on her role as the sole superpower with unprecedented political, economic, military, and cultural clout all over the world.[28] However, due to a proclaimed liberal commitment to promoting "sustainable models of national success" through democracy and free-market policies, the globally dominant United States is perceived as an empire, yet it is also termed a "liberal" empire.[29] Although the old motif of civilizing the illiberal other is unmistakably evident in today's imperial democracy, this "liberal imperialism" is garbed in the rhetoric of freeing people from the tyranny of their own rulers. Meanwhile, it is also being billed as part of the broader strategy of fighting terror and defending America's interests. The liberating project of imperial democracy, thus, is also a "defensive imperialism," claimed to be consistent with human rights objectives and other cosmopolitan liberal values.[30]

Perceived this way, the vision of liberal imperialism seems to embody in a much more pronounced manner what has been termed "the fallacy of liberal internationalism."[31] Thus, it is believed, all good things can be delivered together without any internal tension. They usually cannot, and such efforts

often turn out to be anything but good.[32] The irony of promoting the democratic values of self-determination, human rights, and respect for international law through military intervention—unilaterally if needed and without
the mandate of the United Nations if necessary—is palpably evident and
clearly a source of dilemma for the liberals.[33] Although war may prevent egregious violation of some negative rights, it violates a great many other rights,
both positive and negative.[34] Along with that, the element of national security
in the idea of defensive imperialism sanctifies the highly contentious idea of
preventive warfare that goes against both international law and the traditional
just-war doctrine, raising grave concerns about just distribution of power.
Given the great asymmetry of power and resources among nations today,
powerful countries could more easily be able to keep weaker countries from
gaining military parity and political equality if so-called preventive wars
continue in the name of war on terror, which is open-ended and often self-
serving. The attempt to justify preventive war by blurring the distinction between prevention and preemption with epithets like "gathering threats" does
not make such war any less controversial.[35] Accordingly, critics may well wonder how democratic is "imperial democracy."

In chapter 7, William McBride claims that the current world order needs to
be viewed differently than the way it was understood even in the recent past.
The obvious reason is the terrorist attacks of September 11, 2001, on U.S. soil,
but more fundamentally, according to McBride, the actions of the Bush administration changed the world order when it seized the occasion to curb
democratic liberties at home and to deploy the nation's military and political
power in an imperialistic fashion to exert hegemonic domination over a part
of the world. Although the administration uses the language of democracy
and freedom for its rhetorical justification of its global policies, in reality,
McBride contends, it shows a contemptuous disregard of global institutions
and treaties through its systematic subversion of democratic aspirations and
policies of countries not conforming to the current U.S. priorities of corporate profit over public good. Consequently, a steady devaluation of liberal democracy is a pronounced feature of the emerging world order, due mainly to
America's unilateralism. Almost parallel to all this, McBride points out, as
much as John Rawls's earlier philosophy of liberal domestic justice was an effective blueprint for flourishing liberalism at home, his later venture into international justice has been a disappointment for many who were enthusiastic about his liberal egalitarianism. Paradoxically, Rawls's later ideas also
proved to be a theoretical precursor to actual events leading to the present demise of political liberalism.

McBride claims that as liberalism started to fall out of favor in the prevailing
political culture of the United States and the world, Rawls became progressively

defensive about his earlier liberal ideas so eloquently expressed in *A Theory of Justice* (1971). In his articulation of a theory of international justice in *The Law of Peoples* (1999), Rawls favors an account of distributive justice that rejects the cosmopolitan, egalitarian, and compensatory traits of his earlier domestic theory.[36] His idea of global redistribution of resources for alleviating poverty and helping the distant needy is minimally demanding, prompting McBride to stipulate that Rawls seems to be conveying the message that if some societies are poor or burdened, it is their own fault, due mainly to their own backward and unreasonable social customs and political institutions.[37] This line of thought, for McBride, proved to be a convenient rationale for the subsequent global mission of the Bush administration in pushing U.S.-style democracy and free market around the world—even by force if necessary. After all, Rawls's law of peoples stipulates that "rogue states" are subject to military intervention by a coalition of "decent" and "reasonable" people if the situation arises for such a move. According to McBride, "this late Rawlsian incursion into globalization" rejects liberal cosmopolitan ideals in international justice and shows a very limited understanding of global issues and global history, along with certain naïve assumptions about liberalism and the just-war theory. Accordingly, it is ironic, in McBride's opinion, that the John Rawls who championed the cause of liberal democracy during an atmosphere of robust political liberalism did not quite envisage how his later law of peoples would parallel the trends of the current era of globalization, in which the prospects of liberal democracy are quite dubious. Due to U.S. unilateralism trumping the collective interests of the global public, the demise of political liberalism is now a distinct possibility.

Frank Cunningham echoes a similar theme in chapter 8 by focusing on John Dewey's conception of a "public" and then extending the notion to the idea of a global public. For Dewey, a public's members are cooperative agents who collectively engage in responding to issues of common interest, and if such a public is vital for a flourishing democracy, then Cunningham wonders what the challenges would be to sustaining a global public in a similar fashion for fostering a thriving global culture of democracy. Although there are clear indications of an already-existing interconnected global community, for such an entity to be considered a viable global public, the test has to be how it responds collectively to issues of common interest. For this purpose, Cunningham takes up two problems—environmental degradation and the growing disparity between the rich and the poor. The broad-based support for the Kyoto Protocol on global warming and the 2000 United Nations Millennium Declaration for reducing world poverty are indications to Cunningham of the formation of a global public. Nonetheless, Cunningham proposes to test the effectiveness of a global public in today's divided world by construing four conditions in broadly Deweyan terms—common objectives, peaceful resolution of conflicts, self-awareness, and public institutions. Regarding common objectives, Cunningham claims that, although it would be unreasonable to expect and unlikely to find a transnational unity of civic virtues given the disparity and diversity in the world, it is evident that people do exhibit a broad consensus of moral indignation at the wanton degradation of environmental resources and at the desperate plight of the global poor in a world of unbounded wealth. Likewise, despite the preponderance of violence, there is an underlying global yearning for peace based on both moral and self-interested reasons—a yearning that is embodied in people's realization that, despite their differences, peaceful resolution of conflicts is essential for a public to address its common problems. Different problems may confront different publics and manifest in various ways, but a commitment to peace in resolving problems is the uniting bond that brings together a broader public in shared determination. Accordingly, to the extent that a mobilized public can collectively and peacefully respond to problems of common concern, it also fulfills the third condition of self-awareness. Dewey is well known for his progressive ideas on public education as a means to democratic citizenship leading to a self-aware public.[38] Furthermore, although a champion of direct democracy at the local levels, Dewey sensed the need for political representation through institutional means—also essential for the makeup of a public—for effective and accountable democratic participation on a larger scale. For Cunningham, on the global scene, an emboldened and democratic United Nations is the obvious candidate for such a political institution.

However, according to Cunningham, the Bush administration's manifest hostility toward the United Nations is symptomatic of a wider pattern of systematic undermining of a global public. By its hegemonic policies of world domination that undercut attempts to build representative global institutions, and by disregarding issues of vital public interest as evident, for example, in the sabotaging of initiatives such as the Kyoto Protocol and the UN Millennium Project, the United States has taken a clear stance against the common interests of the global public. The democratic public is sustained through a dynamic and complementary balance between unity and diversity, whereas the Bush administration is pushing for a homogenizing world order of U.S.-style democracy and free-market capitalism on U.S. terms. This approach simultaneously disregards complexities of culture, history, and politics while playing divisive politics in the Islamic part of the world. On the home front, the U.S. government's alignment with the religious right is breeding fanatical nationalism, while its neglect of the poor and pandering to the rich are creating deep divisions across class lines. All this goes against the prospect of forging a U.S. national public as well.

The chapters in this book debate the nature and viability of democratic norms and political institutions in response to the changing nature of the

global order in the twenty-first century. They renew the question of democracy's role in responding to the challenges of modern globalization by span-
ning the range of issues at the foundation of our contemporary political and
social thought, including human rights and cultural diversity, nationalism
and cosmopolitanism, well-being and economic development, as well as the
broader issues of peace and justice in the new world order. These issues have
overlapping concerns and are tied together by a common need for effective
political and institutional directives that would adequately respond to the
challenges of a new global ethic shaped by the emerging democratic norms.
The chapters emphasize the need for a stronger and more effective international legal and political order and a corresponding reevaluation of the normative status of national sovereignty.

This idealized vision of a new world order may raise questions about its prac-
ticality. For instance, the U.S.-led invasion of Iraq, which happened despite
strong opposition by the international community and without the approval of
the United Nations, highlights the importance of a strong democratic global
ethic while also making vivid the need for a realistic assessment of moral pronouncements. This is not unexpected—in reading the chapters in this book, one
sees the authors grappling with this quandary. To their credit, however, as they
try to bring the issues of normative ideal and political reality closer together,
they also emphasize the importance of moral imperatives in world affairs.

Normative claims of justice and fairness have an important role not only
in setting the norm but also in practice. For instance, although international
relations are usually guided by power and self-interest, the concept of fairness
is invariably brought in when there is a dispute. This is not only evident in
international trade agreements, environmental policies, and other mutually
agreed-upon treaties, but in military interventions as well. Although hegemonic interests are often couched under the pretense of moral imperatives,
it is the latter, usually under the broad rubric of a just-war doctrine, that gives
military ventures their perceived legitimacy.[39]

In this collection of chapters, the demand for a new democratic ethic is urgent, although the scope of individual moral responsibility in meeting this demand is placed within limits. Instead, the authors stipulate political responsibilities of nations and institutions. These responsibilities are stringent indeed,
but the authors make room for national self-interest and the emerging political and economic reality of global interdependence in deciding political and
moral obligations. Their demanding moral pronouncements are anchored to
the prevailing global reality—a realistic move that is refreshingly different
from abstract cosmopolitanism.

Accordingly, because the intersection of democracy and globalization does
not automatically lead to global democracy, the quandaries arising out of the

confrontation between globalization and democracy, while defying easy resolution, highlight the importance of grounding claims of moral relevance in the global realities of politics, culture, and communities, thereby bringing norms and institutions closer together. The chapters in this book reflect this effort as they examine the nature, practice, and limits of democracy in global politics, keeping in focus the role of rights at the normative foundations of democracy in a pluralistic world. Through an examination of key topics of current relevance with contrasting views of the leading theorists, this book addresses the most relevant theories and forms of globalization, traditional democratic paradigms and their limits, public deliberation and democratic participation, the moral hazards of imperial democracy, and the future of liberal democracy. By elucidating theoretical concepts through focused study of the important public and political issues and their vast implications for the normative justifications of the democratic ideals, the contributors examine the institutional viability of democracy in a world challenged by globalization and superpower unilateralism. Along the way, they navigate the uncharted water of yet another defining moment of human evolution—modern globalization—that has challenged political philosophy to its core.

Notes

1. Former Czech president Vaclav Havel thinks that the transition to democracy in Central and Eastern Europe and in some countries of Africa, most notably South Africa, "would never have succeeded without the support of a democratically minded world public." See Vaclav Havel, "Strangling Democracy," *New York Times* (Op-Ed), 24 June 2004. Allen Buchanan, however, cites a list of recent literature that contains contrasting views regarding conditions under which democratization may occur, indicating a great deal of uncertainty on this matter. See Allen Buchanan, "Institutionalizing the Just War," *Philosophy & Public Affairs* 34 (2006): 2–38, note 23. On globalization's implications for justice and its impact on media, culture, society, human rights, health, labor, learning, environment, development, and business, see the articles by Amartya Sen, Joseph Stiglitz, Meghnad Desai, Sunil Khilnani, Irene Khan, Y. K. Hamied, Rehman Sobhan, Roman Grynberg, Susan Leubuscher, and others in *The Little Magazine* 5, issues 4 and 5 (2004). On common misconceptions of and a new perspective on globalization, see Saskia Sassen, *Globalization and Its Discontents* (New York: New Press, 1998). Two important books in the proglobalization literature are Jagdish Bhagwati's *In Defense of Globalization* (New York: Oxford University Press, 2004) and Martin Wolf's *Why Globalization Works* (New Haven, CT: Yale University Press, 2004). For a balanced assessment of globalization, see Joseph Stiglitz, *Globalization and Its Discontents* (New York: W. W. Norton, 2002). For an introduction to the various aspects of the globalization debate, see *The Global Transformations Reader: An Introduction to the Globalization Debate*, eds. David Held and Anthony McGrew (Cambridge, UK: Polity Press, 2000).

2. For a strong defense of democracy along this line, see Ian Shapiro, *The Moral Foundations of Politics* (New Haven, CT: Yale University Press, 2003). For an empirical defense of these normative concerns, see Gerry Mackie, *Democracy Defended* (Cambridge, UK: Cambridge University Press, 2003). This point about democracy's virtue is echoed in Amartya Sen's empirical observation that famines do not happen in democracies precisely because of democracy's commitment to human rights and its mechanism for open access to information and public debate. See Amartya Sen, *Poverty and Famines: An Essay on Entitlement and Deprivation* (New York: Oxford University Press, 1981). Needless to say, much of the plausibility of this claim depends on the degree of democratic accountability one has in mind. See Buchanan, "Institutionalizing the Just War," note 17. Both Sen and Shapiro take democracy as a good in its own right. See Amartya Sen, *Development as Freedom* (New York: Knopf, 1999). For a contrasting view, see Richard Arneson, "Democracy Is Not Intrinsically Just," in *Justice and Democracy*, eds. Keith Dowding, Robert Goodin, and Carole Pateman (Cambridge, UK: Cambridge University Press, 2004) and Brian Barry, "Is Democracy Special?," in Brian Barry, *Democracy, Power, and Justice: Essays in Political Theory* (Oxford: Clarendon Press, 1989). Barry's book studies the connection between normative political theory and how political institutions work in practice—a theme that recurs in the chapters of this book. In general, we focus more on the global implications of democratic norms than on democratic theory itself. For an excellent study of democratic theory, especially of the relation between democracy and justice, see Dowding et al., *Justice and Democracy*.

3. Richard Rorty attributes the term "human rights culture" to the Argentinian jurist and philosopher Eduardo Rabossi. See Richard Rorty, "Human Rights, Rationality, and Sentimentality," in *On Human Rights: The Oxford Amnesty Lectures, 1993*, eds. Stephen Shute and Susan Hurley (New York: Basic Books, 1993).

4. For instance, the United Nations Secretary-General Kofi Annan, in a report released on May 1, 2005, has observed that the ingredients of enduring global security lie not necessarily in deploying a nation's military forces for global safekeeping, but more important, in promoting just development and comprehensive human rights. A recent report on the mission of the Dutch soldiers in Afghanistan seems to corroborate this proactive approach. While the United States and British troops are conducting sweeps and raids, the Dutch-led task force has mostly shunned combat. Instead, they are helping the locals in building bridges and setting up schools for children. As the Dutch commander put it: "We're not here to fight the Taliban . . . . We're here to make the Taliban irrelevant." "Dutch Soldiers Stress Restraint in Afghanistan," *New York Times*, 6 April 2007. For ideas of global civil society promoting human rights, nonviolence, and democracy as an antidote to human wrongs in the international arena, see Richard Falk, "The Challenge of Genocide and Genocidal Politics in an Era of Globalization," in *Human Rights in Global Politics*, eds. Tim Dunne and Nicholas J. Wheeler (Cambridge, UK: Cambridge University Press, 1999). For a well-rounded account of basic rights that blur the alleged distinction between negative and positive rights, see Henry Shue, *Basic Rights: Subsistence, Affluence, and U.S. Foreign Policy*, 2nd ed. (Princeton, NJ: Princeton University Press, 1996). For an empirical description of the rejection of the alleged distinction, see Stephen Holmes

and Cass R. Sunstein, *The Cost of Rights: Why Liberty Depends on Taxes* (New York: Norton & Co., 1999).

5. On the perspectives of the developing countries on the international order, see Balakrishnan Rajagopal, *International Law from Below: Development, Social Movements, and Third World Resistance* (Cambridge, UK: Cambridge University Press, 2003) and *The Third World and International Order: Law, Politics, and Globalization*, eds. Anthony Anghie, Bhupinder Chimni, Karin Mickelson, and Obiora Okafor (Leiden, The Netherlands: Brill Academic Publishers, 2003).

6. In chapter 1, David Crocker cites recent studies to augment this claim. For a contrasting view on the liberating power of capitalism and free market, see Robert Wright, "The Market Shall Set You Free," *New York Times* (Op-Ed), 28 January 2005. Of course, the link between economic and political liberty has been the centerpiece of the libertarian ideology for a long time.

7. For an account of how the inequity in the global order and environmental degradation in the poor countries are linked, see Peter Wenz, *Environmental Justice* (Albany: SUNY Press, 1988). For case studies on the global market being a threat to cultural identity, see Helena Norberg-Lodge, *Ancient Future: Learning from Ladakh* (San Francisco: Sierra Club Books, 1991) and Karen Freeman, "Globalization Drives the Economy, But It Still Pays to Be Irish," *New York Times* (Editorial Observer), 23 October 2004.

8. For a report on how national democracy by itself is not enough to foster just economic development in poor countries in the era of economic globalization without a strict democratic regulatory mechanism in the global order itself, see Juan Forero, "Latin America Is Growing Impatient with Democracy," *New York Times* (Op-Ed), 24 June 2004. For a study of how inequitable global trading rules foster unfair labor practices in poor countries, see Christian Barry and Sanjay Reddy, *Just Linkage: International Trade and Labor Standards* (New York: Columbia University Press, forthcoming). See also Barry and Reddy, "The False Dilemma of the Sweatshop," *Financial Times* (Op-Ed), 24 July 2006.

9. See Alistair Macleod, "Free Markets and Democracy: Clashing Ideals in a Globalizing World?," *Journal of Social Philosophy* 37 (2006): 139–62. Interestingly, economists have started speculating whether the unregulated market driven by the forces of globalization may even be holding down market growth worldwide. In other words, questions have been raised whether globalization and market growth may always go together. See Rich Miller and Gregory Viscusi, "Globalization Backlash Seen as Growth Threat," *International Herald Tribune*, 6 March 2006, 1.

10. Shapiro notes this but does not pursue the global dimension. Shapiro, *Moral Foundations*. For an account of the global dimension of the new dynamics of sovereignty based on cross-border constellation of groups and agencies, see Andrew Kuper, *Democracy beyond Borders: Justice and Representation in Global Institutions* (New York: Oxford University Press, 2004).

11. See Amartya Sen, "Elements of a Theory of Human Rights," *Philosophy & Public Affairs* 32 (2004): 315–56.

12. Sen, "Elements." Also, Amartya Sen, "Human Rights and Asian Values," *The New Republic*, July 10 (1997): 14–21 and Henry Shue, "Thickening Convergence: Human

Rights and Cultural Diversity," in *The Ethics of Assistance: Morality and the Distant Needy*, ed. Deen K. Chatterjee (Cambridge, UK: Cambridge University Press, 2004), 217–41.

13. As studies have shown, mere economic empowerment of women may not overcome the gender inequality between women and men. The inequity is due to a complex set of social and political factors that money alone cannot mitigate. See *Gender, Development, and Money*, ed. Caroline Sweetman (Oxford: Oxfam, 2001).

14. Peter Singer examines the implications of this idea in relation to a new global ethic in his *One World: The Ethics of Globalization* (New Haven, CT: Yale University Press, 2002). Portions of what follow are adapted from my reviews of the following books: *Singer, One World*, reviewed in *Journal of Moral Philosophy* 3, No. 1 (2006); Kuper, *Democracy*, reviewed in *Ethics* 116, No. 3 (2006); and Buchanan (cited in note 23 below) in *Ethics and International Affairs* 19, No. 2 (2005); and from "Multiculturalism," *Encyclopedia of Business Ethics and Society*, ed. Robert W. Kolb (New York: Sage Publications, 2007).

15. Cf. Shue, "Thickening Convergence." For an excellent study of identity politics posing a challenge to democratic theory and practice, see *Democracy and Difference: Contesting the Boundaries of the Political*, ed. Seyla Benhabib (Princeton, NJ: Princeton University Press, 1996).

16. Cf. Kuper, *Democracy*, chap. 2.

17. See Monique Deveaux, *Gender and Justice in Multicultural Liberal States* (New York: Oxford University Press, 2007).

18. See Seyla Benhabib, "On the Alleged Conflict between Democracy and International Law," *Ethics & International Affairs* 19 (2005): 85–100.

19. Amartya Sen, "Human Rights and Capabilities," *Journal of Human Development* 6 (2005): 151–66. This portion on Nussbaum and Sen is adapted from my "Capabilities Approach to Distributive Justice," *Encyclopedia of Business Ethics and Society*.

20. Sen, "Human Rights and Capabilities."

21. Sen, "Human Rights and Capabilities." See also his "Elements of a Theory of Human Rights."

22. See Martha C. Nussbaum, "Women's Bodies: Violence, Security, Capabilities," *Journal of Human Development* 6 (2005): 179.

23. See Allen Buchanan, *Justice, Legitimacy, and Self-Determination: Moral Foundations for International Law* (New York: Oxford University Press, 2004); Singer, *One World*; Kuper, *Democracy*; David Held, *Democracy and the Global Order* (Cambridge, UK: Polity Press, 1995); and *Re-imagining Political Community: Studies in Cosmopolitan Democracy*, eds. Daniele Archibugi, David Held, and M. Kohler (Stanford, CA: Stanford University Press, 1998).

24. In recent days, there has been a surge of debate on nationalism, covering such topics as the normative and political legitimacy of nationalism, the ethnic/civic and identity/difference divide, secession, and consequences of nationalism, mostly bad. For a study of these topics and more, see Maurizio Viroli, *For Love of Country: An Essay On Patriotism and Nationalism* (New York: Oxford University Press, 1995); *The Morality of Nationalism*, eds. Robert McKim and Jeff McMahan (New York: Oxford University Press, 1997); *Rethinking Nationalism*, eds. Jocelyne Couture, Kai Nielsen, and Michel Seymour (Calgary: University of Calgary Press, 1998); and Martha C. Nuss-

baum, *For Love of Country?* (Boston, MA: Beacon Press, 2002). What is innovative in Oldenquist's chapter 5 is the link, however contingent, between nationalism and a democratic global order and an analysis of the idea of group loyalty compatible with the broader political globalization.

25. On education, democratic citizenship, and cosmopolitanism, see Martha C. Nussbaum, "Tagore, Dewey, and the Decline of Liberal Education," in *Tagore's Philosophy of Education*, eds. Deen K. Chatterjee and Martha C. Nussbaum (in preparation).

26. For a recent articulation of this view, see Anthony Anghie, *Imperialism, Sovereignty, and the Making of International Law* (Cambridge, UK: Cambridge University Press, 2005), especially chap. 3. See also Dipesh Chakrabarty, *Provincializing Europe: Postcolonial Thought and Historical Difference* (Princeton, NJ: Princeton University Press, 2000) and Susan Marks, *The Riddle of All Constitutions: International Law, Democracy, and the Critique of Ideology* (Oxford: Oxford University Press, 2000).

27. See Uday Singh Mehta, *Liberalism and Empire: A Study in Nineteenth-Century British Liberal Thought* (Chicago: University of Chicago Press, 1999). See also *Critical Race Theory: The Key Writings That Formed the Movement*, ed. Kimberle Crenshaw (New York: New Press, 1995).

28. Michael Ignatieff, "The American Empire: The Burden," *New York Times Magazine*, 5 January 2003. Commenting on the invasions of Iraq and Afghanistan, Rory Stewart observes: "America and its partners have neither the will nor the intention of becoming colonial powers. And they justified the invasions at least partly in terms of democracy. They must, therefore, follow their [those of the elected leaders of Iraq and Afghanistan] instincts, almost regardless of their ability, ideology or methods.... And they [the elected leaders] can succeed only if we respect local politicians, allow them to deal with our enemies, and drop our utopian dreams." Rory Stewart, "Even in Iraq, All Politics Is Local," *New York Times* (Op-Ed), 13 July 2006, A23.

29. Ignatieff, "The American Empire." Also, Crenshaw, *The Key Writings*.

30. See Robert Cooper, "The New Liberal Imperialism," *Observer*, 7 April 2002. Also, Ignatieff, "The American Empire."

31. Stanley Hoffmann, "The Crisis of Liberal Internationalism," *Foreign Policy* 98 (1995): 159–77. "Internationalism," of course, implies more cooperation and less unilateralism than "imperialism."

32. Hoffmann, "The Crisis," 167.

33. See Buchanan, "Institutionalizing the Just War," for an insightful response to this dilemma.

34. Especially when a war is poorly planned and executed for dubious motives, incalculable suffering results. One should ask, for instance, whether creating a failed state in Iraq is tantamount to promoting democracy and human rights.

35. See *Gathering Threats: Moral Perspectives on Preventive War*, eds. Deen K. Chatterjee and Don E. Scheid (Cambridge, UK: Cambridge University Press, 2008).

36. Peter Singer argues that because for Rawls a sound theory of justice has to match our settled intuitions, in addressing the issue of justice beyond borders Rawls offers arguments in a manner that does not disturb the conventional moral intuition of what we owe to the distant needy, although his arguments are "sharply at odds" with

his earlier egalitarian position. See Peter Singer, "Outsiders: Our Obligations to Those beyond Our Borders," in *The Ethics of Assistance: Morality and the Distant Needy*, ed. Deen K. Chatterjee (Cambridge, UK: Cambridge University Press, 2004), 11–32.

37. Thomas Pogge critiques Rawls for seemingly endorsing the "Domestic Poverty Thesis," which holds that "the persistence of severe poverty is due solely to domestic causes." Thomas Pogge, "'Assisting' the Global Poor," in *The Ethics of Assistance*, 260–88. For Pogge, the Domestic Poverty Thesis is "quite far from the truth." Pogge, 265.

38. See Nussbaum, "Tagore, Dewey."

39. This portion is adapted from my "Foreign Policy, Human Rights, and 'Preventive Non-Intervention,'" in *Between Cosmopolitan and State Sovereignty: Studies in Global Justice*, eds. Ronald Tinnevelt and Gert Verschraegen (New York: Palgrave Macmillan, 2006): 234–44. See also A. John Simmons, *Political Philosophy*, chap. 1.5 (New York, Oxford University Press, 2008).

I
DEMOCRACY AND GLOBALIZATION

1

Development Ethics, Democracy, and Globalization[1]

David A. Crocker

G LOBALIZATION AND DEMOCRATIZATION—and their links—are matters of in-
tense and often bitter worldwide debate. How should globalization be
understood and assessed? Is globalization a permanent change in the world
order or an "over-hyped fad of 1990s,"[2] to be replaced by forces—such as terrorism and U.S. unilateralism—that tear the world apart? Is globalization
good or bad? Who should say and in what terms? What should we mean by
democracy? Can and should democracy be "globalized" in the sense promoted
in authoritarian countries, resuscitated in countries in which it is under attack, and installed or deepened in global institutions? Can democracy be "installed" without undermining its moral foundation? This chapter makes a case
that globalization is an important structural change that should be ethically
assessed as well as understood with respect to its causes and consequences.
Moreover, the chapter argues that globalization is ethically justified only if it
promotes and is promoted by a deepening of local, national, and global democracy. What the world needs now, increasingly argue development ethicists, is both a globalization of (a kind of) democracy and a democratization
of globalization.

This chapter has three parts. Part I discusses the nature and practice of development ethics and argues that such an ethics is one resource that can and
should be applied to the ethical evaluation of globalization and democratization. In Part II, I discuss leading theories of globalization and three approaches
to assessing as well as humanizing and democratizing globalization. In Part III,
I show more systematically what I illustrate throughout the chapter—namely,
that the recent work of Joseph Stiglitz contributes to development ethics by

ethically assessing globalization, democratization, and their actual and ideal linkages.

Part I: Development Ethics

Development ethicists assess the ends and means of local, national, regional, and global development. National policymakers, project managers, grassroots communities, and international aid donors involved in development in poor countries often confront moral questions in their work. Development scholars recognize that social-scientific theories of development and underdevelopment have ethical as well as empirical and policy components. Development philosophers and other ethicists formulate ethical principles relevant to social change in poor countries, and they analyze and assess the moral dimensions of development theories and seek to resolve the moral quandaries lurking in development policies and practice.[3]

Areas of Consensus: Questions

Although they differ on a number of matters, development ethicists exhibit a wide consensus about the commitments that inform their practice, the questions they are posing, and the reasonableness of certain answers. Development ethicists typically ask the following related questions:

- What should count as (good) development? What are clear examples of "good" development and "bad" development? How well are various regions, societies, and locales doing in achieving development? Development ethics emerged due to dissatisfaction with conventional wisdom with respect to development, and it thrives on questioning how good and better development should be conceived.
- Should we continue using the concept of development instead of, for example, progress, economic growth, transformation, liberation, "sustainable livelihoods,"[4] or "post-development alternatives to development"[5]? How, if at all, does (good) development differ from modernization, developmentalism, transformational development (USAID), or the Washington Consensus?
- Are development's professed altruistic aims incompatible or coincident with the national self-interest of donor countries? Is professed altruism either a rationalization for Northern and Western economic dominance or invariably undermined by chosen means (or both)?

- If development is defined generically as good socioeconomic change, what basic economic, political, and cultural goals and strategies should a society or political community pursue, and what values or principles should inform their selection?
- What moral issues emerge in development policymaking and practice and how should they be resolved?[6] How should we assess U.S. efforts to install democracy in Afghanistan and Iraq? Should an independent judiciary be viewed as part of the democratic ideal or as relative only to specific (Western) cultures? Another example of a moral question is unusually explicit in a recent U.S. Agency for International Development (USAID) document:

> Is it enough, from a donor's point of view, that the legal and social instruments for inclusion exist and that there are no barriers to participation: Or should they [such instruments] also be concerned about whether the citizenry—indeed all segments of the citizenry—actually participates? And, if so, are they coerced to participate? . . . Should donors support programs to improve actual, not just permissive, participation?"[7]

Does a preoccupation with anticorruption strategies crowd out long-term efforts at poverty reduction and participatory democracy?[8] Should USAID personnel refuse to demote birth control (condoms) to a secondary status compared to policies of abstinence and marital fidelity?[9]

- How should the benefits and harms of development be conceived and distributed? Is the most fundamental category gross domestic product (income), utility, subjective happiness (Graham and Pettinato),[10] social primary goods (Rawls),[11] access to resources (Roemer),[12] basic human needs (Galtung, Max-Neef, and Streeten),[13] negative liberty (Bauer and Nozick),[14] free agency or autonomy (Sen and Ellerman),[15] capabilities and functionings (Nussbaum),[16] or human rights (Pogge and Sen)[17]? If human rights are important, should they include positive socioeconomic rights as well as civil and political rights? Is some composite measure of development success basic, such as economic growth or economic efficiency, or does social justice require maximizing the least well off, getting all above a threshold, or reducing degrading inequality?
- Who (or what institutions) bears responsibility for bringing about development—a nation's government, civil society, or the market? What role—if any—do or should more affluent states, international institutions, nongovernmental associations, and poor countries themselves have in development? What are the obligations of a sovereign state for its

own citizens and are these duties more demanding than its duties to all human beings?[18]

- Regardless of the identity of duty bearers, how should development responsibilities be understood? Are duties based solely on divine commands, social pacts, general positive duties of charity (which permit donor discretion with respect to specific beneficiaries), specific duties to aid (any needy rights-bearer), negative duties to dismantle unjust structures or halt injurious action, or duties to make reparation for past wrongs? Is the duty of "do no harm" enough, or should citizens and development agents also consider positive duties to aid and, if so, how should the duty not to harm be weighed in relation to the duty to do good? Is the duty to aid distant peoples a cosmopolitan duty of justice, which makes no distinction in duties to compatriots and others, or a humanitarian duty to rescue or assist, which is less demanding than a duty to one's fellow citizens (Nagel)?
- What are the virtues and vices of various development agents? How good or obligatory is honesty and how bad or permissible is deception? Should USAID and other donor agencies have a code of ethics or conduct for its personnel? What is the evidence with respect to the role of similar professional codes in improving conduct? Is a code likely to do more harm than good? Would the prohibitions of such a code encourage employees to act in questionable ways just up to the threshold of permissible conduct, thereby encouraging problematic conduct? What would a defensible ethical code look like? Who should decide on such a code and by what process? Should it be imposed from the top or deliberated from the bottom? How should a code be enforced? How does an ethics of professional virtue or conduct relate to an ethics for assessing policy and institutional arrangements?
- What are the most serious local, national, and international impediments to and opportunities for good development? How should blame for development failures be apportioned among global, national, and local agents? What are the most relevant theories and forms of globalization and how should the promise and risks of globalization be assessed from a moral point of view?
- To what extent, if any, do moral skepticism, moral relativism, national sovereignty, political realism, and religious or political fundamentalism pose a challenge to this boundary-crossing ethical inquiry?
- Who should decide these questions and by what methods? What are the respective roles of appeal to authority, philosophical reflection, constitutional constraints, public deliberation, donor deliberation, and "learning by doing"?

Areas of Consensus: Answers

In addition to accepting the importance of these questions, most development ethicists share at least ten beliefs or commitments about their field and the general parameters for ethically based development. First, development ethicists typically agree that—in spite of global progress with respect to outlawing or reducing slavery and achieving higher living standards—there are still grave deprivations for many in contrast to the elevated affluence of a few. Development ethicists start from judgments about what Dewey would call a "problematic situation": many people throughout the world undeservedly and needlessly suffer or die. These deaths may be either agonizingly slow, due to poverty of various sorts, or rapid but brutal due to ethnic and military conflict, repressive governments, or fragile states. In our affluent world, these unacceptable sufferings and deprivations need not continue, should be halted, and people everywhere should have a chance for a decent life. Pogge's cool expression of moral outrage is typical of many who share his sentiments:

> How well are the weak and vulnerable faring today? Some 2,800 million or 46 percent of humankind live below the World Bank's $2/day poverty line—precisely: in households whose income per person per day has less purchasing power than $2.15 had in the United States in 1993. On average, the people living below this line fall 44.4 percent below it. Over 1,200 million of them live on less than half, below the World Bank's better-known $1/day poverty line. People so incredibly poor are extremely vulnerable to even minor changes in natural and social conditions as well as to many forms of exploitation and abuse. Each year, some 18 million of them die prematurely from poverty-related causes. This is one-third of all human deaths—50,000 every day, including 34,000 children under age five. Such severe and extensive poverty persists while there is great and rising affluence elsewhere. The average income of the citizens of the affluent countries is about 50 times greater in purchasing power and about 200 times greater in terms of market exchange rates than that of the global poor.[19]

Moreover, development ethicists contend that development practices and theories have ethical and value dimensions and can benefit from explicit ethical analysis and appraisal. Although important, ascertaining the facts and their likely causes and effects cannot take the place of morally assessing what has been, is, and could be. Ethics or value commitments are lenses that reveal or highlight the valuational or moral dimension of human actions, institutions, and their consequences. It is indispensable to know the causes and consequences of such things as poverty, corruption, repressive governments, and state fragility. It is another thing to evaluate the morally salient features of those phenomena and decide whether alternatives would be morally better. For example, does the economic growth supposedly generated by a given development strategy get translated to expanding valuable freedoms of a nation's most vulnerable citizens? Ethical assessment of past policies and present options enables people who are active in development endeavors to keep their eyes on the ball of reducing remediable and undeserved human death and suffering. Many people work in development in order to make the world better, but the conceptual frameworks that guide them are largely concerned with technical means rather than morally urgent ends. Development ethics is a way of thinking that puts moral questions and answers in the center of thought and action.

In addition, development ethicists tend to see development as a multidisciplinary field that has both theoretical and practical components that intertwine in various ways. Hence, development ethicists aim not merely to understand the nature, causes, and consequences of development—conceived generally as desirable social change—but also to argue for and promote specific conceptions of such change. In backing certain changes, development ethicists assume that choice among alternatives is real and some are better than others.[20]

Furthermore, although they may understand the terms in somewhat different ways, development ethicists are generally committed to understanding and reducing human deprivation and misery in poor countries and regions. Development ethicists persistently remind development agencies that development should be for human beings rather than treating humans merely as tools (or "social capital") for development. Assessment of development policies and projects should emphasize impacts on preventing death as well as relieving suffering and loss of meaning. A consensus increasingly exists that development institutions, projects, and aid givers should seek strategies in which both human well-being and a healthy environment jointly exist and are mutually reinforcing.

Another matter of agreement is that most ethicists are convinced that what is frequently called "development"—for instance, economic growth—has created as many problems as it has solved. Development can be used both descriptively and normatively. In the descriptive sense, development is usually identified as the processes of economic growth and modernization that result in a society's achievement of a high or improving (per capita) gross domestic product (GDP) or gross national product (GNP). So conceived, a "developed" society may be either celebrated or criticized. In the normative sense, a developed society—ranging from villages to national and regional communities as well as the global order—is one whose established institutions realize or approximate (what the proponent believes to be) worthwhile goals. Most centrally, these goals include the overcoming of economic and social deprivation. In order to avoid confusion, when a normative sense of development is meant, the noun is often preceded by a positive adjective such as "good," "authentic," "humane," "just," or "ethically justified."

Development ethicists also agree that development ethics must be conducted at various levels of generality and specificity. Just as development debates occur at various levels of abstraction, so development ethics should assess

- basic ethical principles such as justice, liberty, autonomy, solidarity, and democracy
- development goals and models, such as economic growth, growth with equity, a new international economic order, basic needs, and, most recently, sustainable development, structural adjustment, human development (United Nations Development Programme),[21] and transformational development (USAID)
- specific institutions, projects, and strategies

Most development ethicists also contend that their enterprise should be international or global in the triple sense that the ethicists engaged in this activity come from many societies, including poor ones; that they are seeking to forge a cross-cultural consensus; and that this consensus emphasizes a commitment to alleviating worldwide deprivation.

Although many development ethicists argue that at least some development principles or procedures are relevant for any poor community or polity, most agree that development strategies must be contextually sensitive. What constitutes the best means—for instance, donor aid or withdrawal, state provisioning, market mechanisms, civil society, and their hybrids—will depend on a political community's history and stage of social change as well as on regional and global forces such as globalization and international institutions.

Finally, this flexibility concerning development models and strategies is compatible with the uniform rejection of certain extremes. Ethically based development is not exclusive: it offers and protects development benefits for everyone in a society, regardless of their religion, gender, ethnicity, economic status, or age. Moreover, most development ethicists would repudiate two models: (1) the maximization of economic growth in a society without paying any direct attention to converting greater opulence into better human living conditions for its members, what Amartya Sen and Jean Drèze call "unaimed opulence;"[22] and (2) an authoritarian egalitarianism in which physical needs are satisfied at the expense of political liberties.

Controversies

In addition to these points of agreement, one also finds several divisions and unsettled issues. One unresolved issue concerns the scope of development ethics. Development ethics originated as the "ethics of Third World Development." There are good reasons to drop—as a Cold War relic—the "First-Second-Third World" trichotomy. However, no consensus exists on whether or how development ethics should extend beyond its central concern of assessing the development ends and means of poor or traditional societies. Some argue that development ethicists should criticize human deprivation wherever it exists, including in rich countries and regions since they too have problems of poverty, powerlessness, and alienation and so properly fall within the scope of development ethics. Some argue that perhaps the socioeconomic model that the North has been exporting to the South results in the underdevelopment of both. Moreover, just as the (affluent) North exists in the (geographic) South, so the (poor) South exists in the (geographic) North. Yet others restrict development ethics to poor countries by arguing that attention to Northern deprivation diverts development ethicists and agents from the world's most serious destitution (in poor countries) and the ways in which rich countries benefit from the current global order.

My own view is that restricting development ethics to "developing" countries is defective in three ways. It falsely assumes that the most severe deprivation occurs in poor countries when in fact, as Sen points out, "the extent of deprivation for particular groups in very rich countries can be comparable to that in the so-called third world."[23] Furthermore, Northern and Southern poverty reduction are linked; migrants from the global South making money in the global North send valuable remittances to their families back home, but may also drain the South of able workers and displace workers in the North. Finally, there is the increasing prevalence of applying "best practices" learned from development in the global South to destitution in the global North (as well as vice versa). For example, the USAID has applied—through its Lessons without Borders program—lessons learned abroad to destitute U.S. cities. Development agents in different societies often face similar problems—such as unemployment, racism, violence, and powerlessness—and benefit from innovative ways of solving them.

A second question with respect to the scope of development ethics concerns how wide a net development ethics should cast with respect to the topics it addresses. It is controversial whether development ethicists, concerned with rich country responsibility and global distributive justice, should restrict themselves to official development assistance or whether they also should treat such topics as international trade, capital flows, migration, environmental pacts, terrorism, civil conflict, state fragility, military intervention, humanitarian intervention, and responses to human rights violations committed by prior regimes. The chief argument against extending its boundaries in these ways is that development ethics would thereby become too ambitious and diffuse. If development ethics grew to be identical with all international ethics or even all social ethics, the result might be that insufficient attention would be paid to alleviating poverty and powerlessness in various communities. Both sides agree that development ethicists should assess various kinds of North–South (and South–South) relations and the numerous global forces, such as globalization, that influence poverty as well as economic and political inequality in poor countries. What is unresolved, however, is whether development ethics also should address such topics as trade, security, the Internet, drug trafficking, military intervention, the conduct of war, peacekeeping, and the international criminal court when—or to the extent that—these topics have no causal relationship to absolute or relative poverty or powerlessness.

Development ethicists also are divided on the status of the moral norms that they seek to justify and apply. Three positions have emerged. Universalists, such as utilitarians and Kantians, argue that development goals and principles are valid for all societies. Particularists, especially communitarians and postmodern relativists, reply that universalism masks ethnocentrism and (Northern or Western) cultural imperialism. Prodevelopment particularists either reject the existence of universal principles or affirm only the procedural principle that each nation or society should draw exclusively on its own traditions and decide its own development ethic and path. (Antidevelopment particularists, rejecting both change brought from the outside and public reasoning about social change, condemn all development discourse and practice.) A third approach—advanced, for example, by Amartya Sen, Martha Nussbaum, Jonathan Glover, Seyla Benhabib, as well as myself[24]—tries to avoid the standoff between the first two positions. Proponents of this view insist that development ethics should forge a cross-cultural consensus in which a political community's own freedom to make development choices is one among a plurality of fundamental norms. Furthermore, these norms are sufficiently general to permit and also require sensitivity to societal differences.

One must also ask a further question related to the universalism/particularism debate: to what extent, if any, should development ethicists propose visions committed to a certain conception of human well-being or flourishing, and how "thick" or extensive should this vision be? There is a continuum here: at one end of the range, one finds a commitment to the values of individual choice, tolerance of differences, and public deliberation about societal ends and means; on the other end, one finds normative guidance and institutional guarantees with respect to the good human life, but less tolerance for individual and social choice.

Although I cannot argue for it here, I find most plausible a "threshold" view that identifies a minimal level of agency[25] and well-being that should be open to everyone, regardless of their citizenship. This threshold functions as a "platform" for individuals and communities freely to decide their own conception of the flourishing human life, its elements, and their weightings. One reason for this approach is that it will be easier to obtain cross-cultural consensus for a "moral minimum" than for a robust conception of the good life. Another reason is that such an approach both respects the rights of individuals and communities to determine (within limits set by their respect for the like freedom of others) their own conception of the good and enhances the "domain of public reasoning."[26]

Even supposing that development principles have some substantive content (beyond the procedural principle of self-determination that each society or person should decide for itself), there remain disagreements about that content. If one accepts that societal development concerns human development, one still must explore the moral categories crucial to human well-being and development. Candidates for such fundamental moral notions include, as we have seen, utility (preference satisfaction); subjective happiness; social primary goods, such as political liberty, income, wealth, and self-respect; negative liberty; basic human needs; autonomy or agency; valuable capabilities and functioning; human rights; and compassion or care.

Although many think that a development ethic ought to include more than one of these moral concepts, development ethicists differ about which among these values ought to have priority. The alternative I favor endorses the development of an understanding of sufficient human well-being (not flourishing) that combines, on the one hand, a neo-Kantian commitment to autonomy and human dignity, critical dialogue, and public deliberation with, on the other hand, neo-Aristotelian beliefs in the importance of physical health and social participation. Development duties might then flow from the idea that all humans have the right to a minimal level of well-being and agency, and various institutions have the duty to secure and protect these freedoms as well as restore them when lost. Donor agencies, such as the World Bank and USAID, should consider the merits of a rights-based approach to development.

One also finds an ongoing debate about how development's benefits, burdens, and responsibilities should be distributed within poor countries and between rich and poor countries. Utilitarians prescribe simple aggregation and maximization of individual utilities. Rawlsians advocate income and wealth maximization for the least well-off (individuals or nations). Libertarians contend that a society should guarantee no form of equality apart from equal freedom from the interference of government and other people. Pogge broadens the libertarian notion of harm (and rights) and argues that rich elites and nations should refrain from harming the vulnerable. Singer continues to challenge development ethicists and citizens everywhere with his argument that if affluent nations and individuals can relieve suffering and death without sacrificing anything of comparable moral worth, they are morally obliged to do so. Capability ethicists defend governmental and civil responsibility to enable everyone—even those who are citizens of other countries—to advance to a level of sufficiency (Sen, Crocker) or flourishing (Nussbaum, Little) with respect to the valuable functionings. Nagel distinguishes a stronger duty of justice that governments owe to their own citizens (and fellow citizens owe to each other) and a less stringent duty of beneficence that such governments and citizens owe to citizens of other countries. Unfortunately, distributional questions are conspicuous by their absence from much development policymaking. Development ethics challenges this silence by asking not only who in fact gains and loses, but which distribution of burdens and benefits is most justified morally.

Development ethicists also differ about whether (good) societal development should have—as an ultimate goal—the promotion of values other than the present and future human good. Some development ethicists ascribe intrinsic value—equal or even superior to the good of individual human beings—to such human communities as family, nation, or cultural group. Others argue that nonhuman individuals and species, as well as ecological communities, have equal and even superior value to human individuals. Those committed to "ecodevelopment" or "sustainable development" often fail to agree on what should be sustained as an *end in itself* and what should be maintained as an indispensable or merely *helpful means*. Nor do they agree on how to surmount conflicts among environmental and other competing values. Stiglitz clearly recognizes that these and other value disagreements are sometimes implicit in factual or policy disagreements:

> There are important disagreements about economic and social policy in our democracies. Some of these disagreements are about values—how concerned should we be about our environment (how much environmental degradation should we tolerate, if it allows us to have a higher GDP); how concerned should we be about the poor (how much sacrifice in our total income should we be willing to make, it if [sic] allows some of the poor to move out of poverty, or to be slightly better off); or how concerned should we be about democracy (are we willing to compromise on basic rights, such as the rights to association, if we believe that as a result, the economy will grow faster).[27]

Each development ethic and theory of justice offers insight at both the broad policy level and at the level of specific interventions. Although these moral frameworks seldom provide definitive or specific answers, they do call attention to candidates for fundamental ends in the light of which many current strategies and tactics might turn out to be morally questionable or even morally impermissible. The moral theories provide lenses that enable us to see ourselves, our duties, and others in new and compelling ways. They can reinforce moral motivations and thereby shape both citizen and professional conduct.

An increasingly important disagreement concerns not values directly, but the roles in resolving moral conflicts of, on the one hand, various experts such as judges (and the constitutions they interpret), political leaders, donors and their technical experts, philosophers, and, on the other hand, popular agency. Popular participation and democracy are suspect insofar as majorities (or minorities) may dominate others and insofar as people's beliefs and preferences are deformed by tradition, adapted to cope with deprivation, and subject to demagogic manipulation. Moreover, experts often excel at "know-how" if not "know why." On the other hand, rule by experts or guardians can lead to new tyrannies, and many experts themselves affirm Sen's "agent-oriented view" of development: "With adequate social opportunities, individuals can effectively shape their own destiny and help each other. They need not be seen primarily as passive recipients of the benefits of cunning development programs. There is indeed a rationale for recognizing the positive role of free and sustainable agency—and even of constructive impatience."[28]

Sen rightly, or so it seems to me, calls for development institutions to reorient their approach from one of providing goods and services to passive recipients to one of enabling countries and their citizens genuine opportunities to be authors of their own lives and developmental path. Such an "agency-centered" development perspective implies a deepening and broadening of democracy that includes but goes well beyond a universal franchise coupled with free and competitive elections. Crucially important is the engendering of venues—within both government and civil society—in which citizens and their representatives can engage in deliberative give-and-take to solve common problems.

The theory and practice of deliberative democracy, grounded in the ideals of agency and reciprocity, has much to offer development ethics.[29] Rather than focusing exclusively on free and fair elections, as important as they are, the theory and practice of deliberative democracy emphasizes social choice through public discussion that aims at solutions—solutions that nearly everyone can accept—to common problems. Gutmann and Thompson offer a useful working conception:

> We can define deliberative democracy as a form of government in which free and equal citizens (and their representatives), justify decisions in a process in which they give one another reasons that are mutually acceptable and generally accessible, with the aim of reaching conclusions that are binding in the present on all citizens but open to challenge in the future.[30]

Not only a philosophical normative theory, deliberative democracy is informed by and informs promising experiments in democratic governance occurring in Porto Alegre and almost two hundred other cities in Brazil; Kerala, India (an Indian state of forty million inhabitants); and Chicago, Illinois; among other places.[31]

Finally, controversy also exists with respect to which global or national agents and structures are largely if not exclusively to blame for the present state of global destitution and unequal opportunity. Charles Beitz states the empirical aspects of the issue well: "There is a large, complex, and unresolved empirical question about the relative contributions of local and global factors to the wealth and poverty of societies."[32] Some development ethicists, such as Pogge, emphasize that the global order is both dominated by affluent countries and unjustly tilted against poor countries.[33] This global order and the process of globalization amounts, claims Pogge, to a "strong headwind" against which any poor community must struggle and which is largely responsible for development failures: "national policies and institutions are indeed often quite bad; but the fact that they are can be traced to global policies and institutions."[34] Other development ethicists and policymakers ascribe development failure much less to global and foreign sources and much more to national and local causes—such as elite capture of power, widespread corruption, and the lack of democratic values.

Let us appropriate and develop Pogge's "headwind" metaphor in a way that captures a view more balanced and flexible than the one Pogge usually expresses about the relative and changing weight of external (global structure, rich country role) and internal (developing country role) factors in causing global poverty.[35] Sailors know that the headwind against which they sail is an important but constantly changing and sometimes ambiguous factor, and that getting to their destination requires skill and good judgment as well. The headwind is not always steady. Sometimes it gusts and sometimes it lulls (depending on the wind and whether their boat goes behind an island and is temporarily protected from the wind). Likewise, the impact of the global order and rich countries increases and decreases from time to time and place to place.

Moreover, sometimes there are crosswinds, some of which aid the helmsman and some of which impede progress, and a good sailor must take advantage of the former and adjust to the latter. Likewise, the global order opens up opportunities for poverty reduction and democratization as well as impedes them, and wise leaders and peoples discern the difference. Furthermore, the good sailor tacks back and forth in the face of the wind, taking advantage of it for forward progress and not bucking it directly. Likewise, a developing country can find ways to take advantage of and "manage" normally adverse global factors. For instance, a cutback on U.S. aid in Costa Rica enabled Costa Rica to be less dependent on the United States. Additionally, sometimes a headwind changes and becomes a tailwind. Then the global forces and rich country impacts coincide with and supplement internal development efforts. Finally, just as some boats are better than others with respect to resourcefulness, navigability, and stability, so some countries, owing to such things as natural endowments, governance, and human and social "capital," develop further and faster than others.

The moral of this nautical story is clear: Just as the national development efforts vary from time to time and place to place, so do the impacts of the global order and the rich countries that dominate this order. While the wind is always a factor in sailing (sometimes more, sometimes less, sometimes good, sometimes bad, often both), so is the skill of the captain and crew (and their ability to work together). Empirical investigation is important to determine which way and how hard the wind is blowing and how best to use national skills and resources to reach a society's destination. Pogge recognizes the variability of internal factors; in his less careful formulations, he fails to recognize the variability and complexity of external factors, the changing balance between external and internal factors, and the always important and sometimes crucial role of internal factors.

This debate over the chief causes of development failure is closely linked to sharp disagreements over the moral appraisal of globalization and the identification of "agents of justice."[36] Does globalization doom or guarantee good national and local development? Does globalization offer blessings and opportunities as well as miseries and risks? Is it up to developing nation-states and local communities to seize the good and avoid the bad of a globalizing world? Or should the main agents of justice be the rich nations, transnational corporations, and global institutions? In the following sections, I shall follow Stiglitz and argue that "today, the challenge is to get the balance right . . . between collective action at the local, national, and global levels."[37]

Part II: Globalization and Democratization

Development ethics faces the new and pressing task of understanding and ethically evaluating "globalization" and proposing ethically appropriate institutional responses to this complex and contested phenomenon. The debate about globalization since the late 1990s reminds one of earlier controversies about development. Like the term "development" in the 1960s through mid-1990s, globalization has become a cliché and buzzword that the mainstream celebrates and dissenters condemn. Moreover, like development, globalization challenges ethicists to move beyond simplistic views—such as "globalization is (exceedingly) good" or "globalization is (terribly) bad"—and to analyze leading interpretations of the nature, causes, consequences, and the value of globalization. Development ethicists, committed to understanding and reducing human deprivation, will be especially concerned to assess (and defend norms for assessing) globalization's impact on individual and communal well-being and to identify those types of globalization that are least threatening to or most promising for human development.

It is important to ask and sketch out the answers to four questions about globalization:

- What is globalization?
- What are the leading interpretations of globalization? What explains globalization and how unique is it in relation to earlier forms of integration? Does globalization result in the demise, resurgence, or transformation of state power? Does globalization eliminate, accentuate, or transform the North/South divide?
- How should (different sorts of) globalization be assessed ethically? Does globalization (or some of its different varieties) undermine, constrain, enable, or promote ethically defensible development?
- Can and should globalization be resisted, contested, modified, or transformed? If so, why? And, finally, how, if at all, should globalization be humanized and democratized?

What Is Globalization?

First, what should we mean by globalization? Just as it is useful to demarcate development generically as "beneficial social change" prior to assessing particular normative approaches to the ends and means of development, so it is helpful to have a (fairly) neutral concept of globalization. David Held, Anthony McGrew, David Goldblatt, and Jonathan Perraton have suggested an informal definition useful for this purpose: "Globalization may be thought of as the widening, deepening and speeding up of worldwide interconnectedness in all aspects of contemporary social life, from the cultural to the criminal, the financial to the spiritual."[38] More rigorously, the same authors characterize globalization as "A process (or set of processes) which embodies a transformation in the spatial organization of social relations and transactions—assessed in terms of their extensity, intensity, velocity and impact—generation of transcontinental or interregional flows and networks of activity, interaction, and the exercise of power."[39]

Three Interpretations of Globalization

Interpretations or theories of globalization—which all contain historical, empirical, and normative components—differ with respect to (1) the number, variety, and relation of processes or flows, for example, tokens (money), physical artifacts, people, symbols, and information; (2) causation: monocausal or reductive (economic or technological) approaches versus multicausal or nonreductive approaches; (3) character: inevitability versus contingency and open-endedness; (4) consequences, for example, the impact on state sovereignty and the division of countries into North or South; and (5) desirability (and criteria for assessment).

Although no one generally accepted theory of globalization has emerged, at least three interpretations or models of globalization are offered. Following Held et al., I label these approaches (1) hyperglobalism, (2) skepticism, and (3) transformationalism.[40]

Hyperglobalism, illustrated by journalist Thomas L. Friedman[41] and trade economist Jagdish Bhagwati,[42] conceives of globalization as a qualitatively unique global age of economic (capitalist) integration characterized by open trade, global financial flows, "outsourcing" of work to producers in other countries, and multinational corporations. Driven by capitalism, communications, and transportation technology, integration into one world market is increasingly eroding state power and legitimacy. The hierarchical North–South dichotomy will be rapidly replaced by a "flat" global entrepreneurial order structured by a "level playing field" and new global "rules of the game," such as those of the World Trade Organization (WTO). Although hyperglobalism concedes that there are short-term losers as well as winners, it insists that the rising global tide will eventually lift all national and individual boats—except for those who resist the all-but-inevitable progress. *Newsweek* editor Fareed Zakaria, sympathetically reviewing Thomas Friedman's recent book *The World Is Flat*, observes

> He [Friedman] ends up, wisely, understanding that there's no way to stop the [globalization] wave. You cannot switch off these forces except at great cost to your own economic well-being. Over the past century, those countries that tried to preserve their systems, jobs, culture or traditions by keeping the rest of the world out all stagnated. Those that opened themselves up to the world prospered.[43]

Commenting on Bhagwati, economist Richard N. Cooper exactly captures the normative dimension of hyperglobalism:

> His [Bhagwati's] main thesis is that economic globalization is an unambiguously good thing, with a few downsides that thought and effort can mitigate. His sec-

ondary thesis is that globalization does not need to be given a "human face"; it already has one. . . . His conclusion: that the world, particularly its poorest regions, needs more globalization, not less.[44]

At least when development is identified with economic growth, "global integration," as Dani Rodrik observes, "has become, for all practical purposes, a substitute for a development strategy."[45] According to this view, governmental attention and resources should be focused on rapidly (and often painfully) removing tariffs and other devices that block access to the globalizing world. Tony Blair succinctly expresses the hyperglobalist faith:

> [We] have an enormous job to do to convince the sincere and well-motivated opponents of the WTO agenda that the WTO can be, indeed is, a friend of development, and that far from impoverishing the world's poorer countries, trade liberalization is the only sure route to the kind of economic growth needed to bring their prosperity closer to that of the major developed economies.[46]

Skepticism rejects hyperglobalism's view that global economic integration is (or should be) taking place and that states are (or should be) getting weaker. Skeptics argue that regional trading blocs are (or should be) getting stronger; resurgent fundamentalisms either insulate themselves from or clash with alien cultures, including those shaped by North American consumerism; and national governments are (or should be) getting stronger. These skeptics of hyperglobalism include Stephen Krasner,[47] Paul Hirst and Grahame Thompson,[48] and Samuel Huntington.[49] In a more explicitly normative version of skepticism, Herman Daly concedes that hyperglobalist trends exist, but argues that states should be "brought back in," should resist economic openness, and should emphasize national and local well-being.[50] Instead of extinguishing the North–South divide, skeptics argue that economic integration, cross-boundary financial investment, the digital revolution, and multinational power mire poor countries in the South in even greater poverty. Rodrik, for example, argues that

> By focusing on international integration, governments in poor nations will divert human resources, administrative capabilities, and political capital away from more urgent development priorities such as education, public health, industrial capacity, and social cohesions. This emphasis also undermines nascent democratic institutions by removing the choice of development strategy from public debate.[51]

Marxist skeptics contend that the hyperglobalist thesis is a myth that rich and developed countries perpetrate to maintain and deepen their global dominance over poor countries. Countries—especially poor and transitional ones—must resist the Sirens of economic and cultural openness; instead, they should aim for national or regional sufficiency and develop themselves by their own lights. Authoritarian skeptics endorse efforts—such as those of Fidel Castro in Cuba or Hugo Chavez in Venezuela—to centralize power, bring top-down improvement in living standards, and weaken civil society. Liberal skeptics emphasize that national sovereignty, with its demanding duties of justice, cannot and should not be replaced by global economic or political institutions that either lack sovereignty or threaten global tyranny. Democratic skeptics promote dispersed and local control, target health and education, and promote public deliberation about development ends and means. The variants of skepticism conceive of globalization as something inimical to genuine development.

Transformationalism, such as Held and his colleagues advocate, conceives of recent globalization as a historically unprecedented and powerful set of processes (with multiple causes) that is making the world more interconnected and organizationally multileveled. They argue that it is too simple to say that states are either being eroded or reinforced; it is more accurate to conclude that states are (and should be) reconstituting themselves in a world order increasingly populated by global and regional economic, political (regulatory), cultural institutions, and by social movements.

Transformationalists insist that globalization is not one thing—and certainly not merely economic—but many processes with diverse consequences. The new economic (trade, finance, multinational corporations), political, cultural, criminal, and technological global processes proceed on multiple, sometimes interlinked, and often uneven tracks. Rather than being inexorable and unidirectional, globalization is contingent, open, and multidirectional. Rather than uniformly integrating communities, globalization results in new global and regional exclusions as well as novel inclusions, new winners, and new losers. The nation-state is increasingly reconstituted in relation to regional, hemispheric, and global institutions; the old North–South dichotomy is being replaced by a trichotomy of elite/contented/marginalized that cuts across the old North–South polarity (and justifies development ethics confronting poverty wherever it exists):

> North and South are increasingly becoming meaningless categories: under conditions of globalization distributional patterns of power and wealth no longer accord with a simple core and periphery division of the world, as in the early twentieth century, but reflect a new geography of power and privilege which transcends political borders and regions, reconfiguring established international and transnational hierarchies of social power and wealth.[52]

Just as development ethicists have stressed that development—while complex and multicausal—is a pattern of institutionalized human activity that can and should be a matter of voluntary, humanizing, and democratic collective choice, so transformationalists emphasize that globalization can and should be civilized and democratized. Transformationalists are both less enthusiastic than hyperglobalists and less pessimistic than skeptics. Transformationalists insist that a globalizing world shows neither the uniform good that the hyperglobalists celebrate nor the unmitigated evil that worries the skeptics. Instead, globalization at times impedes, and at times enables, good human and communal development.

Ethical Assessment of Globalization

Regardless of how globalization—its nature, causes, and consequences—is understood, development ethics must evaluate it ethically. Throughout its history, development ethics has emphasized ethical assessment of the goals, institutions, and strategies of national development and constructively proposed better alternatives. In a globalizing world, development ethics takes on the additional task of offering an ethical appraisal of globalization and suggesting better ways of managing new and evolving global interconnectedness.

How is this evaluation to be done? There are both empirical and normative aspects of inquiry. Globalization's multiple, often uneven, and frequently changing influences on individuals and communities admit of empirical investigation, while deciding which consequences are ethically significant requires the application of ethical criteria and a theory of global as well as national justice. Absent from much investigation into globalization are precisely the efforts to clarify and defend criteria to identify whether and in what ways globalization is good or bad for human beings, enhances or limits freedom, violates or respects human rights, and/or unfairly or fairly distributes benefits and burdens within and between nations. It is not enough to inquire how or why globalization affects human choice and institutional distribution. One must also have a reasoned normative view of what counts as beneficial and deleterious consequences, and how justice should be understood.[53]

The most promising approach to such explicitly normative dimensions of development ethics is, I believe, the "agent-oriented" capability perspective discussed briefly above. Applying a conception of the human as agent and of human well-being as a plurality of capabilities and functionings that humans have good reason to value, the capability development ethicist can inquire into the effects different kinds of globalization have on everyone's agency and capabilities for living lives that are—among other things—long, healthy, secure, socially engaged, and politically participatory. Because these valuable capabilities (or functionings) are the basis for human rights and duties, a development ethic will also examine how globalization is a help or a hindrance as individuals and institutions fulfill their moral duties to respect rights. The long-term goal of good national and global development must be to secure an adequate level of agency and morally basic capabilities for everyone in the world—regardless of nationality, ethnicity, age, gender, or sexual preference.

With a multifaceted notion of globalization, some kinds of globalization, for instance, such global phenomena as a worldwide network of illegal drug distribution, sex tourism, forced migrations, and HIV/AIDS are bad and should be resisted. Other kinds of globalization, such as the global dispersion of human rights and democratic norms, are good and should be promoted. Most kinds of globalization, such as open trade, financial liberalization, foreign direct investments, outsourcing of work, and multinationals, are a mixed blessing. The extent to which these sorts of globalization enhance, secure, or restore agency and human capabilities will depend on context and especially on a reform of global institutions and how a national polity integrates and shapes global forces.

I contend that an agency and capability approach judges both hyperglobalism and skepticism as empirically one-sided and normatively deficient. Nation-states are neither obsolete entities of the past nor possess a monopoly on global agency. A globalizing world weakens some states and strengthens others, and all states find themselves interconnected. The capability approach challenges national and subnational communities to protect, promote, and restore human capabilities, among them the capabilities for political participation. The energy-focused capability approach also challenges both territorial and nonterritorial political communities in two related ways. First, territorial political communities and transnational agencies—the European Union, UN, WTO, World Bank, International Commission of Human Rights, Human Rights Watch, and International Criminal Court (ICC)—are responsible for setting policies that improve the chances of all persons to live decent lives. Second, these overlapping political communities should themselves be "civilized and democratized."[54] These communities must be venues in which people exercise their agency and have substantive freedoms, including some kind of political participation and democratic deliberation. They should also be imaginatively restructured so as to achieve greater democratic accountability:

> National boundaries have traditionally demarcated the basis on which individuals are included and excluded from participation in decisions affecting their lives; but if many socioeconomic processes, and the outcomes of decisions about them, stretch beyond national frontiers, then the implications of this are serious, not only for the categories of consent and legitimacy but for all the key ideas of democracy. At issue is the nature of a political community—how should the proper boundaries of a political community be drawn in a more regional and

global order? In addition, questions can be raised about the meaning of representation (who should represent whom and on what basis?) and about the proper form and scope of political participation (who should participate and in what way?)[55]

As Held and his colleagues insist, the new normative challenge is "how to combine a system of territorially rooted [and deepened] democratic governance with the transnational and global organization of social and economic life."[56] Part of this challenge is that of deciding each governance level's responsibilities, whether unique or shared.

Humanizing and Democratizing Globalization: Three Projects

Development ethicists have identified three projects that respond to the normative challenges presented by globalization. If development ethics has the task, as Denis Goulet once observed, of "keeping hope alive," one way to do so is to identify best practices and promising projects for globalization with a human and democratic face.

1) *Liberal internationalism.* One project—expressed for example in the Commission on Global Governance's *Our Global Neighbourhood*—aims at incremental reform of the existing international system of sovereign nation-states and international organizations and regimes.[57] Popular governance takes place in nation-states in which democracy is either initiated or made more robust. In addition, argues Nagel, sovereign governments have unique duties to protect not only the civil and bodily but also the socioeconomic rights or their citizens.[58] In the face of cross-border threats of various kinds, nation-states can and should cooperate in regional and global trade, and in financial, military, legal, environmental, and cultural institutions. To protect national self-interest and sovereignty, national governments try to negotiate favorable loans and loan forgiveness with international financial institutions (IFIs). The ICC came into being in early 2002 when a treaty, which national delegates signed in Rome in 1998, was ratified by over sixty national governments. The ICC has jurisdiction over war crimes and other violations of internationally recognized human rights only when a nation-state is unwilling or unable to try its own citizens for war crimes or crimes against humanity. It is anticipated that, with the existence of the ICC, the UN will increasingly represent the will of the majority of participating states and not (so much) the members of the Security Council. Although human individuals have rights and responsibilities and international bodies have responsibilities, the rights and duties of nation-states are the most fundamental.

2) *Radical republicanism*, expressed systematically by Richard Falk's *On Humane Governance: Toward a New Global Politics* and more fervently by many

antiglobalizers, seeks to weaken—if not dismantle—existing nation-states and international institutions in favor of self-governing alternatives and largely local communities committed to the public good and harmony with the natural environment.[59] The current global order is inherently unjust, for it systematically favors affluent nations and corporations and is stacked against poor nations, peoples, and individuals. Giving priority to the empowerment of grassroots and indigenous communities that resist and struggle against the many forms of globalization, this bottom-up approach (ironically enough) utilizes communications technology to enable grassroots groups to become a global civil society of concern and action. One can anticipate or hope that institutions such as the World Bank will become obsolete or decentralized. An elite-dominated ICC would be no better and perhaps worse than national judicial processes. Indigenous communities, whether or not located within only one nation-state, should govern themselves according to their own rules and traditions. Democracy, largely direct and local, must operate on the basis of consensus.

3) *Cosmopolitan democracy* seeks to "reconstitute" rather than reform (liberal internationalism) or abolish (radical republicanism) the current system of global governance. This reconstitution, to be guided by an evolving "cosmopolitan democratic law," consists in a "double democratization."[60] First, nation-states should either initiate or deepen and widen both direct and representative democratic rule. Such internal democratization will include some devolution of power to constituent territorial units and civil society. Rather than merely periodic voting, democracy should include public debate and democratic deliberation from top to bottom.[61] Second, one can anticipate that nation-states would come to share sovereignty with transnational bodies of various sorts (regional, intercontinental, and global), and these bodies themselves would be brought under democratic control. Although the details will vary with the organization, this cosmopolitan democratizing will institutionalize popular and deliberative participation in institutions such as the UN and the WTO, in regional development banks and IFIs, and in the ICC and such bodies as North Atlantic Free Trade Agreement.[62]

Necessary for this institutional democratization will be new and complex individual moral identities and a new ideal of multiple citizenship.[63] People would no longer view themselves as nothing more than members of a particular local, ethnic, religious, or national group, but rather as human beings with responsibilities for all people. And one can anticipate that citizenship will become multilayered and complex—from neighborhood citizenship, through national citizenship (often in more than one nation-state), to regional and world or "cosmopolitan" citizenship":

> Citizenship in a democratic polity of the future . . . is likely to involve a growing mediating role: a role which encompasses dialogue with the traditions and discourses of others with the aim of expanding the horizons of one's own framework of meaning and increasing the scope of mutual understanding. Political agents who can "reason from the point of view of others" will be better equipped to resolve, and resolve fairly, the new and challenging trans-boundary issues and processes that create overlapping communities of fate.[64]

Regardless of scope, citizenship is neither trivial nor absolute. Each kind of citizenship is partially constituted by a commitment to human rights, including the right of democratic participation, and the duty to promote human development at every level of human organization:

> Democracy for the new millennium must allow cosmopolitan citizens to gain access to, mediate between and render accountable the social, economic and political processes and flows that cut across and transform their traditional community boundaries. The core of this project involves reconceiving legitimate political authority in a manner which disconnects it from its traditional anchor in fixed borders and delimited territories and, instead, articulates it as an attribute of basic democratic arrangements or basic democratic law which can, in principle, be entrenched and drawn on in diverse self-regulating associations—from cities and subnational regions, to nation-states, regions and wider global networks.[65]

How should we assess these three political projects for humanely responding to globalization and what might be the relations among them? Each of the three projects has different emphases and normative commitments. One task of development ethicists and others is to weigh the advantages and disadvantages of each approach and to examine whether the three projects are mutually exclusive or, in some way, may be combined. Liberal internationalism has current institutional salience and can become a starting point and platform for (as well as a constraint on) the more substantive changes that local and cosmopolitan democracy require. Radical republicans rightly insist on the importance of local and deep democracy. Cosmopolitan democrats share many democratic and participatory values with radical republicans, but the former judge the latter as too utopian about grassroots reform that is not accompanied by "double democratization" and too pessimistic about the democratic potential of transnational institutions. On the agenda for development ethicists and others is the pressing question of whether national government—in contrast to both subnational and global institutions—has distinctive duties of justice with respect to protecting the socioeconomic rights of their citizens.

Insofar as the globalization processes are neither inexorable nor fixed, development ethics must consider, then, the kinds of globalization most likely to benefit human beings as well as the best ways to humanize and democratize it. Such an inquiry, we have seen, requires that one have criteria for normative appraisal as well as a basis for assigning duties to the various agents of development and globalization. The challenges of globalization expand—rather than narrow—the agenda of development ethics. Interdisciplinary and cross-cultural dialogue and forums of democratic deliberation allow development ethics to understand and secure genuinely human development at all levels of political community and in all kinds of regional and global institutions. As Sen remarks in concluding "How to Judge Globalism":

> The central issue of contention is not globalization itself, nor is it the use of the market as an institution, but the inequity in the overall balance of institutional arrangements—which produces very unequal sharing of the benefits of globalization. The question is not just whether the poor, too, gain something from globalization, but whether they get a fair share and a fair opportunity. There is an urgent need for reforming institutional arrangements—in addition to national ones—to overcome both the errors of omission and those of commission that tend to give the poor across the world such limited opportunities. Globalization deserves a reasoned defense, but it also needs reform.[66]

Part III: Stiglitz as Ethicist of
Development, Globalization, and Democratization

Joseph E. Stiglitz, like Sen, is both a Nobel Laureate in economics and has addressed the moral dimensions of development in a globalizing world. In two recent books and several articles, Stiglitz criticizes mainstream (Washington Consensus) commitments to free-market liberalism and offers "a new paradigm for development," which he calls "development as transformation."[67] In defending this new approach, Stiglitz formulates answers to some of the basic questions in development ethics. He also seeks to resolve some of its controversies, applies his normative vision to assess the goods and bads of globalization, and proposes a development strategy to "reshape" both globalization and democratization so as to make them more "humane, effective, and equitable."[68] In very broad strokes, which will miss many nuances in his position, I sketch Stiglitz's views on each of these issues and begin the assessment that his approach deserves.

Development as Transformation

Considered descriptively, development "represents a transformation of society"[69]: "It embraces a movement from traditional relations, traditional cultures and social norms, traditional ways of dealing with health and education, traditional methods of production, to more 'modern' ways."[70] Rather than accepting the world as it is, the modern perspective acknowledges "that we, as individuals and societies, can take actions that, for instance, reduce infant mortality, extend lifespan and increase productivity."[71]

Considered normatively, ethically based development assumes that individuals should engage in collective action that results in "sustainable, equitable, and democratic growth"[72]: "Development is about transforming societies, improving the lives of the poor, enabling everyone to have a chance at success and access to health care and education."[73] Such transforming action will require, among other things, a "systematic change" in global, national, and local institutions.

Ethical Principles

What values and moral commitments should inform this new vision and guide this transforming practice? What should be the most fundamental goals of development policies in a "world of globalization"?[74] To answer these questions, Stiglitz engages in a form of development ethics, which he designates as "practical ethics" about matters of development. It is practical in three senses. First, Stiglitz sets forth five ethical principles but only minimally clarifies or defends them. For instance, he explicitly says that he will not attempt to derive his principles from higher-order principles, although he states "one could articulate these views within a Rawlian [sic] framework, but I shall not do so here."[75] Unlike Sen who painstakingly explains and defends his normative concepts of agency, capability, and functioning as alternatives to utilitarian and Rawlsian theories, Stiglitz quickly gets down to the work of applying his principles. Second, Stiglitz explains that he has designed the ethical principles for the world as it is, assuming that people are often selfish and that human institutions are always imperfect. One implication of this view is that Stiglitz—although he insists that narrow self-interest and moral imperatives often diverge—seeks incentives for individuals to do the right thing. Another implication is that political institutions should include checks and balances.[76] Third, Stiglitz's ethic is pragmatic in the tradition of American pragmatism; in selecting and seeking implementation of ethical principles, he takes their likely consequences into account.

I noted in Part I that development ethicists sometimes differ with respect to the content of the ethical principles they use to evaluate current development policies and practices and advocate alternatives. For Stiglitz, when development agents at local, national, and global levels seek to transform a society, they have five fundamental obligations or should aim for five high-priority goals: "honesty, fairness, social justice (including a concern for the poor), externalities, and responsibility."[77] Not wedded to virtues, goals, or duties, Stiglitz alternatively formulates his moral vision in terms of first- and second-generation rights.[78] In what follows, I have reordered the list, subsumed "externalities" under a more general principle (protection of life and promotion of security), and added a sixth principle increasingly prominent in Stiglitz's writing—namely, the duty to promote democracy and respect a person's right to participate in decisions that affect her life.

First, Stiglitz affirms the ethical norm of responsibility: "Responsibility is the ethical norm that individuals should take responsibility for their own actions and for the consequences of those actions."[79] I suggest that this principle is best understood as the moral companion to Stiglitz's assumption that persons can act individually and collectively so as to make a difference in the world. Not only is it true that "we, as individuals and societies, can take actions" that have good or bad effects, but we should be held morally accountable—praised or blamed—for voluntary actions and their foreseeable consequences. Individuals and groups, not condemned to be the pawns of impersonal forces or the designs of others, are agents who can and should take charge of their own destiny.[80] Stiglitz's emphasis on persons as morally responsible accords with Sen's conception, referred to above, of citizens as agents and his participatory, "agent-oriented" ideal of development:

> The need for broadening the instruments for sustainable development is certainly strong: participatory ethics and citizenship are clearly important in this broadening. But ethics not only has instrumental importance—it can change what we have reason to value. To see a person as a citizen is to take a particular view of humanity—not to see the person just as a creature whose well-being is of relevance; we have to understand a person as a reasoning being who thinks and values and decides and acts. . . . The idea of citizenship brings out the need to see people as reasoning agents, not merely as beings whose needs have to be fulfilled or whose standard of living must be preserved. It also identifies the importance of public participation not just for its social effectiveness, but also for the value of that process in itself.[81]

Second, implicit in Stiglitz's writings is that institutions and especially national governments have a duty to protect human life and property and to provide security against standard threats—for instance, the state itself and the depredations by the rich and powerful. This duty to protect subsumes a duty that Stiglitz explicitly asserts—a development agent's version of the Hippocratic oath: "This above all else: We should do no harm."[82]

Third, development agents have a duty of social justice in the sense of reducing poverty, especially that of the poorest of the poor. Although Stiglitz could deepen his account by following Sen and distinguishing various forms of capability deprivation from income poverty, both Stiglitz and Sen insist that everyone should be able to live—and have the right to live—a minimally decent life. Like Sen, Stiglitz emphasizes that for most persons this "equality of opportunity" requires employment options as well as the provision of education and health. Stiglitz unremittingly criticizes both IFIs and national governments for insufficiently attending to the impact of policies on the poor and not adequately emphasizing poverty alleviation. For example, development agents, contends Stiglitz, should find the right balance between proemployment and anti-inflation policies, but the Washington Consensus overemphasizes the latter and pays too little attention to the former—with the result of increasing the misery of the poor.

Fourth, Stiglitz embraces fairness as an ethical principle. Whereas justice, for Stiglitz, concerns the capability of all to attain an absolute threshold, fairness is a comparative notion. Development agents have the duty not to discriminate on the basis of morally irrelevant features such as gender, race, caste, and religious affiliation. Moreover, development agents at every level should ensure both that development policies and institutions benefit the poor more than the rich and that the rich share more burdens and risks than the poor (because they can afford it more than the poor). Again, the Washington Consensus turns things upside down. The International Monetary Fund's (IMF's) insistence on developing country deficit reduction and loan repayment unfairly benefits rich lending institutions more than it does developing countries. It is poor borrowers and not rich lenders that bear the greatest risks in loan agreements. The rich countries keep their own trade barriers high, especially with respect to agriculture, but unfairly and hypocritically require poor countries to open their markets to rich country exports.[83] The United States wants other countries to abide by the "rule of law" but accepts another standard for itself: "It is in favor of the rule of law, as long as the outcomes conform with what it wants."[84]

Fifth, development agents at all levels—whether public or private—have the duty to be honest and transparent. Citizens and other individuals affected have the right to know what governments and other public institutions are doing and why. Most governments and IFIs thrive on secrecy, for secrecy is a useful way to hide mistakes, avoid criticism, give inappropriate favor to special interests, and give officials undue discretion.[85] Stiglitz's technical work in the economics of asymmetric information (in which people's having unequal information results in inefficiency and unfair disadvantage results) enables him to see the importance of governmental openness. Not only does secrecy open the door to corruption, but it also undermines confidence in government and democracy itself. Rule by the people is impossible if citizens are kept in the dark: "Meaningful participation in democratic processes requires informed participants."[86] How could the American (and other) people have deliberated adequately the pros and cons of the U.S. invasion of Iraq if the U.S. government misrepresented the threats involved with Iraq's (nonexistent) weapons of mass destruction? The IFI (such as the World Bank and the IMF) advisors to developing countries are morally obligated to indicate how much their advice is dependent on forecasts based on sketchy evidence. Necessary are not merely legal or moral codes and sunshine laws, but also a "culture of openness, where the presumption is that the public should know about and participate in all collective decisions."[87] Important means to such transparency are, for Stiglitz, "an active and free press"[88] and venues for public discussion (including discussion on the legitimate limitation of openness).

Stiglitz's "openness" principle points back to his social justice principle and ahead to his democracy principle. More openness in the national governments as well as IFIs are likely to result in decisions that are more favorable to the poor than at present and lend less cover to the interests of the rich and powerful: "More open and representative deliberation, more open and fuller discussion, would most likely have led to different policies being pursued [during the East Asian economic crisis of 1997], policies that would at the very least have subjected the poor and vulnerable to less risk."[89] The duty of honesty and the right to know is both valuable in itself and contributes to democratic processes, for "secrecy reduces the information available to the citizenry, hobbling their ability to participate meaningfully."[90]

Although Stiglitz does not include it in his formal list of principles, he suggests elsewhere that government leaders and development agents have the duty to empower individuals "to participate meaningfully in the decisions concerning the collective actions that have such profound effects on their lives and livelihoods."[91] We can call this the duty to promote and protect democracy, for Stiglitz agrees with John Dewey, Amartya Sen, and deliberative democrats, among others, that democracy is public discussion as well as voting: "Democracy is more than just periodic elections; it entails ensuring that all voices are heard, and there is a deliberative process"[92] "in which different views and voices are heard and taken into account"[93] and in which "you must persuade others of the rightness of your views, not bully them."[94] Democracy is a process that enables individuals to exercise their right to run their own lives. They do so in and through dialogue with each other as they seek more or less consensus about some policy or action that will affect them all. Without inclusive participation and democratic deliberation, governments and IFI experts impose their wills from above and outside, creating resentment and divisiveness. With inclusive and deliberative participation, citizens are likely to forge a just policy suitable to their circumstances. Participatory processes are also likely to result in "ownership," that is, to "elicit commitment and demo-cratic involvement that is necessary for development to be socially acceptable and sustainable."[95]

One implication of this democracy principle is that IFIs and their economic advisors should not authoritatively prescribe from above the "right choice" let alone "impose" change from the outside. Rather, outsiders should identify an array of options for a developing country, always honestly pointing out likely benefits and burdens—especially those for the poor. Stiglitz defends this view by remarking that people "cannot be forced to change their hearts or minds; or, indeed, their basic attitudes and values."[96] A strategic implication is the im-portance of education, including civic education, security, and health if citi-zens are to be informed, safe, and sufficiently healthy to participate politically.

These six ethical principles form the abstract normative component of Stiglitz's paradigm of development as transformation. They also provide the basis for his ethical evaluation of globalization, his critique of the Washington Consensus, and his design of alternative institutions and strategies for "glob-alization with a more human face."[97]

Globalization

How does Stiglitz interpret and evaluate globalization? By "globalization," Stiglitz means not only "the removal of barriers to free trade and closer inte-gration of national economies,"[98] but also closer links and more rapid inter-actions among the "peoples of the world."[99] The less impeded and faster "flows" between countries and peoples include not only goods, services, capi-tal, and peoples, but also knowledge and values. Among the causes of global-ization are reduced costs of boundary-crossing transportation and communi-cation and the reduction of "artificial" restrictions such as trade barriers, immigration restrictions, and intellectual property rights.

Where does Stiglitz stand with respect to the debate, described in Part II above, among hyperglobalists, skeptics, and transformationalists? Stiglitz is fundamentally a transformationalist—that is, he believes that globalization is neither the unalloyed good that "hyperglobalists" celebrate nor the unmiti-gated evil that antiglobalist skeptics condemn. Sometimes Stiglitz expresses his third way by saying that "globalization itself is neither good nor bad."[100] He formulates his view more perspicuously, however, when he asserts that—from the standpoint of his moral principles—globalization is a mixture of good and evil. Although it has yielded some good and has the power to bring about much more that is beneficial, integration (of countries and peoples) in its cur-rent form has resulted in widespread and unconscionable harm. These nega-tive consequences are largely—but not exclusively—due to the fact that rich countries have shaped globalization for their own benefits or, more precisely, for the benefit of their powerful elites.

Informing and justifying this global dominance is a dogmatic "mind-set," which Stiglitz variously terms the "Washington Consensus," "free market ideology,"[101] and "market fundamentalism."[102] This approach puts great emphasis on markets and significantly reduces and even demonizes the role of governments. As a condition for loans and bailouts, IMF prescribes one (and only one) package: a country should cut government spending or raise taxes, balance its budget (cut deficits and attack inflation), raise interest rates, cut wages, liberalize trade, deregulate capital markets, encourage foreign investment, sell off government-owned enterprises, and pay back its loans.[103]

This kind of increasing economic integration, argues Stiglitz, has enabled some nations and peoples to find markets for their goods and gain access to more, better, and cheaper imported goods. With cheaper and faster communication and travel, remote regions have overcome their isolation and taken advantage of new commodities and ideas. A global civil society has helped diffuse and institutionalize human rights as well as improve approaches to poverty alleviation and democratization.

In spite of these and other benefits, Stiglitz argues that globalization has a "darker side."[104] The particular package of policies pushed by IMF and the U.S. Treasury Department has contributed—knowingly if not intentionally—to innumerable but unnecessary harms.

What is the bad of globalization?[105] The number of income-poor people in the 1990s has increased by more than one hundred million people (to 1.31 billion). Unemployment and poor health is high and growing, with Russia and many African countries as the most painful examples. Even if Friedman—in his book *The World Is Flat*—is right and globalization is "flattening the world," Stiglitz, in his review of Friedman's book, insists that when we disaggregate, it is painfully clear that not every individual or locale in the North or the South is better off:

> While free trade may ultimately make every country better off, not every individual will be better off. There are winners and there are losers; and while, in principle, the winners could compensate the losers, that typically does not happen. Among other things, a flatter world means a less flat America—more inequality.
>
> The playing field may be getting more level, but not everyone is equipped to play on it. On . . . [a recent] trip to India, I spent more than half my time in the countryside surrounding Bangalore, where traveling 10 miles was like traveling back 2,000 years. Peasants were farming as their ancestors must have. What has enabled Bangalore to become a high tech success story is that companies like Infosys have removed themselves from what is going on nearby. They communi-

cate directly by satellite with the United States, and in a place where local newspapers list the number of brownouts the previous day, these companies can have their own sources of power. And while new technologies may close the gap between parts of India and China and the advanced industrial countries, they will also increase the gap between those countries and Africa.

Mr. Friedman is right that there are forces flattening the world, but there are other forces making it less flat. At issue is the balance between them.[106]

Even when the poor become less poor, they often do not attain a minimally decent level that justice requires, and the gap between the poor and their rich fellow citizens is increasing. To repay debts to foreign lenders and balance country budgets, state provisioning for health, education, and job creation are cut. Forced privatization results in government-owned enterprises sold at favorable prices to the rich and well connected—who, in turn, either strip the enterprises of their assets or set up mafia-linked monopolies. Lack of a regulatory framework opens the door to corruption. Given the upsurge in drug traffickers, sex traders, and crony capitalists, crime increases and human security decreases. Urban and ethnic conflicts erupt when people are hungry and powerless. Democracy is undermined or never has a chance to emerge when foreign experts or national elites make the crucial decisions.

Suppose that Stiglitz is correct that the current shape of globalization has had these bad consequences.[107] Whom or what does he hold morally culpable? How does he address the controversy, which I noted in Part I, among development ethicists and economists with respect to both responsibility for failed development and duties to address the problems? Stiglitz happily avoids one-sided views that ascribe the ills of globalization exclusively to either internal or external factors. He vigorously indicts the Washington Consensus, but he believes that this ideology is shared by both external and internal development agents and financial decision makers. He finds much fault with national leaders and entrepreneurs not only when they implement—sometimes enthusiastically—neoliberalism, but also when they engage in corrupt or criminal practices. (Stiglitz also praises China, which resisted IMF prescriptions and "following its own course, showed there was an alternative path of transition which could succeed both in bringing the growth that markets promised and in markedly reducing poverty."[108]) Stiglitz lays the greatest blame, however, on the IFIs, the rich countries that control the IFIs, and the elite interests that often call the shots in rich countries: "Governments of the advanced industrial countries have tried to manage globalization in ways which benefit themselves, or more particularly special interests within their boundaries"[109] Even worse, these rich governments and special interests have not only been the dominant shapers of globalization, but have also unfairly reaped globalization's goods at the expense of poor countries and peoples.

If rich countries and IFIs are to be guided by ethics, they must recognize that sometimes—especially when there is an asymmetry of information and power between actors—what is right and just diverges from the advantaged actor's (short-termed) self-interest: "When one is in such a situation, do not necessarily do what is in your own self-interest. Think about the moral dimensions of our actions, how the poor and weak are likely to suffer or benefit."[110]

Appealing here to his ethical principles, Stiglitz concludes:

In the way they have sought to shape globalization, the advanced industrial countries have violated some basic ethical norms.[111]

It [U.S. global strategy] was based on pressuring countries in the Third World to adopt policies that were markedly different from those that we ourselves had adopted—to adopt the market fundamentalist policies that represented everything at home that the Clinton administration was fighting against. It was based on our putting aside principles—principles of social justice, equity, fairness, that we stressed at home—to get the best bargain we could for American special interests.[112]

Humanizing and Democratizing Globalization

Given his ethical principles and his diagnosis of the source of globalization's harms and benefits, Stiglitz advocates a "new framework" for—and the radical reform of—global and national institutions. Stiglitz is a transformationalist (in Held's sense) because globalization has brought about the economic and cultural interdependence of hitherto more or less closed societies, and globalization—unlike the one-sided views of either the hyperglobalists or skeptics—is a mixture of goods and bads. He does not, however, fully qualify as a transformationalist in Held's sense. Whereas Stiglitz sees scant global "political integration," Held sees ways in which sovereign states are already being supplemented by global civil society and global quasi-political institutions. For Stiglitz, full transformationalism is a vision to be accomplished rather than institutions in the making. Stiglitz believes it is precisely because "economic globalization has outpaced political globalization"[113] that the world's nations and peoples through "collective action" can and should create "a polity in which shared values of democracy, social justice, and social solidarity play out on a global scale."[114]

How does Stiglitz propose that globalization "be radically rethought,"[115] "reshaped,"[116] and given "a more human face"[117]? How does Stiglitz's alternative to the Washington Consensus relate to the three humanization "projects" I discussed in Part II: liberal internationalism, radical republicanism, and cosmopolitan democracy?

Although Stiglitz's alternative vision shares features of each of these three projects, I believe Stiglitz's recommendations fit best within liberal internationalism. Stiglitz shares liberal internationalism's assumption that the global order is and will be composed of sovereign nation-states, global institutions (whose members represent nation-states), transnational corporations, and an emerging global civil society. Stiglitz's aim is to *reform* this global architecture. His recommended reforms are a good deal more than those current World Bank or IMF "reforms" that tend to be merely rhetorical, "half-hearted or half-baked,"[118] and pretty much carry on business as usual. Like liberal internationalism, however, Stiglitz does not propose that the current global order be abolished or radically "reconstituted." Incremental, slow-paced, and sequenced changes (and not "shock therapy") are called for because incremental change enables societies to transform themselves without destroying their cultural identity. Stiglitz's watchword is "get the balance right." There should be a gradual and incremental power shift from collective action at the local and nation-state level to collective action in global institutions,[119] but Stiglitz does not address adequately—as do Held et al. and Nagel in very different ways—the question of whether national sovereignty is being and should be reduced in favor of higher and lower centers of relative or quasi-sovereignty.

For Stiglitz, IFIs should not only reshape their tables and rearrange the chairs of those who come to the table, but they also should give more voice—if not voting rights—to representatives from poor countries. IFIs should also get the balance right between (1) respecting a recipient nation's right to decide its own path and (2) promoting a general strategy (within which the nation can make its own decisions). Instead of imposing economic reforms from above, IFIs should offer alternative strategies and honestly estimate each strategy's costs and benefits, especially for the poor and powerless. IFIs proactively also should adopt Stiglitz's paradigm of development as transformation and assist nation-states in getting their own balance right between the roles of state and market.[120] One way to do so is to forgive or alleviate a poor country's—often crushing—debt owed to private banks and IFIs. Rather than insist on loan repayments or relying on bailouts, IFIs should forgive debts, especially when banks made these loans to now-ousted dictators (who absconded with the money) or lent monies they knew were unlikely to be repaid. Another way is to reject the coercive offers and fungibility problems connected to tied or conditional aid in favor of selecting for assistance those countries that have taken development into their own hands and have performed well in the past.[121]

It should be stressed, however, that in Stiglitz's judgment both national governments and IFIs have responsibilities. Recognizing the dangers of completely unregulated capital markets and trade policy, IFIs should recommend and states should establish appropriate regulatory frameworks. Rejecting both left-wing

and right-wing views that see states and markets as mutually exclusive and exhaustive alternatives, Stiglitz argues that both IFIs and nation-states are obliged
to "get the balance right between government and market."[122] Although he does
not address Nagel's question of whether national governments have a unique
duty of justice with respect to their own citizens, Stiglitz consistently insists that
a responsible state should address market failures and promote social justice.[123]
Economic growth must be made "pro-poor" through state (and public/private)
provision of jobs, health care, and education. Although inflation hurts the poor,
job creation, poverty reduction, and low interest rates should be of greater
concern—except in cases of hyperinflation.

The "reformist" character of Stiglitz's proposal to humanize globalization
comes out clearly when we compare it with "radical republicanism," which advocates the elimination of nation-states and IFIs in favor of noncoercive networks of local, self-determining communities. Stiglitz does recognize the importance of what he calls "localization." This "demand for greater political,
fiscal, and administrative autonomy," he contends, is often an appropriate reaction to globalism and is "tied to the upsurge of participatory politics that
has given many people a voice and provided foci for organization."[124] But, for
Stiglitz, local improvements such as land reform and local governance require
the right kind of national infrastructure as well as supportive and regulative
polices. Stiglitz could bolster his argument by referring to the likelihood that
without the right kind of regulatory and democratic framework, local elites
would capture grassroots institutions.[125]

Yet Stiglitz's account is only beginning to make adequate room for the
role that grassroots, municipal, and province-wide innovations may play—
sometimes in partnership with national or international interventions.[126]
Moreover, some local groups show more ingenuity and resourcefulness than
others in taking advantage of the goods and avoiding the bads of globalization. In turn, these local experiments may set good examples for other communities at home and abroad. National and international institutions may
embrace and assist these local experiments and in turn promote them on
other local levels. Porto Alegre and other Brazilian cities' striking successes
with participatory budgeting, and Kerala, India's, renovation of the Pan-
chayet system are having impacts far beyond their locations of origin.[127]
Stiglitz could improve his framework by getting a better balance between
local and national/international transformation.

Recall that Held and his colleagues identified and endorsed cosmopolitan
democracy as a third project for humanizing globalization. This approach re-
tains a role—albeit diminished— for national governments but describes and
advocates more robust subnational and supranational collective action and
governance structures. Held et al. call for a "double democratization" in which

both global and national institutions install a "global democratic law" and consolidate democratic decision making that is more inclusive and deliberative than current exercises in collective choice. It might be better to call this project "multiple democratization" instead of cosmopolitan democracy, for Held et al. envisage transnational corporations and global civil society as additional venues for democratization.

Increasing indications exist that Stiglitz is taking steps toward this third approach to humanizing and democratizing globalization. In his most recent book, he calls his vision "democratic idealism," and as we have seen, his sixth ethical principle is that of inclusive and deliberative democratic decision making. Just as all people have a right to know, so they have a right to (help) decide those matters that affect them, to be the authors of their individual and collective destinies. Democracy should be deepened and broadened in both developed and developing countries. On the last page of *Globalization and Its Discontents*, Stiglitz goes beyond his liberal internationalism, saying that global institutions should become venues for a more inclusive and deeper democracy:

> Development is about transforming societies, improving the lives of the poor, enabling everyone to have a chance at success and access to health care and education.
>
> This sort of development won't happen if only a few people dictate the policies a country must follow. Making sure that democratic decisions are made means ensuring that a broad range of economists, officials, and experts from developing countries are actively involved in the debate. It also means that there must be broad participation that goes well beyond the experts and politicians. Developing countries must take charge of their own futures. But we in the West cannot escape our responsibilities. . . .
>
> The developed world needs to do its part to reform the international institutions that govern globalization.[128]

What more specifically does Stiglitz propose? Unfortunately, very little. Just when one expects that he will make his vision more determinant and describe how democracy might be deepened and broadened in our current international and national institutions, Stiglitz falls largely silent. He does make the general point that "governments must be willing to accept bounds on their sovereignty and act in concert" and that "to reap the benefits of globalization, it is necessary to have international institutions that put in place commonly agreed on and widely observed rules."[129] He does tell us that the World Bank and IMF should broaden voting rights or, short of that, include more nonvoting members at the table.[130] He does urge that IFIs fund independent think tanks in developing countries.[131] And, as noted above, Stiglitz recommends that IFIs do less prescribing and more offering of options (without strings attached).[132] But more attention is needed as to both the shared and the unique responsibilities of various development agents and how democratic decision making at all levels might—and should—be promoted, consolidated, deepened, and broadened. In Stiglitz's defense, it is not as if anyone (even Held and associates) has gone much further in specifying a vision of cosmopolitan democracy as a way of humanizing globalization. The challenge is one for Stiglitz and the rest of us who have been stimulated by his call to make globalization more democratic and more "humane, effective, and equitable."

To Stiglitz's credit, he does underscore a point that many (including Held et al.) either ignore or downplay: "Globalization also forces us to address issues of social justice at the global level."[133] Although Stiglitz does not take up Nagel's challenge to consider whether nation-states have more demanding duties of justice with respect to their own citizens than to those of other countries, Stiglitz does remark that "with globalization, principles of fairness and justice will increasingly need to guide our attitudes towards how we treat members of our global community."[134] We (citizens, developed nations, IFIs) are obligated not to harm poor nations and peoples, even or especially when such harm will benefit us. Moreover, when we have so much and others have so little, global social justice compels us to assist poor nations and peoples, especially when we can do so at no great sacrifice of our own opportunities. Furthermore, we should be cautious in assuming that what is good for us necessarily promotes global justice: "processes in which each nation attempts to push for those policies which are narrowly in their own self-interest are not likely to produce outcomes which are in the general interest."[135] Finally, Stiglitz reminds us that in global matters a wider and enlightened concept of self-interest may sometimes converge with what ethics requires:

> We may, in the short run, be able to make progress in winning the physical war on terrorism. But in the long run, the battle is for the hearts and minds of the young people around the world. If they are confronted by a world of despair, of unemployment and poverty, of global hypocrisy and inequity, of global rules that are patently designed to advance the interests of the advanced industrial countries—or more accurately, special interests within those countries—and disadvantage those who are already disadvantaged, then the young will turn their energies from constructive activities, to building a better world for themselves and their children, to destructive activities. And we will all suffer as a consequence.[136]

Globalization presents both opportunities and dangers. Development ethicists, such as Stiglitz, improve public discussion by challenging global citizens to improve development policies and global institutions so that globalization can be more democratic and, thereby, less of a curse and more of a blessing.

Notes

1. The first two parts of this chapter were adapted from "Development Ethics and Globalization," *Philosophical Topics* 30, 2 (2002): 9–28, earlier versions of which appeared as "Development Ethics," in *Routledge Encyclopedia of Philosophy*, vol. 3, ed. Edward Craig (London: Routledge, 1998), 39–44; and as "Globalization and Human Development: Ethical Approaches," in *Proceedings of the Seventh Plenary Session of the Pontifical Academy of Social Sciences*, eds. Edmond Malinvaud and Louis Sabourin, the Vatican, 25–28 April 2001 (Vatican City: Pontifical Academy of the Social Sciences, 2001), 45–65. For helpful comments, I thank Deen Chatterjee, Roger Crisp, David P. Crocker, Edna D. Crocker, Nigel Dower, Jay Drydyk, Arthur Evenchik, Des Gasper, Verna Gehring, Denis Goulet, Xiaorong Li, Toby Linden, Nasim Moalem, Jerome M. Segal, and Roxanne Walters.

2. Moisés Naím, *Surprises of Globalization* (Washington, DC: Carnegie Endowment for International Peace, 2003), 3.

3. For treatments of the history of development ethics, see David A. Crocker, "Toward Development Ethics," *World Development* 19, 5 (May 1991): 457–83; David A. Crocker, "Development Ethics and Globalization," 10–11; Denis Goulet, *Development Ethics*, Preface, Introduction, and Part I; and Des Gasper, "Development Ethics: An Emergent Field? A Look at Scope and Structure with Special Reference to the Ethics of Aid," *Ethics and Development: On Making Moral Choices in Development Cooperation*, ed. C. J. Hamelink (Kampfen, The Netherlands: Kok, 1997), 25–43.

4. Richard M. Clugston and John A. Hoyt, "Environment, Development, and Moral Values," *Ethics and Development*, ed. C. J. Hamelink.

5. Arturo Escobar, *Encountering Development: The Making and Unmaking of the Third World* (Princeton, NJ: Princeton University Press, 1995). See also Wolfgang Sachs, ed. *The Development Dictionary* (London: Zed, 1992).

6. For a sample of such moral dilemmas in development practice and cooperation, see David A. Crocker, "Toward Development Ethics" 461–64; ed. C. J. Hamelink, *Ethics and Development: On Making Moral Choices in Development Cooperation*, and Des Gasper, *Ethics of Development* (Edinburgh: Edinburgh University Press, 2004).

7. USAID, "Conducting a DG Assessment: A Framework for Strategy Development," 23.

8. Although anticorruption strategies sometimes encompass the objectives of poverty reduction and participatory democracy, a focus on controlling corruption often eclipses these larger development goals and becomes the only end considered. See, for example, Moisés Naim, "Bad Medicine," *Foreign Policy* (March/April 2005): 95–96.

9. See Nicholas D. Kristof, "When Marriage Kills," *New York Times*, 30 March 2005, A27.

10. Carol Graham and Stefano Pettinato, *Happiness and Hardship: Opportunity and Insecurity in New Market Economies* (Washington, DC: Brookings Institution Press, 2002).

11. John Rawls, *A Theory of Justice* (Cambridge, MA: Belknap Press of Harvard University Press, 1971; rev. ed., 1997).

12. John Roemer, *Theories of Distributive Justice* (Cambridge, MA: Harvard University Press, 1996).

13. Johann Galtung, "The New International Order and the Basic Needs Approach," *Alternatives* 4 (1978/1979): 455–76; Manfred Max-Neef, *Human Scale Development: Conception, Application, and Further Reflections* (London: Apex Press, 1993); Paul Streeten with S. J. Burki, Mahbub ul Haq, Norman Hicks, and Frances Stewart, *First Things First: Meeting Basic Needs in Developing Countries* (London: Oxford University Press, 1981); Len Doyal and Ian Gough, *A Theory of Need* (London: Macmillan, 1991); Des Gasper, *The Ethics of Development*, chap. 6, among many others.

14. P. T. Bauer, *Dissent on Development* (London: Weidenfeld & Nickolson, 1971); Robert Nozick, *Anarchy, State, and Utopia* (New York: Basic Books, 1974).

15. Amartya Sen, *Development as Freedom* (New York: Knopf, 1999); Onora O'Neill, *Bounds of Justice* (Cambridge, MA: Cambridge University Press, 2000); David Ellerman, *Helping People Help Themselves: From the World Bank to an Alternative Philosophy of Development Assistance* (Ann Arbor: University of Michigan Press, 2005).

16. Martha Nussbaum, *Women and Human Development: The Capabilities Approach* (Cambridge, UK: Cambridge University Press, 2000).

17. Thomas W. Pogge, *World Poverty and Human Rights* (Cambridge, UK: Polity Press, 2002). See also Amartya Sen, "Elements of a Theory of Human Rights," *Philosophy & Public Affairs* 32, 4 (2004): 315–56.

18. Thomas Nagel argues that duties of socioeconomic justice are the exclusive concern of sovereign states (and their citizens) in relation to their own (fellow) citizens. In relation to citizens of other countries, a sovereign state only has negative duties not to enslave, coerce, or violate civil liberties as well as the positive duties of humanitarian assistance and rescue. See Thomas Nagel, "The Problem of Global Justice," *Philosophy & Public Affairs* 33, 2 (2005): 113–47.

19. Nagel, "The Problem of Global Justice," 2. Compare with Nagel, 118.

20. Des Gasper is particularly eloquent in articulating the widely shared assumption that development agents face alternative paths and that development ethics emphasizes "value-conscious ways of thinking about and choosing between alternative paths and destinations" (Gasper, *The Ethics of Development*, xi).

21. United Nations Development Programme, *Human Development Report* (Oxford: Oxford University Press, 1990–2006). These *Human Development Reports* operationalize the capability approach and address such themes as consumption, globalization, human rights, technology, democracy, the Millennium Development Goals, cultural liberty, international cooperation, and water supplies. See *Readings in Human Development: Concepts, Measures, and Policies for a Development Paradigm*, eds. Sakiko Fakuda-Parr and A. K. Shiva (Oxford: Oxford University Press, 2003); Asunción Lera St. Clair, "The Role of Ideas in the United Nations Development Programme," *Global*

Institutions and Development: Framing the World? eds. Morten Bøås and Desmond McNeill (London: Routledge, 2004), 178–92.

22. Amartya Sen and Jean Drèze, *Hunger and Public Action* (Oxford: Oxford University Press, 1989).

23. Sen, *Development as Freedom*, 21.

24. See Martha Nussbaum and Jonathan Glover, eds., *Women, Culture and Development: A Study of Human Capabilities* (Oxford: Oxford University Press, 1995).

25. By "agency," I follow Sen and not institutional economics:

The expression "agent" is sometimes employed in the literature of economics and game theory to denote a person who is acting on someone else's behalf (perhaps being led on by a "principal") and whose achievements are to be assessed in the light of someone else's (the principal's) goals. I am using the term "agent" not in this sense, but in its older—and "grander"—sense as someone who acts and brings about change, and whose achievements can be judged in terms of her own values and objectives, whether or not we assess them in terms of some external criteria as well. This work [*Development as Freedom*] is particularly concerned with the agency role of the individual as a member of the public and as a participant in economic, social and political actions (varying from taking part in the market to being involved, directly or indirectly, in individual or joint activities in political and other spheres. (Sen, *Development as Freedom*, 18–19)

26. Amartya Sen, "Elements of a Theory of Human Rights," 333, n. 31.

27. Joseph E. Stiglitz, *Globalization and Its Discontents* (New York: W. W. Norton, 2002), 218–19.

28. Sen, *Development as Freedom*, 11.

29. See, for example, Amy Gutmann and Dennis Thompson, *Democracy and Disagreement* (Cambridge, MA: Harvard University Press, 1996); *Why Deliberative Democracy?* (Princeton, NJ: Princeton University Press, 2004); and David A. Crocker, "Sen and Deliberative Democracy," in *Capabilities Equality: Basic Issues and Problems,* ed. Alexander Kaufman (New York: Routledge, 2006), and *Ethics of Global Development: Agency, Capability, and Deliberative Democracy* (Cambridge, UK: Cambridge University Press, forthcoming), among other contributions.

30. Gutmann and Thompson, *Why Deliberative Democracy?*, 7; n. 3 on 189 (referring to key works in deliberative democracy) omitted.

31. The most important source for case studies and ethical assessments of deliberative democracy in both developing and developed countries is Archon Fung and Erik Olin Wright, eds., *Deepening Democracy: Institutional Innovations in Empowered Participatory Governance* (London: Verso, 2003).

32. Charles R. Beitz, "Does Global Inequality Matter?" *Global Justice*, ed. Thomas W. Pogge (Oxford: Blackwell, 2001), 113.

33. Pogge, *World Poverty*, 15, 21, 112–16, 141–45.

34. Pogge, *World Poverty*, 143.

35. Pogge himself formulates a more balanced view in hypothetically discussing Brazil: "If a particular underfulfillment of human rights—hunger in Brazil, say—comes about through the interplay of global and national factors and could be remedied

through global as well as through national institutional reforms, then the responsibility for this underfulfillment lies with both institutional schemes and therefore also with both groups of persons: with all those involved in upholding the global or the Brazilian basic structure" (Pogge, *World Poverty*, 50).

36. Onora O'Neill, "Agents of Justice," in *Global Justice*, ed. Thomas W. Pogge (Oxford: Blackwell, 2001), 188–203.

37. Joseph E. Stiglitz, *The Roaring Nineties: A New History of the World's Most Prosperous Decade* (New York: W. W. Norton, 2003), xii.

38. David Held, Anthony McGrew, David Goldblatt, and Jonathan Perraton, *Global Transformations* (Stanford, CA: Stanford University Press, 1999), 2.

39. Held et al., *Global Transformations*, 16.

40. Held et al., *Global Transformations*, 2–16.

41. Thomas L. Friedman, *The Lexis and the Olive Tree: Understanding Globalization* (New York: Farrar, Straus & Giroux, 1999); *The World Is Flat: A Brief History of the 21st Century* (New York: Farrar, Straus & Giroux, 2005).

42. Jagdish N. Bhagwati, *Free Trade Today* (Princeton, NJ: Princeton University Press, 2002); *In Defense of Globalization* (New York: Oxford University Press, 2004).

43. Fareed Zakaria, "The Wealth of Yet More Nations," *New York Times Book Review*, May 1, 2005, 11.

44. Richard N. Cooper, "A False Alarm: Overcoming Globalization's Discontents," *Foreign Affairs* 83, 1 (January/February 2004): 152–53.

45. Dani Rodrik, "Trading in Illusions," *Foreign Policy* (March/April 2001), 55.

46. Dani Rodrik, "Trading in Illusions," 57.

47. Stephen Krasner, *Sovereignty: Organized Hypocrisy* (Princeton, NJ: Princeton University Press, 1999).

48. Paul Hirst and Grahame Thompson, *Globalization in Question: The International Economy and the Possibilities of Governance* (Cambridge, UK: Polity Press, 1996).

49. Samuel P. Huntington, *The Clash of Civilizations and the Remaking of the World Order* (New York: Simon & Schuster, 1996).

50. Herman E. Daly, "Globalization and Its Discontents," *Philosophy and Public Policy Quarterly* 21, 2/3 (2001): 17–21. See also Herman E. Daly, "Globalization's Major Inconsistencies," *Philosophy and Public Policy Quarterly* 23, 4 (2003): 22–27.

51. Rodrik, "Trading in Illusions," 55.

52. Held et al., *Global Transformations*, 429.

53. In addition to the present book, a recent interdisciplinary volume—with essays by religious leaders, politicians, business people, and scholars (but no philosophers)—promises to help fill this void. See John H. Dunning, ed., *Making Globalization Good: The Moral Challenges of Global Capitalism* (Oxford: Oxford University Press, 2003).

54. John H. Dunning, *Making Globalization Good*, 444.

55. John H. Dunning, *Making Globalization Good*, 446–47.

56. John H. Dunning, *Making Globalization Good*, 431. See also, Amartya Sen, "Justice across Borders," in *Global Justice & Transnational Politics*, eds. Pablo De Greiff and Ciaran Cronin (Cambridge, MA: MIT, 2002), 37–55. For the notion of global as well as national civil society, see David A. Crocker, "Truth Commissions, Transitional Justice, and Civil Society," in *Truth v. Justice: The Morality of Truth Commissions*, eds.

Robert I. Rotberg and Dennis Thompson (Princeton, NJ: Princeton University Press, 2000), 99–121.

57. Commission on Global Governance, *Our Global Neighborhood* (Oxford: Oxford University Press, 1995).

58. Nagel, "The Problem of Global Justice," 113–47.

59. Richard Falk, *On Humane Governance: Toward a New Global Politics* (Cambridge, UK: Polity Press, 1995).

60. Held et al., *Global Transformations*, 450.

61. See Crocker, "Sen and Deliberative Democracy."

62. Ngaire Woods, ed., *The Political Economy of Globalization* (New York: Palgrave Macmillan, 2000); David Held, *Models of Democracy*, 2nd ed. (Stanford, CA: Stanford University Press, 1996); *Democracy and the Global Order: From the Modern State to Cosmopolitan Governance* (Stanford, CA: Stanford University Press, 1995); James Bohman, "International Regimes and Democratic Governance," *International Affairs* 75 (1999): 499–514; "Citizenship and Norms of Publicity: Wide Public Reason in Cosmopolitan Societies," *Political Theory* 27 (1999): 176–202; *Democracy across Borders* (Cambridge, MA: MIT Press, 2007).

63. For the idea of open and flexible personal identity, see Amartya Sen, "Reason Before Identity," Romanes Lecture, given in Oxford, 17 November 1998; "Beyond Identity: Other People," *The New Republic* 223/25 (December 18, 2000): 23–30; *Identity and Violence: The Illusion of Destiny* (New York: W. W. Norton, 2006). For the ideal of global citizenship, see Dower, *An Introduction to Global Citizenship* (Edinburgh: Edinburgh University Press, 2003).

64. Held et al., *Global Transformations*, 449.

65. Held et al., *Global Transformations*, 450.

66. Amartya Sen, "How to Judge Globalism," *The American Prospect* 13, 2 (January 2002): 1–14.

67. Joseph E. Stiglitz, "Towards a New Paradigm for Development," in *Making Globalization Good*, ed. John H. Dunning, 76–107.

68. Stiglitz, *Globalization*, xvi.

69. Stiglitz, "Towards a New Paradigm," 77.

70. Stiglitz, "Towards a New Paradigm," 5.

71. Stiglitz, "Towards a New Paradigm," 5.

72. Stiglitz, *Globalization*, xi.

73. Stiglitz, *Globalization*, 252.

74. Joseph E. Stiglitz, "Development Policies in a World of Globalization," a paper presented at the seminar New International Trends for Economic Development, Rio Janerio, Brazil, September 12–13, 2002.

75. Joseph E. Stiglitz, "Ethics, Market, and Government Failure, and Globalization," 19, n. 3.

76. Joseph E. Stiglitz, "On Liberty, the Right to Know, and Public Discourse: The Role of Transparency in Public Life," in *Globalizing Rights: The Oxford Amnesty Lectures 1999*, ed. Matthew J. Gibney (Oxford: Oxford University Press, 2003), 149.

77. Stiglitz explicitly sets forth five "ethical principles" or "widely held ethical precepts" in "Ethics, Economic Advice, and Economic Policy," 2, a paper presented in the

International Meeting on Ethics and Development, Inter-American Development Bank, December 6–7, 2002.

78. See Stiglitz, *Roaring Nineties,* 304–5.

79. Stiglitz, "Ethics, Economic Advice, and Economic Policy," 2.

80. Stiglitz, *Globalization,* xii, 88, 186, 248, and 251.

81. Amartya Sen, "Reanalyzing the Relationship between Ethics and Development," Ethics and Development Day, Inter-American Initiative on Social Capital, Ethics, and Development, Inter-American Development Bank, January 16, 2004, 5, 8.

82. Stiglitz, *Globalization,* 192. See *Ethics, Market and Government Failure,* 17.

83. Stiglitz, *Globalization,* 60–61, 172.

84. Stiglitz, *Roaring Nineties,* 312; see also 333–34.

85. Stiglitz, "Liberty," 130–36.

86. Stiglitz, "Liberty," 135.

87. Stiglitz, "Liberty," 152.

88. Stiglitz, *Globalization,* xx.

89. Stiglitz, "Liberty," 154.

90. Stiglitz, "Liberty," 125.

91. Stiglitz, "Liberty," 156.

92. Stiglitz, *Roaring Nineties,* xxii.

93. Stiglitz, *Roaring Nineties,* 301.

94. Stiglitz, *Roaring Nineties,* 239. Stiglitz makes brief but suggestive remarks about "development as democratic transformation," "government by discussion as the key to democracy," and "economic democracy in the workplace" in "Democratic Development as the Fruits of Labor," in *Joseph Stiglitz and the World Bank: The Rebel Within,* ed. Ha-Joon Chang (London: Anthem, 2001): 279–315. He approvingly cites Dewey, one of the pioneers of deliberative democracy: "In theory, the democratic method is persuasion through public discussion carried on not only in legislative halls but in the press, private conversations and public assemblies. The substitution of ballots for bullets, of the right to vote for the lash, is an expression of the will to substitute the method of discussion for the method of coercion" (John Dewey, *Freedom and Culture* [New York: Capricorn, 1939], 128; cited by Stiglitz in "Democratic Development as the Fruits of Labor," 309, n. 34). Cf. Jean Drèze and Amartya Sen, *India: Development and Participation,* 2nd ed. (Oxford: Oxford University Press: 2002), 23–33, 347–79; Amartya Sen, "Democracy and Its Global Roots," *The New Republic,* October 6, 2003; David A. Crocker, "Sen and Deliberative Democracy."

95. Stiglitz, "Towards a New Paradigm," 88.

96. Stiglitz, "Towards a New Paradigm."

97. Stiglitz, *Globalization,* 247.

98. Stiglitz, *Globalization,* ix; see also 9. Also see Stiglitz, *Roaring Nineties,* x and xv.

99. Stiglitz, *Globalization,* 9.

100. Stiglitz, *Globalization,* 20

101. Stiglitz, *Globalization,* 13.

102. Stiglitz, *Roaring Nineties,* 284.

103. Stiglitz, *Globalization*, 12–13. For a clear analysis, see Benjamin M. Friedman, "Globalization: Stiglitz's Case," *New York Review of Books* 49/13 (August 15, 2002), 48–53.

104. Stiglitz, "Ethics, Market and Government Failure," 1.

105. See, for example, Stiglitz, "*Globalization*," 8, 20.

106. Joseph Stiglitz, "Global Playing Field: More Level, but It Still Has Bumps," *New York Times*, 30 April 2005, A22.

107. It is beyond the scope of this chapter to evaluate Stiglitz's claims with respect to the effects of globalization and the IFIs' role in producing them. Benjamin Friedman is correct to challenge someone such as Stanley Fischer or Lawrence Summers (premier economists involved in IMF or Treasury Department decisions) to assess Stiglitz's account. Another candidate would be Stiglitz's colleague at Columbia, Jagdish Bhagwati.

108. Stiglitz, *Roaring Nineties*, 21. See also, *Globalization*, 181–88.

109. Stiglitz, "Ethics, Market, and Government Failure," 18.

110. Stiglitz, "Ethics, Market, and Government Failure," 18.

111. Stiglitz, "Ethics, Market, and Government Failure," 1.

112. Stiglitz, *Roaring Nineties*, 28.

113. Stiglitz, "Ethics, Market, and Government Failure," 18. See also *Roaring Nineties*, 313.

114. Stiglitz, "Ethics, Market, and Government Failure."

115. Stiglitz, *Globalization*, x.

116. Stiglitz, *Globalization*, 22, 215.

117. Stiglitz, *Globalization*, 247.

118. Stiglitz, *Globalization*, 251.

119. Stiglitz, *Roaring Nineties*, xiii.

120. Stiglitz, *Roaring Nineties*, xi, 283, 294.

121. Stiglitz, *Globalization*, 46–47. Stiglitz explains fungibility as "the fact that money going in for one purpose frees up other money for another use; the net impact may have nothing to do with the intended purpose" (*Globalization*, 46). See also *Globalization*, 49–50, 242–43, and Paul Collier, "Making Aid Smart," The IRIS Discussion Papers on Institutions and Development, Paper No. 02/08 (College Park, MD: Center for Institutional Reform and the Informal Sector, University of Maryland, 2004).

122. Stiglitz, *Roaring Nineties*, xi.

123. Stiglitz, *Globalization*, 54, 218; *Roaring Nineties*, xi.

124. Shahid Yusuf and Joseph E. Stiglitz, "Development Issues: Settled and Open," in *Frontiers of Development Economics: The Future in Perspective*, eds. Gerald M. Meier and Joseph E. Stiglitz (New York: Oxford University Press, 2001), 237.

125. In *Human Development Report 2003*, United Nations Development Programme argues for greater decentralization, but most of the examples given seem to have been subject to elite capture. An important challenge is to identify municipal and other local development institutions that have been able to resist domination by local elites. See James Manor, *The Political Economy of Democratic Decentralization* (Washington, DC: World Bank, 1999); and eds. Philip Oxhorn, Joseph S. Tulchin, and An-

drew D. Selee, *Decentralization, Democratic Governance, and Civil Society in Comparative Perspective: Africa, Asia, and Latin America* (Baltimore, MD: Johns Hopkins University Press/Woodrow Wilson Center Press, 2004).

126. His most suggestive remarks about the potential of local governance occur in Yusuf and Stiglitz, "Development Issues," 236–38, 243–47.

127. See Fung and Wright, eds., *Deepening Democracy.*

128. Stiglitz, *Globalization,* 252.

129. Yusuf and Stiglitz, "Development Issues," 244.

130. Yusuf and Stiglitz, "Development Issues," 225–27.

131. Yusuf and Stiglitz, "Development Issues," 227.

132. Yusuf and Stiglitz, "Development Issues," 251.

133. Stiglitz, *Roaring Nineties,* 315.

134. Stiglitz, *Roaring Nineties,* 315.

135. Stiglitz, "Ethics, Market and Government Failure," 18.

136. Stiglitz, *Roaring Nineties,* 316.

2

Negotiating the Global and the Local: Situating Transnational Democracy and Human Rights

Carol C. Gould

POLITICAL THEORISTS HAVE RECENTLY DEVELOPED frameworks for increasingly global applications of democracy and human rights, such that these norms can be given institutional expression in cross-border or transnational contexts. The new projection of these norms is meant to contrast with older views in which democracy and human rights are regarded as embodied in national constitutions and understood as having application exclusively within nation-states. In this older perspective, while human rights documents are thought to have some force internationally, they are said to gain effectiveness through their institutionalization at the national level; similarly, democracy is held to be primarily a matter of forms of government at the level of particular political societies. The extension in transnational contexts of both the ideas of democracy and human rights is a salutary one in my view, and I have myself presented a conception along these lines in my book *Globalizing Democracy and Human Rights*.[1] Such approaches have called for new cross-border forms of democratic decision making and the introduction of regional (as in the European Union) or even fully global, human rights courts or institutions of global governance that could give these rights truly cosmopolitan force.

However, such globalizing recommendations raise new questions of the appropriate application of normative frameworks to diverse localities with differing cultural, social, political, and economic formations. And while it is easy enough to insist that the application of cosmopolitan norms of democracy and human rights should take this diversity of localities into account, more significant problems arise if we want to open these basic concepts themselves to diverse cultural interpretations and if we attempt to leave space for local divergence in the very forms of democracy and human rights and for some "empowerment" of localities in this emergent context.

In this chapter, I want to make some progress in considering this rather confusing issue of the "situatedness" of transnational democracy and human rights by first analyzing some of the possible meanings of the local or of localities in contemporary terms. Whereas the status of the national has been frequently articulated—though much remains to be done on the question of varying national interpretations of the universalist concepts of democracy and human rights—far less attention has been given to the idea of the local. I will focus on the analysis of this latter concept in the first part, in view of the growth in global interconnectedness, but some of what I have to say will be applicable to national delimitations of these cosmopolitan ideas as well. In the second part, I will turn to some of the efforts to make room for the local within the new frameworks of global democracy and human rights and will consider ways in which localities can play a role not only in the application of these concepts, but also in their interpretation and even in their constitution. Finally, I will suggest that there is an important distinction to be drawn between democracy and human rights in regard to the degree of transnational agreement that is required for these norms to be viable and to serve a useful heuristic and critical function.

Part I: Puzzles of Locality

Older definitions of the local have been drawn from a model of local communities understood in the first instance as territorially based. Often identified with a neighborhood within a larger city or with a small village, the local connotes a highly delimited geographical sphere in which it is relatively easy to have face-to-face interactions with the members of the community. In modern discussions of such local communities, their situatedness within a given nation-state is most often taken for granted. Accordingly, even the rather recent phrase, "Think globally, act locally" makes appeal to an idea of a relatively small, geographically specific and delimited community. Newer discussions of the local have indeed gained prominence in regard to the political significance of ecology and sustainable development. And there is now consideration of the relation of localities to the concept of autonomy, to which I will return at a later point.

However, if a sense of a small community with its associated friendliness or neighborliness is taken to be definitive of locality, as it is in most of the earlier uses of the concept of the local and in some of the recent ones, then we can observe the accelerated emergence of what can only be called cross-border or even *transnational localities.* This phenomenon is perhaps most evident in Internet forums or similar online discursive communities in which people interact with select others on a regular basis and know them, if not in face-to-face ways (absent video connections), then in relatively immediate ways in which they may even become friends at a distance. In these online forums, *temporally contemporaneous* discussions or those transpiring within short time delays establish connections between people that to some degree replace *the spatial proximity* afforded by geographically contiguous old-fashioned localities. Of course, these online communications still lack many of the features of face-to-face interaction, especially the visual dimension, but they are often experienced as having an immediacy and a meaningfulness of their own.

Other contemporary examples of emergent transnational localities can be found in the interactions within and among far-flung nongovernmental organizations, as well as among activists in new political and social movements, in the latter case often interacting and reaching decisions through the medium of the Internet. An important example of the latter is the burgeoning social forum movement, which has held several world conferences and an increasing number of local ones. Furthermore, individuals may form into local but cross-border communities where they share ongoing ecological concerns, for example, regarding acid rain or toxic dumping. Alternatively, such cross-border communities may form around economic interests, especially regarding production or trade, and these may look for ways to make or to influence collective decisions concerning these issues. And of course, immigrant groups may constitute communities at borders, as in the case of some localities at the U.S.-Mexico border.

However, if the local can now be cross-border or even transnational in these ways, then various puzzles arise. It becomes unclear how we can demarcate the local from the global, in which case the concept of the local loses any clear reference. Yet, small-scale geographical localities or neighborhoods in the traditional sense clearly retain significance for us. Furthermore, the "local" must still matter if we are concerned with the empowerment of individuals and small groups with their diverse ways of life within increasingly globalized networks of interaction. Nonetheless, we must admit that the concept of the local has become blurred in the present situation because of the increasing role of cross-border small communities, particularly on the Internet. If local communities can indeed be cross-border, then we may wonder what happens to such oft-cited and important desiderata as "subsidiarity," or the idea that democratic decisions should be made at the most local level possible. Moreover, if new transnational "local" communities sometimes matter more to us than the ones in which we are territorially situated, then perhaps political philosophy needs to replace its emphasis on geographical localities with such newer cross-border localities. Clearly, the observation that in contemporary societies it is sometimes the case that the local is in fact global, or at least transnational, suggests that the concept of the local needs to be clarified and rescued from its apparent paradoxical status.

Defining the Local

To explicate the local, we can consider several possible interpretations of it in contemporary globalizing contexts:

1. The primary sense noted above—the local as a territorially bounded small community. In this conception, it must be possible for people to meet each other in person in their daily lives, although they may not in fact do so. In addition, they share a small geographical place or space.
2. The local as a nonterritorially based small community, in which temporal proximity replaces a spatial one. As above, people can meet each other daily and recognize each other as members of the same community, even if their interactions are not face to face.
3. The local as an affiliative or affective community, in which people are bound together by common feelings for each other. This sort of community requires direct interactions among individuals, which may be either face to face or mediated by technologies or other modalities.
4. The local as a group or community bound by shared goals, which are at least partly constitutive of the group.
5. The local as a particular discursive community, where there is recognition among the members of each other as possible interlocutors in an ongoing discourse.
6. The local as a community determined by a shared understanding of a set of cultural or ethnic factors that make it a single community.
7. Whatever is nonregional or nonglobal (i.e., the local defined purely negatively).

It is evident that in most of these meanings, the local is not given but constituted or constructed. In these uses, it involves an intentionalistic constitution of a group or a shared space through the joint action or understanding of the people who make it up. Only the first of these meanings, where locality is taken to essentially require a delimited geographical area, partly avoids the intentionalistic reading, although even here the scope and specific borders of the local is undoubtedly variable and dependent on social construction and convention. It is also apparent that several of the above conceptions overlap and it is likely that local communities will instantiate several of them at once. In particular, the first sense above, as a small territorially defined community, has often been thought to involve features of the third sense, or care for each of the members. But these may be separated in theory and, indeed, often in practice as well.

The Local and the Idea of Self-Determination

We can observe that a crucial feature is missing from the above list, a feature often emphasized in contemporary discussions of the significance of the local. This consists of a tie between the local and some conception of power or autonomy. In this use, autonomy refers to self-determination or, sometimes, to self-governance. Contemporary emphases on the local, where they are not concerned primarily with sustainability or the environment more generally, focus on the idea that autonomy is more likely and more essential at the level of local community.[2]

Some advocates of local autonomy remain with the idea of self-determination, familiar as a basis for nonintervention in the internal affairs of nation-states. Such internal affairs are not necessarily conducted in democratic ways. Increasingly, however, important emphasis has been placed on democratic decision making within local contexts as a basis for a new type of "empowered participatory governance."[3] Visions of such autonomy may see such relatively self-determining localities as bound together in networks of increasingly global interconnections with other localities. Such a network model of globalization has been proposed as an alternative to the current more thoroughgoing, centralized, and homogenizing globalization of economic, political, social, and cultural life, which seems to threaten the viability of diverse forms of cultural and social organization.[4] To the degree that these networks extend to civil society's organizations, they have been thought to give rise to the desirable phenomenon of "globalization from below."[5]

From the standpoint of organized forms of political decision making or governance, some who seek greater autonomy for individuals within such processes have argued for the devolution of power from nation-state levels to more local communities, following such models as the participatory budgeting of Porto Allegre in Brazil, or in neighborhood policing in some American cities, where supervision is retained at higher levels.[6] Other theorists have looked to the introduction of regional bodies, whether within or across nation-states, that may permit more cooperation among traditional localities and may mitigate the effects of powerful interests, especially in terms of corporations or trade, that themselves operate in increasingly transnational ways.[7] Nonetheless, these regional associations are often interpreted as linkages among traditional localities. By contrast, the new cross-border localities that I have characterized are often omitted from these discussions. They represent a new form of community, the impact of which is currently somewhat unclear, that is of growing importance in economic, cultural, and perhaps political terms.

In order to steer this analysis of the concept of the local to bear on the question of interpreting and institutionalizing democracy and human rights, we need to clarify further the significance that should be accorded to democratic autonomy in these and other local contexts. It can largely be taken for granted here that there is value both in preserving at least a certain degree of local autonomy and also in recognizing and even enhancing local sorts of diversity—whether cultural, social, economic, or otherwise. While it is probably unnecessary to give a justification for these claims, we can note—without pursuing the argument in any depth—that they can be derived from the norms of freedom and democracy themselves. Thus it is apparent that people tend to value their distinctive cultural traditions and social practices; the importance of preserving these therefore follows from the recognition of the equal freedom of individuals. Likewise, local autonomy itself can be seen to be a form of democratic self-determination in the sense of people's joint control over their daily lives in community with others, free from the imposition of such determinations on them by groups who do not share their goals or activities and who have less of a stake in the decisions in question.

Thus, there is a connection, sometimes overlooked, between the norm of democracy as entailing equal rights of participation in decision making concerning what I have called common activities and that of self-determination. The latter has been developed primarily in the rather different context of an international right of sovereign nation-states against nonintervention in their internal affairs, or in terms of the rights of cultural or national minorities to secession or other types of legal recognition. Yet, as I have argued elsewhere, rights of self-determination gain much of their justification when they are conceived as rights of social self-determination of the people who make up a state,[8] or in Walzer's terms, as rights of the political community.[9] But as such, the self-determination ought to be understood as a democratic right on the part of those making up the collectivity to codetermine their own activities, where these decisions are themselves subject to human rights constraints.[10] Yet, in contrast to some cosmopolitan readings, the normative requirement for democracy here, understood as closely related to the idea of self-determination, does not in itself legitimate intervention by others to produce such democracy in other political communities, except in delimited contexts where such help is clearly requested by majorities of the community in question and where the appeal is to the legitimate authority of a relevant international organization. Of course, difficulty arises when no democracy is in place, as in that case it is obviously difficult for the will of the majority to gain clear expression. Yet it would be wrong, I think, to take a small minority's expression of such a will as sufficient grounds for intervention.

In view of the constraints posed on such intervention to ensure the freedom and democratic rights of others, it is worth noting that other modalities, especially financial support and diplomacy, may be of some help in assisting others in their efforts at self-transformation. The relevant disposition needed in such cases is neither charity nor a will to domination, but what we can call solidarity. Indeed, I have suggested elsewhere that this disposition importantly links relatively autonomous communities with each other (whether these be local in the traditional sense or new cross-border ones). The idea of solidarity requires new theorizing to show the importance of standing with others, understanding the specificity of their situation and their demands, supporting them in their struggles, yet yielding to the others the leading role in dealing with their own situation. Although its original home was in the labor movement, especially in the idea of workers and their supporters expressing solidarity by, for example, not crossing picket lines, the idea of solidarity points to a new relation between actors and those who support them at a distance. The support given need not only be moral support, but can extend also to concrete modalities of aid. The idea suggests, however, that those immediately engaged are the ones to determine the extent of such aid and its nature, in terms of their own understanding of their specific situation.[11]

Part II: Local Interpretations and Universalist Norms

We can now address the central question concerning how much scope should be given to local interpretations and instantiations of the increasingly globalized human rights frameworks and of democracy itself, and on what grounds one can propose recognizing these distinctively local interpretations and applications. Here, I will not focus primarily on the standard question regarding the ways in which various national constitutions embody (or fail to embody) human rights nor on the frequently discussed issue of the optimal institutional forms of democracy in the context of nation-states. As suggested, my concern is different: namely, the significance that should be accorded to democratic autonomy and to conflicting human rights interpretations on the part of sub-global units, where these relatively local communities are over time becoming increasingly cross-border, though they may encompass also traditional local, regional, or even national entities. After considering the issue of giving recognition to diverse interpretations of democracy, I shall take up some of the ways in which human rights may in fact differ from democracy in this respect.

We can begin by noting a few of the leading ways of construing the issue of local interpretations. It is indeed relatively uncontroversial that (putatively) universal human rights need to be given more specific interpretations depending on the local and national context and traditions.[12] These differing interpretations reflect differences in the conditions for establishing equal freedom and dignity, as protected by human rights, in various cultural and social contexts. However, there is considerable disagreement on whether the very idea of human rights (and the list of the recognized human rights) can themselves be permitted to vary according to local cultures and practices. This reluctance to admit variability into the concepts pertains even more to the idea of democracy itself, which, as we have clearly witnessed lately, tends to be subject to very strict limits in the readings given of it. Thus democracy is most often thought to be limited to the procedural forms of majority rule and elections, themselves often given a U.S. interpretation, with a nod to European parliamentary alternatives.

To cast further light on these issues, we need to consider—at least briefly— the question of the genesis and justification of these universalist norms and see what role is given here to diverse cultures and local communities. One prevalent approach—whether tacit or explicitly appealed to—endorses some distinction between "thick" and "thin" readings of these norms. Whatever universal and common ground is possible is construed as a thin or minimalist one that in turn enables some agreement across cultures and localities, where these latter are understood to have their own thicker and incommensurable approaches to these and other norms. On this view, there is no possible substantial ground for the thin morality except one expressive of a thick morality. A minimal morality abstracted from the thick one supports a certain vicarious and solidaristic identification with others, but this thin morality does not approach any genuine universality.[13]

Alternatively, appeal may be made to a conception of an overlapping consensus in which norms such as human rights and democracy may (hopefully) be found in the overlap among otherwise divergent approaches. However, while the thin approach may leave the norms without any critical basis beyond an unexplained appeal to common sense or common humanity, it is not clear that a political appeal to consensus can provide a critical ground either. It may in fact equally be confronted with dissensus instead of consensus, or with important sets of local groupings of people who fall outside the requisite consensus.

The theory of discursive or deliberative democracy importantly adds to the idea of consensus formation an account of the conditions and the procedures that can permit such a genuine consensus to emerge. But as I have argued elsewhere, some of these accounts may be question-begging in presupposing among these conditions the very rights to freedom and equality (at least the freedom and equality of interlocutors to enter into and participate in the discourse), which they in turn see as emerging from the consensus.[14] Furthermore, while placing helpful emphases on the role of reasoning and openness in the process of coming to agreement, these theories have sometimes been overly rationalist and have disregarded the role of emotions in this process, especially the helpful emotions of empathy and solidarity. There has also been a tendency, somewhat corrected by more recent theorists,[15] to neglect the diversity of voices or the impediments of such a pure discourse for those who have traditionally lacked voice. Likewise, a greater role for conflict and its engagement probably needs to be given within such discursive processes.

The approach I have argued for elsewhere[16] differs from all of these in some important ways. It calls for supplementing abstractly universalist conceptions of norms like democracy and human rights with what I have called a conception of concrete universality. With the abstract universalists, this view places weight on certain general or universal norms, which it specifically sees as having emerged from and being grounded in people's practical activities of self-transformation, whether individual or collective—that is, in the human capacity for change and self-change. To the degree that the very capacity for self-transformative activity is possessed by everyone and comes to be recognized as such, it supports norms of freedom and of equal human rights. Thus, inasmuch as such capacity for self-transformation has as among its conditions the meeting of certain basic economic and social needs and requires the absence of political interference, it provides a basis for the recognition of equal human rights that allow for and facilitate its expression (though these human rights may in turn have somewhat differentiated applications for diverse groups and cultures).

Yet, in contrast to traditional approaches, the view here sees a purely general characterization of universal norms as insufficient, inasmuch as it disregards the ways in which these norms emerge from a social and historical process of interaction among and across diverse cultural localities and through social networks of both cooperation and conflict. In these processes, confrontation with the different and sometimes conflicting approaches of others plays an essential role, as does the ability to engage in criticism, and especially self-criticism, in light of an awareness of these alternative perspectives.

Through practical interactions among people and localities that have become more wide ranging and increasingly universalistic in scope over time, new perspectives come into play and can be incorporated within the emerging norms. Existing conceptions can come to be scrutinized, such that their limitations or one-sidedness may become apparent and be criticized. This criticism and the potential widening of the social and normative understanding that it can bring about is most successful when those who hold one-sided perspectives are willing to be self-consciously critical about the limitations of their own views and seek to develop broader, more comprehensive understandings. Whereas in actuality these broader agreements have sometimes been imposed on recalcitrant others, the agreements are more resilient and more firmly grounded when they are freely adopted by all concerned, as the deliberative tradition has emphasized.

Furthermore, inasmuch as these understandings emerge from the practices of people who are self-transformative and in this sense free, the diversity of their creations is essential to the process, and they rightly seek recognition of these differences. They can also legitimately expect from others a certain empathic or solidaristic grasping of the distinctiveness of their social situations and standpoints. Obviously, this empathy and solidarity require considerable strengthening for the further expansion and elaboration of the normative ideas discussed here.

When applied to the norms of human rights and democracy, this approach does not then see them as thin or purely political. Rather, these norms emerge in part through the interactions—whether cooperative or confrontational—of diverse cultures and people. And, to the degree that they have been imposed by some powerful local communities on others, they need to be subjected to social critique to attempt to rectify their one-sided or ideological character. Nonetheless, inasmuch as these norms give expression to the very self-transformative agency of people and are based on a recognition of this individual and social agency (where people are increasingly linked in a variety of cross-border ways), the norms have important core significances that can come to be articulated in universalist or cosmopolitan terms. In my view, these norms express the valid claims that people make on each other for the recognition of their freedom (as this power of self-transformation) and for the conditions necessary for its realization, including among these rights of democratic participation and the other human rights. Of course, although these claims may be very general when taken abstractly, they most often require practical implementation through more delimited institutional frameworks, including social, economic, and political institutions. In this view, then, the interpersonal or social claims people can make on each other for the conditions of agency necessitate the development of local, national, or in some cases transnational institutions that can realize them.

From this expanded perspective of concrete universalism, the abstract norms of democracy and human rights are indeed seen as having a critical function of their own. But this approach also holds that these universalist norms must be rid of the one-sided, limited interpretations that derive from the experiences of only one set of cultural and social localities.

Further, beyond its emphasis on the critique of one-sided perspectives, the concrete universality approach adds to the idea of the equal recognition of persons a more affiliative notion of empathy or solidarity with the situation of others, in which common problems, along with the distinctively different ones that vary with social circumstance, can be taken into account. New cross-border relationships and networks among individuals and groups lay the groundwork for empathic understanding of the situation of others, which entails not only the possibility of a cognitive grasping of their perspective but also a more feelingful identification with the specifics of their concrete situation and with their suffering and their struggles to alleviate it. This understanding can give rise to solidarity with them, in the sense of standing with them and supporting them, even at a distance. So far, these sorts of empathy and solidarity have been rather haphazard, depending on the particular others who are singled out for attention by the increasingly global (and corporate) media. However, it seems possible that a disposition to solidarity might be developed and that more disciplined and widespread forms of empathy could be cultivated. These modalities of understanding and communication with others might then in fact conduce to the equal recognition of persons required by the human rights conception, and might bring with it more appreciation—or at least recognition—of the differences of others.

Beyond this, to the degree that the political form of empathy or solidarity requires actually hearing from others at a distance about their concerns and interests, and requires taking their views seriously into consideration, it would seem to require democratic input from these others, including in cross-border or transnational contexts.[17] In *Globalizing Democracy and Human Rights*, I proposed a new criterion for determining when such input is required, as an interpretation of the idea that those affected by a decision have a right to participate in making it. Such a criterion would be a necessary supplement to the rights of participation that attend equal citizenship or more generally the equal right to participate in decisions concerning the common activities in which people are engaged, where this provides a fundamental justification for a rather extensive account of democratic rights of participation.

In regard to the explication of the idea of "being affected" by a decision, we cannot say that everyone even remotely affected globally has a right to participate in the decision.[18] However, for the many contexts in which decisions increasingly affect those far away, I have proposed the following criterion: If a decision at a distance *affects people's basic human rights and their fundamental ability to fulfill them,* then these people have a right to participate in a significant way in the decisions in question. If, for example, a decision by a multilateral economic institution affects the ability of people at a distance to realize their right to means of subsistence, then these people have a right of significant input into that decision. Clearly, democratic theory and practice have quite far to go in devising and implementing institutions or in reforming existing ones such that this sort of participation is taken seriously and made practicable. New forms of transnational representation in the institutions of global governance will likely need to be constructed in order to facilitate this input.

Part III: Making Room for the Local in Understanding Democracy and Human Rights

Returning to our issue of negotiating the local and global at the level of interpretations of norms, I want to suggest that the broader conception of concrete universality discussed here opens the way for taking more seriously the idea of intercultural interpretation and, to a degree, intercultural constitution of the norms of democracy and human rights. Insofar as agreement is needed on a global human rights framework, it has to emerge from cross-cultural networks of relations and dialogue among people from different localities (and not only among governments).[19] We can observe that the content of the human rights, if not their form, has in fact partly emerged from an interchange to some degree of this sort, as I have argued elsewhere.[20] At least the United Nations Declaration of Human Rights, and indeed many of the subsequent covenants, reflected the contributions not only of the United States and Western Europe, but also the emphases of Eastern European, Soviet, and developing countries with regard to economic rights and cultural and development rights.[21]

In an approach in which differences among communities and local autonomy are respected, we can also see that a multiplicity of forms of democratic organization as well as of instantiations of human rights is required. However, in my view, this need not extend to the sort of local control currently advocated by some antiglobalization theorists who favor a return to self-governance by small local communities, more or less as traditionally understood.[22] In fact, the analysis I gave earlier of contemporary local communities as increasingly cross-border or transnational suggests that this preference for a return to traditional communities is in this respect arbitrary (if not also romantic). I would further argue that there is no ground in the concept of the local or of democratic community itself for requiring this sort of return, even leaving aside the impact it would have on economic efficiency and on the growing social interrelations with people at a distance. (We should note, however, that recognizing the limitations of the ground for a return to traditional communities does not yet address the question of whether or not there are ecological grounds for urging upon us such a focus on the territorially local.)

Nonetheless, despite these reservations concerning proposals to return to earlier smaller-scale and geographically limited communities, we can see that there is a need to recognize greater diversity in the forms of democracy applicable to decision making in local communities, keeping in mind that some of these local communities will be cross-border or transnational. Leaving aside the issue of the cross-cultural constitution of an adequate norm of democracy referred to above, this diversity of forms of democracy would entail an openness to alternative versions of democratic decision making such as those based on consensus. In this way, democracy would not necessarily be limited to its familiar forms of elections and representative government.[23]

Along these lines, Kwasi Wiredu has argued for the democratic status of consensus or near-consensus types of decision making found in certain traditional African communities such as the Bugandans in Uganda, the Zulu in South Africa, and the Akans in Ghana. In his description, participation among tribal members at lower levels is combined with representatives who meet at a council level, where these representatives consult with community members to solicit their views on the issues under discussion and then try to reach consensus within the council on what is to be done, a consensus that often involves compromise by all involved.[24] Again, in the case of some of the indigenous peoples of the Americas, relatively autonomous communities exist in which people exercise control over their political, economic, and cultural affairs, and this can serve as an example of democracy in the sense of codetermination of joint activity. An example of this is the Aymara with the ayllu system of government, developed before the Inca and Spanish conquests in what is presently Bolivia, and currently advanced by some as a model to be reintroduced there and more widely.[25] Another case is the Haudenosaunee, or the Iroquois Confederacy, with its own democratic model and its Great Law of Peace, which existed prior to the period of colonization.[26] Consensus decision making has also been attempted within certain alternative social movements today functioning within and across larger liberal democracies, usually with a large Internet component. In these diverse cases, democracy is often direct and, although it sometimes involves representation, is neither electoral nor majoritarian. Of course, democracy is hardly complete within such communities and it remains an ideal not fully realized in practice. However, such a gap evidently exists elsewhere as well, even in the fully representative liberal nation-states that constitute the dominant models of democracy.

There are several aspects to the argument for recognizing diversity in the forms of democracy, which can be only pointed to here. First, if the idea of democracy requires popular control or shared decision making concerning matters of common activity or common concern, then as long as people do not give up their power of deciding to others without limit, multiple forms of

such decision making are possible as interpretations of the democratic concept. We could also continue to require that some conception of equality be
included in the concept, especially as equal rights of participation in decision
making. Second, it is important that such democratic decision making extend
to local communities, if it should not also be ultimately based there. The argument for some degree of local autonomy is grounded in the root idea of democracy itself, inasmuch as those most directly active and involved in a potential course of action should participate in making decisions about it and in
determining its course. Yet, people may well have discrepant ideas, often based
in a variety of traditions and accepted practices, about how to give force or application to this local autonomy. As previously noted, however, a distinction
needs to be drawn between traditional conceptions of local, community-
based decision making and more contemporary versions, where local communities may encompass those living at a distance from each other. To the degree that members of these emergent communities share goals, interests,
dialogue, and feelings for each other, they may well seek to define new democratic ways to come to agreement about how to direct their interactions over
time. Speaking ideally as well, they may additionally seek to establish cooperative and potentially democratic relations with other communities with which
they are networked. A new democratic theory for such networked cross-border localities remains to be developed.

At the outset of this chapter, I suggested that the cases of situating global
democracy and global human rights may in fact differ in important ways. We
have seen the argument for allowing a fairly wide variety in instantiations of
democracy in diverse contexts, consistent with its root notion, and in some
ways a similar argument could be made for human rights. But the two cases
differ in important ways, in my view. Although both the norms of democracy
and human rights can benefit from cross-cultural interpretation and perhaps
even intercultural constitution as I proposed earlier, there is more of a need
for coming to agreement on a single cosmopolitan framework of human
rights, or at least on a delimited set of regional frameworks. Thus, it would
seem that the conception of human rights cannot ultimately range as broadly
as that of democracy, and that there is more urgency for agreement about
human rights across borders. The reason for this is the importance of arriving
at transnational frameworks of human rights that can serve as a ground for
appeal against the actions of nation-states that violate them. The strengthening of the status of human rights in international law can only be salutary
inasmuch as it will permit such appeals for the enforcement of these rights
across borders, even by citizens against the decisions of their own governments. This direction has already been well-developed in Europe, in both the
European Court of Human Rights and more recently in the European Union.

Even the Inter-American Court of Human Rights has moved to recognize the preeminence of such a transnational human rights framework. The further development and strengthening of transnational courts that frame human rights at a regional level thus promises a more serious implementation of human rights if existing nation-states provide an inadequate basis for their protection, and they also exert pressure on nation-states to enforce them on their own. Moreover, to the degree that they gain authority and legitimacy in their domain, such courts and other modes of rights enforcement may be able to provide an alternative to violence in preventing and rectifying human rights abuses.

At the present time, effective regional frameworks, rather than fully global ones, might well suffice for these purposes, with the advantage of allowing for some continuing local diversity in rights interpretations. It should be clear too that, were such regional human rights instruments to be introduced widely (beyond the borders of the European Union), these instruments would not replace constitutional protections of human rights at the national level, but rather would reflect new agreements across a given range of nation-states. Nonetheless, it would be a mistake to conceive of the agreements that are required in cases such as these as permitting the imposition of a favored framework of one nation-state on others. Consistent with the recognition that has already been given to human rights in international law and morality, these further agreements will hopefully emerge on the basis of open dialogue and intercultural respect, such that the understandings of the norms will lose much of their one-sided character and will be responsive to the new networks of interrelations that mark one of the positive aspects of contemporary globalization.

Notes

1. Carol C. Gould, *Globalizing Democracy and Human Rights* (Cambridge, UK: Cambridge University Press, 2004), especially chaps. 7–9.

2. For formulations along these lines, see Amory Starr and Jason Adams, "Anti-Globalization: The Global Fight for Local Autonomy," *New Political Science* 25, 1 (2003): 19–42, and Balakrishnan Rajagopal, *International Law from Below* (Cambridge, UK: Cambridge University Press, 2003), especially chap. 8.

3. See the discussion of some new institutional directions along these lines in Archon Fung and Erik Olin Wright, eds., *Deepening Democracy* (London: Verso, 2003).

4. Michael M'Gonigle, "Between Globalism and Territoriality: The Emergence of an International Constitution and the Challenge of Ecological Legitimacy," *Canadian Journal of Law and Jurisprudence* 15, 2 (2002): 159–74.

5. Richard Falk, *On Humane Governance: Toward a New Global Politics* (Cambridge, UK: Polity Press, 1995); and "Global Civil Society and the Democratic

Prospect," in *Global Democracy: Key Debates*, ed. Barry Holden (London: Routledge, 2000), 162–78.

6. See Fung and Wright (2003).

7. See, for example, David Held, who in fact takes this cooperation to include not only regional, but also more global levels of decision making, *Democracy and the Global Order* (Stanford, CA: Stanford University Press, 1995).

8. Carol C. Gould, *Rethinking Democracy* (Cambridge, UK: Cambridge University Press, 1988), chap. 12.

9. Michael Walzer, *Just and Unjust Wars* (New York: Basic Books, 1977), esp. 53–55, and "The Moral Standing of States," *Philosophy and Public Affairs* 9, 3 (1980): 209–29.

10. For a development of this point, see Carol C. Gould, "Self-Determination beyond Sovereignty: Relating Transnational Democracy to Local Autonomy," Special Issue on *Democracy and Globalization*, eds. Carol C. Gould and Alistair Macleod, *Journal of Social Philosophy* 37, 1 (Spring, 2006): 44–60.

11. See Carol C. Gould, "Transnational Solidarities," Special Issue on *Solidarity*, eds. Carol Gould and Sally Scholz, *Journal of Social Philosophy* 38, 1 (Spring 2007): 146–62.

12. See, for example, Martha Nussbaum, "Human Capabilities, Female Human Beings," in *Women, Culture, and Development*, eds. Martha Nussbaum and Jonathan Glover (New York: Oxford University Press, 1995), 93.

13. Michael Walzer, *Thick and Thin* (Notre Dame, IN: University of Notre Dame Press, 1994), 9–11.

14. See Carol C. Gould, "Diversity and Democracy: Representing Differences," in *Democracy and Difference*, ed. Seyla Benhabib (Princeton, NJ: Princeton University Press, 1996), 171–86, and *Globalizing Democracy and Human Rights*, chap. 1.

15. See, for example, Iris Marion Young, *Inclusion and Democracy* (Oxford: Oxford University Press, 2000), and Seyla Benhabib, *The Claims of Culture* (Princeton, NJ: Princeton University Press, 2002).

16. Carol C. Gould, "The Woman Question: Philosophy of Liberation and the Liberation of Philosophy," in *The Philosophical Forum* 5, 1–2 (Fall/Winter 1973–74), Special Issue on Women and Philosophy, eds. Carol C. Gould and Marx W. Wartofsky, published with a new introduction as *Women and Philosophy: Toward a Theory of Liberation*, eds. Carol C. Gould and Marx W. Wartofsky (New York: G. P. Putnam's, 1976), 5–44; and *Globalizing Democracy and Human Rights*, chaps. 2 and 4.

17. I have developed this connection further in *Globalizing Democracy and Human Rights*, especially chapters 9 and 12.

18. Carol C. Gould, *Globalizing Democracy and Human Rights*, chap. 7.

19. John Dryzek has characterized the arena for this interchange in terms of the idea of an "international public sphere" in his *Democracy in Capitalist Times* (Oxford: Oxford University Press, 1996), chap. 4.

20. Carol C. Gould, *Globalizing Democracy and Human Rights*, chap. 2.

21. The issue of whether these latter should be taken as group rights or individual human rights is an interesting one; I take up this question in "Cultural Identity, Group Rights, and Social Ontology," in *Globalizing Democracy and Human Rights*, chap. 5. See also the discussions in Will Kymlicka, *Multicultural Citizenship* (Oxford: Oxford Uni-

versity Press, 1995) and Will Kymlicka, ed., *The Rights of Minority Cultures* (Oxford: Oxford University Press, 1995).

22. See, for example, Starr and Adams, "Anti-Globalization."

23. The material in this paragraph and the one that follows draws on my discussion to similar effect in *Globalizing Democracy and Human Rights*, chapter 1.

24. Kwasi Wiredu, "Society and Democracy in Africa," *New Political Science* 21, 1 (1999): 33–44. But see also the criticisms of Wiredu's approach developed in Emmanuel Chukwudi Eze, "Democracy or Consensus? Response to Wiredu," *Postcolonial African Philosophy: A Critical Reader*, ed. Emmanuel Eze (Oxford: Blackwell, 1997), 313–23.

25. Taller de Historia Oral Andina, *Ayllu: Pasado y Futuro de los Pueblos Originarios*. La Paz: Aruwiyiri, 1995; Marcia Stephenson, "The Impact of an Indigenous Counterpublic Sphere on the Practice of Democracy: The Taller de Historia Oral Andina in Bolivia," Working Paper #279 (September 2000), Kellogg Institute, University of Notre Dame, http://kellogg.nd.edu/publications/workingpapers/WPS/279.pdf, accessed April 14, 2007; and Silvia Rivera, "Liberal Democracy and *Ayllu* Democracy in Bolivia: The Case of Northern Potosí," *Journal of Development Studies* 26, 4 (1990): 97–121.

26. See John Mohawk, "The Great Law of Peace," as cited in *Communitarianism: A New Public Ethics*, ed. Markate Daly (Belmont, CA: Wadsworth, 1994), 165–78.

II

HUMAN RIGHTS, CAPABILITIES, AND DEMOCRATIC ACCOMMODATION

3

Relativism, Self-Determination, and Human Rights

James Nickel and David Reidy

E FFORTS TO ESTABLISH AND ENFORCE universal human rights have often been resisted by advocates of some form of relativism. The "Asian values" argument, for example, poses a relativist challenge to any international human rights agenda that includes individual liberties and democratic institutions (see Bauer and Bell 1999). Such challenges have led many to see current controversies about human rights as rooted in a fundamental conflict between moral relativism and moral universalism. The aim of this chapter is to suggest a particular resolution of this conflict, one that does not sacrifice either the universality of fundamental human rights or the respect for and tolerance of diversity sought by those who advocate relativism. It sees respect for national self-determination as interacting with respect for universal human rights to produce a doctrine of accommodation. In the final section, we apply our position to the human right to democratic institutions (International Covenant on Civil and Political Rights 1996, Article 25).

Developments in the field of human rights since the end of the Cold War suggest that the idea of a relativist challenge to human rights is now out of date. As Anne Bayefsky writes, "Every UN member state is a party to one or more of the six major human rights treaties. 80% of states have ratified four or more" (Bayefsky 2001, xiii).[1] Furthermore, all countries now use similar political institutions (e.g., bureaucratic government, law, courts, police, prisons, taxation, public schools, military forces) and these institutions carry with them similar problems and abuses (Donnelly 1999; Nickel 2006). Beyond this, the banner of cultural relativism is often carried by states with extremely bad human rights records and this gives the idea itself a bad odor (Bayefsky 1996).

We suggest, however, that these developments have changed the nature of the relativist challenge without making it obsolete. If the challenge was once *Is the very idea of universal human rights plausible in light of cultural and political diversity?* perhaps it is now changed to *In spite of their amazing successes in finding acceptance around the world, do lists of human rights still need to be understood and interpreted in ways that allow governments to accommodate local self-understandings, traditions, problems, and financial and institutional resources?*

This chapter addresses the second formulation of the relativist challenge. It explores and defends a view we call "modest prescriptive relativism," the idea that there are good moral and political reasons for valuing and accommodating the self-determination of peoples and countries, even when some of the accommodation must be made at the expense of human rights.

Relativisms

There are several different relativist theses that are important to distinguish. One, which we call "descriptive relativism," holds that as a matter of fact there are no moral norms shared by all people alive today. Although the world obviously contains considerable diversity of moral belief and practice, descriptive relativism is not obviously true—and the widespread acceptance of human rights treaties certainly challenges it. Differences over freedoms and rights are often exaggerated (Sen 2004, 253), and it is very likely that there are some universally shared moral norms. But in any case descriptive relativism is a purely descriptive claim and by itself entails no normative conclusions. To put the point differently, even if universally shared moral norms do not now exist, it could still be true that they ought to exist and that the international human rights movement is justified as a political effort to bring them into existence. Those who seek to resist the normative globalization threatened by universal human rights initiatives must argue from stronger premises than descriptive relativism.

A second relativist thesis, which we call "skeptical relativism," holds that the explanation of why our world has so much moral diversity is that there are no rational or objective cross-cultural bases for resolving moral disagreements. Without access to such grounds for assessing the truth or falsity of conflicting moral claims, there can be no good reasons for imposing our values on other countries. Defenders of skeptical relativism often maintain that tolerance is the appropriate response. It is unclear, however, how they could defend their preference for tolerance against those urging intolerance. Although there are no good grounds on this view for imposing one's values on another country, it is equally true that there are no good grounds for refraining from doing so.

Like descriptive relativism, skeptical relativism entails no normative conclusions. At most it suggests, with the help of the ought implies can principle, that one ought not to try to resolve moral disagreements through appeals to rational, objective, cross-cultural methods since none exist. Whatever the normative implications of skeptical relativism, it is unlikely we shall be driven to endorse them any time soon, for determining whether the thesis is true is a task even more Herculean than determining whether descriptive relativism is true.

Of course, if descriptive relativism could be established, then skeptical relativism might be put forward as the best explanation of the fact that there are no universally shared moral norms. The trouble is that there are so many other obvious and plausible explanations of moral diversity and disagreement, and thus of the descriptive relativism (were it to turn out to be true), that it is hard to see how one would go about vindicating this skeptical relativist thesis as the best explanation of it. And if the descriptive relativist thesis is hard to vindicate, then the possibility of there being—and of humans having access to—some rational, objective, and cross-cultural method for resolving moral disagreements would seem a likely explanation of such moral and legal consensus as does exist. Against those who object here that humans have yet to reach any consensus on the nature or content of any such method, it is worth noting that even if this objection is true, it does not entail that no such method exists, either as yet undiscovered or perhaps as latent but not yet articulated within human moral discourse and practice. Those who seek to resist the normative globalization of universal human rights initiatives must argue from more than skeptical relativism.

A third relativist thesis, which we call "prescriptive relativism," is that there are good cross-cultural reasons for claiming that tolerance ought universally to govern the relations between morally diverse peoples. On the strongest version of prescriptive relativism, tolerance of moral diversity is the only value or norm for which there are good objective moral reasons of universal application. Weaker versions of prescriptive relativism allow for additional universally binding values or norms, but insist that they are few in number and sufficiently narrow or abstract that they do not undermine the commitment to tolerating a very wide range of morally diverse value systems, cultures, ways of life, and legal and institutional arrangements.

Prescriptive relativism is incompatible with both descriptive and skeptical relativism. It rejects them in favor of a substantive moral view about the content and reach of universally binding values or norms and the rational, objective, cross-cultural methods deployed in their justification. Weaker versions of prescriptive relativism embody commitments to (1) a wide but not unlimited tolerance between peoples, (2) national sovereignty and self-determination constrained only by some basic international norms (apart from those positively undertaken by voluntary ratifications of human rights and other treaties), and (3) a global political order that does not stifle local cultures and traditions.

Prescriptive relativism aspires to offer a principled resolution of the conflict between those who seek, often rightly in our view, to resist the normative globalization threatened by some conceptions of universal human rights and those who reject, also rightly in our view, skeptical relativism in favor of a substantive and cosmopolitan ethic defended through appeal to rational argument and objective reasons. Prescriptive relativism may also be useful in debates over economic globalization. Those resisting economic globalization often argue for taking steps to ensure that diverse cultures, peoples, ways of life, and possibilities for local self-determination are not swamped by a tidal wave of economic, cultural, and political influences. But opponents of globalization typically appeal to substantive moral values or norms alleged to be universally binding. Their defense of moral and cultural diversity and local self-determination against the forces of economic globalization stems from a commitment to neither a descriptive nor a skeptical relativism; it is rather rooted in something like prescriptive relativism.

Tolerance and Self-Determination at the International Level

International tolerance can be supported by appealing to the value of diversity in the world's cultures and political institutions. There is such value, no doubt, but it does not extend to deeply unjust practices or institutional arrangements. It is wildly implausible to suggest that the world would be made better because more diverse if slavery were restored in Brazil or the United States, apartheid rebuilt in South Africa, or male-only voting reestablished in Switzerland. As part of any argument for international tolerance, the value of cultural and institutional diversity will be restricted to cultural and institutional patterns judged already to be just or acceptable to some requisite degree but threatened nonetheless by an international order insufficiently attentive to the demands of tolerance (as economic globalization is alleged by its critics to threaten some cultural or institutional patterns).

There are several good grounds for international tolerance beyond any commitment to the value of cultural and institutional diversity. One is the relationship between tolerance and international peace and stability. Tolerance is one dimension of civility, and as such it helps to reduce international friction and avoid war. If countries tolerate each other's problems and misdeeds—within limits, of course—the international political environment is likely to be safer and more stable.

Another ground for international tolerance is the fragility of our moral knowledge. It is normal to be confident of our moral beliefs and to have strong feelings about practices that violate them. But our moral capacities are limited, require factual knowledge that we often lack, and are subject to distortion and bias. Trade-offs between competing values are particularly difficult (Rawls 1996, 57). Given all this, we ought to exhibit an appropriate humility with respect to our moral judgments. Such humility will be expressed as tolerance for practices about which we have reason to think our views might be hasty, biased, poorly founded, or insensitive to differences in circumstance (Sen 2004, 250).

A third ground for international tolerance is respect for the autonomy or self-determination of peoples and countries. Countries able to act on the global stage and to assert their claims there think of themselves not just as corporate agents, but as corporate moral agents with rights and responsibilities. (Otherwise, they would neither claim nor be willing to extend fair treatment to others.) As corporate moral agents, they claim for themselves, and recognize in their peers, a right to self-determination. If we imagine peoples or countries coming together and trying to find reasonable and mutually acceptable terms to govern their interactions, it is not hard to see the attractions of a principle of tolerance. As mentioned above, each has an interest in reducing international friction and the prospects of war and this is one reason why such a principle would be proposed and accepted. But there are deeper reasons as well. Tolerance within limits is a reasonable policy for states to apply to each other. A principle of toleration requiring respect, within limits marked by basic norms of international law and fundamental human rights, for the self-determination and territorial integrity of states is a principle all states will or should find mutually acceptable.

Thinking about reasonable norms to govern interaction at the individual level requires us to work up and use a conception of the human person or individual moral agent. It is common to suggest that human persons (i.e., normal individual human adults) are (1) physical beings whose survival and welfare require protection and provision; (2) agents in the sense that they are able to act to promote their survival and welfare and to form, revise, and pursue a particular conception of their own good; and (3) moral beings in the sense that they are able to develop and act in accordance with moral standards, including standards of fair cooperation.

Like individual human persons, states are (1) physically embodied beings whose survival and welfare requires protection and provision. They are embodied in their human members, their territories, and their developed infrastructures. They are also (2) agents in that they are able to act to promote and protect their survival and welfare and in that they are able to form, revise, and pursue a conception of their national interests. And they are (3) moral beings in that they are able to identify and act in accordance with moral standards of reasonable interaction, including standards of justice.[2] Just as an individual human being need not possess these capacities and dispositions to any great or ideal degree to qualify as a person, so too a state or people need only possess them to some appropriate minimum and imperfect degree to qualify as a corporate artificial person.

Two problems with conceiving of states in this way should be addressed at once.

First, there is greater variety in size and power between states than there is between individual human persons. The differences in size and power between China and San Marino are greater than the differences between healthy adult humans. Even from within a moral point of view shared by all states as corporate moral agents, these differences in size and power might be thought to undermine the idea that reasonable terms of interaction require equal rights for all states. A sound normative theory of international relations will ground itself in both the common moral point of view shared by all states as corporate moral agents as well in an accurate empirical account of the scope of differences that may distinguish any one state from another.

Second, there is the question of whether states are capable of becoming and acting as moral agents and so constraining themselves by reasonable principles of interaction. The realist tradition in international relations has made skepticism about the ability of states to become or act as moral agents in this way its defining theme. At a minimum, the realist challenge requires us to emphasize that states, like individual persons, often engage in criminal and self-serving behavior. A sound normative theory of international relations will recognize the persistent moral and legal failings of states.

If countries were to think of themselves in accordance with the three-part conception sketched above and were to proceed to deliberate about reasonable terms of coexistence and interaction, some familiar principles would emerge and find acceptance. Among these would be the broad ideas of forbidding aggressive war, permitting war in self-defense, honoring international agreements, and allowing countries to pursue their interests as long as they do not harm other countries or impose serious costs or risks on them. These principles, found in the UN Charter (United Nations 1945), require all countries to tolerate at least some practices and institutions in other countries of which they disapprove. As an independent corporate moral agent, every state may be expected to claim for itself a substantial freedom or autonomy with respect to its own internal affairs, and thus to extend that same freedom or autonomy to other states. This implies mutual affirmation of a principle of toleration.

Countries say to each other: "We conceive of ourselves as moral agents, and as such we demand for ourselves and are willing to extend to one another—within reasonable limits—respect for our choices about how to organize ourselves and to conceive of and pursue our conceptions of the good." The result is a principle that gives states substantial liberty of action domestically and internationally. This principle limits what can be done, apart from the rights and duties created by treaties, to promote human rights at the international level. In this way, it requires tolerance between states.

Limits on Self-Determination and Tolerance

The appeal to reasonable terms of interaction between countries both supports the principle of self-determination and limits it. If reasonable terms of interaction between countries include a principle requiring respect for human rights, then tolerance will be limited, or at least balanced, by human rights. But in what way is a country's respect for the human rights of its citizens a requirement of its interacting reasonably with other countries? These seem to be different matters.

One answer, emerging from the experience of Hitler's human rights violations and found in the Universal Declaration of Human Rights (United Nations 1948), is that large-scale human rights violations are serious threats to international peace and accordingly can warrant—depending on their severity—international concern, scrutiny, diplomacy, pressure, and intervention. The Preamble of the Universal Declaration asserts that recognition of the dignity and rights of all people is the foundation of international peace. Respect for human rights eliminates many of the conditions likely to generate armed rebellion. Large-scale human rights violations within a country impose on other countries risks of instability and war.

Another answer appeals to the human rights treaties that most countries have accepted. In the last half-century, most of the world's states have agreed to be bound by the UN Charter and by human rights treaties, thereby voluntarily accepting limits on their freedom to order their domestic affairs as they wish. Commitment to the UN Charter and to human rights has become a prerequisite to good standing in the community of nations. States that repudiate human rights are outlaw states. A third way of explaining how human rights justifiably limit the tolerance principle draws on the demands of consistency in moral reasoning. As artificial corporate moral agents, countries or states seek to identify and make operative reasonable terms of interaction between themselves.[3] Consistency then demands that they treat reasonably the individual human agents that constitute their membership and govern them in accordance with a reasonable conception of justice. Once reasonableness is introduced as a governing idea for relations between persons as moral agents, it cannot be restricted simply to the relations between states as artificial corporate moral agents; it must be extended also to the relations of states with individual human persons. Indeed, respect for the most basic demands of reasonableness with regard to its treatment of its own citizens or residents is a condition each state must meet to merit respect from other states. Every state must respect and protect the fundamental interests of its members. And since every state has an interest in seeing all states honor this obligation, they are likely to be willing to see it enforced internationally. Furthermore, as secondary participants in the international debate over the terms of reasonable international relations, the individual human persons populating each of the world's states would affirm this reasoning, since it is crucial to their most fundamental interests being secured. Thus, the deliberations that yield the rights of every person also yield the idea of human rights as limits on the sovereignty or self-determination of states. Of course, the main requirements of reasonableness in how states treat their residents need to be identified and formulated, and that is what theorists of human rights as well as the authors of the Universal Declaration and subsequent treaties have attempted to do.

Rawls recognizes the apparent inconsistency in decent peoples demanding fair treatment from other peoples while being unwilling to extend fair treatment to their own members, but holds that the inconsistency is only apparent: "Some may object that treating the representatives of peoples equally when equality does not hold within their domestic societies is inconsistent, or unfair" (Rawls 1999, 69–70). He rejects this objection as follows:

> Equality holds between reasonable or decent, and rational, individuals and collectives of various sorts when the relation of equality between them is appropriate for the case at hand. An example: in certain matters, churches may be treated equally and are to be consulted as equals on policy questions—the Catholic and Congregational churches, for instance. This can be sound practice, it seems, even though the first is hierarchically organized, while the second is not. A second example: universities may also be organized in many ways. Some may choose their presidents by a kind of consultation hierarchy including all recognized groups, others by elections in which their members, including undergraduates, have a vote. . . . But the fact that universities' internal arrangements differ doesn't rule out the propriety of treating them as equals in certain circumstances.

Rawls's analogy here is weak for three reasons. First, churches and universities are effectively constrained in how they treat their members by the domestic law of liberal societies, but decent nonliberal countries are not constrained by (international) laws that are as effective and comprehensive. Second, churches and universities in liberal societies typically have less impact on a person's prospects than do a country's basic political institutions and practices. Third, people can typically leave abusive churches and universities with less cost than is involved in leaving one's country. It remains far from obvious why the injustice of the domestic institutions of decent societies does not undermine their claims to full equality at the international level.[4]

Decisions made by national governments sometimes go against human rights principles. Should we give any weight to these decisions even when they are incompatible with human rights? We think the answer is affirmative, that some weight should be given even in these cases. This weight will rarely if ever be sufficient to justify respect or tolerance for a governmental decision that runs roughshod over the core of a fundamental human right. But it may sometimes be sufficient to justify at least partial respect or tolerance for good faith decisions about how to understand the core of a right, about which institutions are essential to implementing this or that right, about how to deal with scarcity of resources, and about how to make the transition to fuller compliance with the full range of human rights. Societies that use slavery or apartheid or that purposefully deny subsistence or security or the rule of law to some or all of their citizens or residents ought not be tolerated because they violate systematically the cores of fundamental human rights. But peaceful and internally stable indigenous societies living in traditional ways marked by some illiberal customs and practices, or states that decide, not unreasonably in light of their own local conditions and challenges, to make limited provision for democratic participation, perhaps ought to be tolerated.

There are several reasons for thinking that particular human rights should sometimes yield to an exercise of sovereignty or self-determination. One possible reason is that the moral standing of states is of sufficient weight to preclude any hard and fast rule giving priority to each and every human right over the right of states to determine for themselves how to act, both domestically and internationally. Another is that the only way to decentralize and disperse political power is to empower various national and subnational agencies to exercise their own judgment. These agencies will not be able to fulfill their assigned roles unless we give them considerable latitude.

Clarifying Prescriptive Relativism

We are now in position to define more clearly the position we call "modest prescriptive relativism." Strong prescriptive relativism, which endorses only the principle of toleration and thereby gives unlimited scope to self-determination, is not plausible. Many things are required of countries, and of the international community, besides toleration. The strong claim that tolerance is the only objective and universally binding moral value is too close to abdication of our capacities for moral judgment and responsibility to pass any test of moral justification in which reflective equilibrium figures prominently (Rawls 2001, 29). Furthermore, it is not plausible to imagine that one could provide normative grounds that would support a requirement of tolerance and nothing more. For example, if one grounds tolerance in a principle of respect for persons and their cultures and religions, this principle will also support protecting people against violence and respecting their liberties to pursue and develop their cultures and religions. Solid grounds for international tolerance are sure to provide grounds for some individual human rights as well.

Our proposed version of modest prescriptive relativism urges tolerance within limits as a way of respecting the self-determination of countries. We endorse the familiar view that the lists of human rights found in today's human rights treaties help set the outer limits of self-determination. Just as criminal law limits self-determination at the individual level, human rights— along with some other basic principles of international morality and law— specify the areas where national self-determination runs out, or at least loses much of its power. Let's describe this as giving human rights a limiting role in relation to the self-determination of peoples and countries. Human rights clearly play this limiting role, but we think that there should be room for considerable flexibility and compromise at the margins, at the points where conflicts between self-determination and human rights permit more than one reasonable resolution.

Tolerance is a complicated idea. Suppose that Canada tolerates Burma's lack of democracy. To understand this relationship between the two countries, there are a number of questions that need to be answered. First, what does Canada find bad about Burma's lack of democracy? Why does Canada dislike or disapprove of it? Does it go against Canada's interests? Does Canada believe as a matter of principle that it is bad or wrong? Second, what are the reasons or grounds for Canada's policy of tolerance? Is it that doing anything about the lack of democracy in Burma is too costly or dangerous, or is it that Canada has reasons of principle for toleration? And third, which specific actions fall under tolerance? Does tolerating Burma's lack of democracy mean not invading or sanctioning Burma over this, not criticizing it about this publicly or privately, or not dissociating fully or partially from it?

In the present context, we will be concerned entirely with tolerance of a country's behavior that (1) is based on the belief that the behavior is wrong, unjust, or in violation of human rights, but is nevertheless the behavior of a state capable of considering seriously and binding itself to the demands of reasonableness with respect to its domestic order; (2) is grounded in principle rather than (or in addition to) a desire to avoid the costs of intolerance; (3) excludes using force to stop the country from the action or policy; and (4) does not view the country as an outlaw state that does not deserve full membership in the community of nations. Tolerance is compatible with criticizing the country about the action or policy and using diplomacy to try to persuade it to change. It is also compatible with refusing to promote or undertake certain interactions with the country being tolerated, even when this distancing imposes some costs on that country. It is not compatible with treating the tolerated country as if it were an outlaw state or otherwise fully outside the international community.[5]

The connection between tolerance and self-determination or autonomy is not hard to explain. If Canada and all other countries tolerate Burma's lack of democracy in the way described above, Burma is not forced to become democratic. Burma remains free, autonomous, and self-governing in regard to the use of democratic institutions. Still, as a member of an international moral community, it cannot escape moral criticism or other forms of informal censure.

We now need to specify which human rights we have in mind and offer a view of how we see decisions about the priority, interpretation, and implementation of these rights being made.

Which Rights?

Possible views of which human rights are important enough fully and always to limit the self-determination of states range from minimal to grand. At the minimal end, a plausible view might use the Rome Statute of the International Criminal Court (United Nations 1998) to identify a short list of fundamental human rights. Setting aside war crimes and aggression, the human rights in the Rome Statute fall into two categories, the first dealing with genocide and the second with crimes against humanity. Genocide is directing against a national, ethnic, racial, or religious group actions such as killing, harming, preventing births, and transferring children with the intent of destroying the group (Article 6). Crimes against humanity are defined both by their scale—they involve a "widespread or systematic attack"—and by their content. They involve actions such as murder, torture, rape, enslavement, deportation or forcible transfer of a population, and imprisonment in violation of the fundamental rules of international law (Article 7).

At the maximal end of the continuum a plausible view might include as fundamental all of the rights found in the Rome Statute of the International Criminal Court and in the International Covenant on Civil and Political

Rights (United Nations 1966a), and a few of the rights (particularly subsistence, minimal health services, and education) found in the International Covenant on Economic, Social, and Cultural Rights (United Nations 1966b). Taking this approach would yield the six families of human rights: (1) security rights including rights against genocide and crimes against humanity; (2) due process rights such as the right to a fair trial; (3) rights to fundamental freedoms such as belief, expression, and association; (4) rights to political participation and democratic institutions; (5) equality rights such as equal citizenship, equality before the law, and nondiscrimination; and (6) economic and social rights such as subsistence, minimal health care, and education.

Our position lies at this maximal end of the continuum. But we do not hold the view that each and every right belonging to any one of these six families fully and always limits the self-determination of states. Thinking about tolerance and self-determination cannot be conducted entirely at the level of what sort of tolerance between countries or peoples is most reasonable, most respectful, or best. As soon as we recognize that toleration has substantive limits, we will have to examine the reasons or justifications for the particular principles or rights that are taken to provide those limits. To know whether a particular democratic or due process right should limit tolerance, we have to consider the strength and generality of the justifications for that right. Because of this, the extent to which any particular right limits tolerance cannot be determined without working up an account of the justification and weight of the right in question.

That job is beyond the scope of this chapter. Our tentative view, however, is that once such justifications are tendered, we will find that there are good reasons to preserve the main items in all six families and to treat them as fundamental limits on the international norm of tolerance. Thus, we do not favor attempts to eliminate any of the six families of human rights listed above. Such wholesale cuts are neither necessary nor useful. The conception of human rights suggested by these six families and derived from the Universal Declaration of Human Rights is now so well entrenched in treaties and in international organizations that the time for completely rethinking it as a blueprint for human rights has passed.

Priority, Interpretation, and Implementation

Human rights norms are formulated in broad language that gives countries considerable latitude to decide what they mean, what their weight is in relation to other considerations, and how they are to be implemented. This latitude is reduced, of course, when there is an international court that is authorized to issue binding interpretations of human rights norms. Within the

European human rights system there is the European Court of Human Rights that has such authority and uses it to adjudicate complaints that member countries are not living up to their commitments (Council of Europe 1950). Even there, however, the Court gives considerable deference to the longstanding practices of governments under the "margin of appreciation" doctrine (Steiner and Alston 2000, 554 f). Human rights treaties within the United Nations do not have courts, but rather have quasi-judicial committees whose job it is to receive reports from participating countries, discuss and evaluate those reports, make interpretive suggestions, and—in some cases—receive and attempt to mediate complaints.

The interpretive principles we set forth below are ones that apply apart from the requirements of particular treaties. But they also describe, we suspect, the position that countries are in after they have ratified the International Covenants (United Nations 1966a, 1966b). We propose that

1. The self-determination of countries and peoples should be viewed as a norm that extends into the area of human rights. This means that conflicts between self-determination and human rights will sometimes have to be resolved by balancing each against the other.
2. Countries should be permitted to develop interpretations and justifications of human rights that fit their cultures and circumstances. These national understandings of human rights will have implications for both the priority and the content of particular rights.
3. Countries acting in good faith should have space to develop their own views about which part of a right is the core, which the margin, and which parts are useful but lower-priority prophylactic measures and supporting institutions. For example, a country would unacceptably abandon due process rights if it rejected the principle in the International Covenant on Civil and Political Rights that "all persons deprived of their liberty shall be treated with humanity and with respect for the inherent dignity of the human person (Article 10:1)," but it might reasonably decide to view as a lower-priority prophylactic measure the principle, immediately following, that "accused persons shall, save in exceptional circumstances, be segregated from convicted persons" (Article 10:2(a)).
4. Countries acting in good faith should have latitude to formulate their own plans for the implementation of human rights, even if this means that some rights will not be adequately realized in the near term. This principle is made explicit in the clause of the International Covenant on Economic, Social, and Cultural Rights that permits progressive implementation (Article 2:1). But for poorer countries, at least, a similar view

of the implementation of some civil and political rights is appropriate. This would not extend, however, to the rights found in the Statute of the International Criminal Court because there are no reasonable grounds for any state not to honor these rights fully and immediately.

5. Countries acting in good faith should be free to trim specific rights within any of the several families of human rights (e.g., liberty rights, due process rights, economic rights, etc.) so long as the most central rights in each family are retained. For example, a country could permissibly trim its view of economic and social rights to the most basic ones— namely, rights to subsistence, minimal health care, and basic education.

The Case for Rights to Political Liberties and to Democratic Institutions

To illustrate these principles, we consider a case in which a country without democratic institutions decides to delay its transition to democracy. In thinking about this issue, it is useful to distinguish rights to political liberties and rights to democratic institutions. We distinguish these two categories because we suspect they have different degrees of importance. The International Covenant on Civil and Political Rights addresses rights to political liberty in three articles:

Article 19. (1.) Everyone shall have the right to hold opinions without interference. (2.) Everyone shall have the right to freedom of expression; this right shall include freedom to seek, receive and impart information and ideas of all kinds, regardless of frontiers, either orally, in writing or in print, in the form of art, or through any other media of his choice.

Article 21. The right of peaceful assembly shall be recognized. No restrictions may be placed on the exercise of this right other than those imposed in conformity with the law and which are necessary in a democratic society in the interests of national security or public safety, public order (ordre public), the protection of public health or morals or the protection of the rights and freedoms of others.

Article 22. (1.) Everyone shall have the right to freedom of association with others, including the right to form and join trade unions for the protection of his interests. (2.) No restrictions may be placed on the exercise of this right other than those which are prescribed by law and which are necessary in a democratic society in the interests of national security or public safety, public order (ordre public), the protection of public health or morals or the protection of the rights and freedoms of others. This article shall not prevent the imposition of lawful restrictions on members of the armed forces and of the police in their exercise of this right.

These fundamental liberties are individual rights, justified at least in part by their importance to the ability of individuals to have and lead lives of their own. These liberties extend to the political realm, and indeed have particular importance there. To deny these rights is to wrong particular individuals. Rights to democratic institutions are addressed in Article 25:

> Every citizen shall have the right and the opportunity, without any of the distinctions mentioned in article 2 and without unreasonable restrictions: (a) To take part in the conduct of public affairs, directly or through freely chosen representatives; (b) To vote and to be elected at genuine periodic elections which shall be by universal and equal suffrage and shall be held by secret ballot, guaranteeing the free expression of the will of the electors; (c) To have access, on general terms of equality, to public service in his country.

Wholesale suppression of fundamental freedoms in the political area creates an authoritarian and unaccountable state. It is possible, however, for a country to allow considerable scope to these freedoms in the political sphere without having democratic institutions in the sense of genuine periodic elections in which political leaders are chosen. There are two possible scenarios to consider:

> Scenario 1. A-land engages in wholesale suppression of the liberties of thought, expression, association, and assembly in the political sphere and refuses to adopt democratic institutions.
> Scenario 2. B-land does not engage in wholesale suppression of the liberties of thought, expression, association, and assembly in the political sphere but does refuse to adopt democratic institutions in the sense of periodic elections of political leaders.

B-land allows considerable freedom in the political area and, hence, citizens are free to engage in political thought, communication, and meetings. Through these permitted actions, residents can influence government officials and leaders in various ways, and there are some established channels for doing this.

It is easy to reach the conclusion that B-land is a better candidate for international toleration than A-land.[6] But we still need to explain why wholesale rejection of democratic institutions (Article 25) is a less serious violation of human rights than rejection of liberties of thought, expression, association, and assembly in the political sphere. It should be said, however, that it is not easy for a country to respect fundamental freedoms in the political area without moving in the direction of democracy. If people are free to speak and write publicly about political issues, to associate for political purposes (such as the formation of political parties and movements), and to assemble peaceably in political rallies and protests, they will be able to put a lot of pressure on the government. Unless a government responds to such pressure with suppression of these fundamental freedoms, it will likely be pushed in the direction of democratic institutions. A great advantage of democratic institutions is that they provide a facility or platform for the exercise of fundamental political freedoms. Indeed, democratic institutions are usefully seen as making positive provision for the largely negative political liberties.

There are at least four reasons for tolerating countries like B-land. First, movement away from nondemocratic forms of government and to democracy is usually gradual and may take decades. Countries may reasonably introduce democracy by starting with elections of local officials and then extending electoral politics to top leadership positions.

Second, democratic institutions do not work in some situations. Perhaps the country has too low a level of education or is too ethnically divided for democratic institutions to be effective. Because judgments of this sort are so frequently self-serving, governments who make them should not go unchallenged internationally (and the systems of implementation that go with United Nations human rights treaties provide good opportunities for making such challenges). But self-serving judgments are sometimes correct nonetheless.

Third, refusing democratic institutions does not directly harm individuals (unlike violations of fundamental political freedoms). At most, the absence of democratic institutions increases the likelihood that other rights are violated. But, as suggested earlier, it is helpful to distinguish the core of a right, its margins, and institutions and prophylactic measures needed or likely to protect it. Institutions and prophylactic measures are generally the parts of a right that are most appropriately sacrificed in order to accommodate other rights and other values. To the extent that democratic rights function as institutional means for making good on more fundamental political liberties, they may have less weight than the rights to the more central political liberties and in the end insufficient weight in some cases to outweigh the moral demands of tolerance and respect for the self-determination of states.

A fourth reason, of a somewhat different character, for thinking that the rights to democratic institutions might sometimes justifiably yield to respect for the self-determination of states or peoples pertains to tribal and indigenous peoples that have authoritarian and hierarchical forms of governance deeply embedded in their cultural traditions. Here the question is not merely what works best; it is also one of what form fits the culture and helps preserve some of its key features or at least does not constitute a radical and immediate threat. Rejection of standard forms of democratic institutions, at least for some period of time, can sometimes be defended on these grounds. All human beings have a fundamental interest in a cultural order sufficiently secure and stable to permit a meaningful life. And within some groups, an immediate transition to democracy would be so culturally disruptive that it would be at odds with that fundamental interest (Kymlicka 1989). It should be said, however, that once a people has adopted all of the institutions of the modern state, it also needs the protections developed to make states safer for citizens to live with. It needs rule of law, due process rights, and eventually democratic institutions in one form or another. Appeals to traditional forms of governance are often anachronistic and politically naïve.

States refusing democratic institutions sometimes have a claim to tolerance. They can plausibly argue that the reasons for adopting democratic institutions are not so strong and universal that they require every country to immediately adopt such institutions. With that we agree. Even justified tolerance, however, should not be uncritical. Tolerating a country's decisions to stick with non-democratic political institutions does not mean that criticism is out of order. Diplomatic pressure from other countries and from nongovernmental organizations to promote democratic institutions is not excluded.

The sort of analysis of political liberties and democratic institutions that we have offered can be extended to other rights in any of the six families of human rights. In each case, the limits of tolerance can be marked only after a careful analysis of the rights and values in question. There is no moral algorithm to be used to mechanically resolve such issues in any routine fashion. There is only the general idea that each of the six families of rights contains one or more core rights that mark a fundamental limit on international tolerance and on the self-determination of states. It is important to remember here that human rights generally, and the core human rights most especially, function not as a morality of aspiration but rather as a morality of minimum requirements (Nickel 2006; Shue 1996). Thus affirming some human rights as fundamental limits on international tolerance and the self-determination of states ought not be viewed as encroaching substantially on the values of either tolerance or self-determination.

Conclusion

Modest prescriptive relativism offers an attractive way of harmonizing universal human rights with the right to self-determination and with respect for cultural diversity. Tolerance within limits set by human rights is a very defensible and widely accepted principle. Our approach to characterizing those limits proposes preserving the core rights in all of the six families of human rights while allowing considerable scope for balancing and trimming within them. There is room, we think, for accommodation and self-determination within a human rights agenda that takes universality seriously.

Notes

1. We recognize that countries often have reasons other than sincere acceptance for ratifying human rights treaties. For example, they may wish to make themselves look good to the international community.

2. Just as natural persons include sociopaths who are seriously deficient in their moral capacities, artificial corporate persons include states and organizations that are seriously deficient in their moral capacities because of disorganization or tyrannical leadership. Thomas Nagel has recently speculated that "the path from anarchy to justice must go through injustice" (Nagel 2005, 147).

3. The idea of reasonableness used here is similar to that of Scanlon (1998, 191 f) and Rawls (1996, 50 f).

4. For a sympathetic reconstruction and defense of Rawls's view, see Reidy (2004).

5. John Rawls, in *The Law of Peoples*, defines tolerance as follows: "To tolerate means not only to refrain from exercising political sanctions—military, economic, or diplomatic—to make a people change its ways. To tolerate also means to recognize these nonliberal societies as equal participating members in good standing of the Society of Peoples" (Rawls 1999, 52).

6. What we propose here is reasonably close in spirit, although very different in how it is described, to the view proposed by Rawls in *The Law of Peoples* (1999).

Bibliography

Bauer, J. and Bell, D., eds. 1999. *The East Asian Challenge for Human Rights* (Cambridge, UK: Cambridge University Press).

Bayefsky, A. 2001. *The UN Human Rights Treaty System: Universality at the Crossroads* (Ardsley, NY: Transnational).

———. 1996. "Cultural Sovereignty, Relativism, and International Human Rights: New Excuses for Old Stategies," *Ratio Juris* 9: 42–59.

Council of Europe. 1950. European Convention on Human Rights. www.hrcr.org/docs/Eur_Convention/euroconv.html (accessed April 5, 2007).

Donnelly, Jack. 1999. "Human Rights and Western Values: A Defense of 'Western' Universalism," in Bauer and Bell, *The East Asian Challenge for Human Rights*, 1999.

Gould, C. 2004. *Globalizing Democracy and Human Rights* (Cambridge, UK: Cambridge University Press).

Kymlicka, W. 1989. *Liberalism, Community, and Culture* (Oxford: Clarendon Press).

Nagel, T. 2005. "The Problem of Global Justice," *Philosophy & Public Affairs* 33: 113–47.

Nickel, J. 2006. *Making Sense of Human Rights.* 2nd ed. (Oxford: Blackwell Publishing).

Rawls, J. 2001. *Justice as Fairness* (Cambridge, MA: Harvard University Press).

———. 1999. *The Law of Peoples* (Cambridge, MA: Harvard University Press).

———. 1996. *Political Liberalism* (New York: Columbia University Press).

Reidy, D. 2004. "Rawls on International Justice: A Defense," *Political Theory* 32: 291–319.

Scanlon, T. 1998. *What We Owe to Each Other* (Cambridge, MA: Harvard University Press).

Sen, A. 2004. "Elements of a Theory of Human Rights," *Philosophy & Public Affairs* 32: 315–56.

Shue, H. 1996. *Basic Rights: Subsistence, Affluence, and US Foreign Policy* (Princeton, NJ: Princeton University Press).

Steiner, H. and Alston, P. eds. 2000. *International Human Rights in Context* (Oxford: Oxford University Press).

United Nations. 1998. Rome Statute of the International Criminal Court. www.prevent genocide.org/law/icc/statute (accessed April 5, 2007).

———. 1966a. International Covenant on Civil and Political Rights. http://193.194.138 .190/html/menu3/b/a_ccpr.htm (accessed April 5, 2007).

———. 1966b. International Covenant on Economic, Social, and Cultural Rights. http://193.194.138.190/html/menu3/b/a_cescr.htm (accessed April 5, 2007).

———. 1948. Universal Declaration of Human Rights. www.un.org/rights/50/decla.htm.

———. Charter, 1945. www.un.org/aboutun/charter/ (accessed April 5, 2007).

4

Constitutions and Capabilities

Martha C. Nussbaum[1]

I. The Capabilities Approach and Social Justice

FOR MANY YEARS, APPROACHES TO POVERTY in the international development and policy-making world were obtuse in human terms. They focused on economic growth as the primary goal of development and measured quality of life simply by looking at gross national product (GNP) per capita. That crude measure, of course, did not even take distribution into account, and thus was utterly useless in confronting nations with a lot of poverty and high rates of inequality. Actually, it was worse than useless because it gave high marks to nations that contained huge inequalities, encouraging people to think that such nations (for example, South Africa under apartheid) had done things right. Moreover, as that example shows, the GNP approach also failed to take cognizance of other aspects of the quality of life that are not well correlated with economic advantage, even when distribution is factored in: aspects such as health, education, gender, and racial justice. And once again, by suggesting that things were well done when nations increased their GNP, it positively distracted attention from these factors.

Today, a different approach is prominent: the capabilities approach, also known as the "human development approach," represented in the *Human Development Reports* of the United Nations Development Programme. As the late Mahbub Ul Haq wrote in the first of those reports, in 1990, "The real wealth of a nation is its people. And the purpose of development is to create an enabling environment for people to enjoy long, healthy, and creative lives. This simple but powerful truth is too often forgotten in the pursuit of material and financial wealth." Economist Amartya Sen, of course, has been the primary architect of this approach; I have also developed it, focusing particularly on women's poverty and the relationship between poverty and sex inequality. More recently, the international Human Development and Capability Association, founded in 2004, has brought together researchers from many nations (eighty-six were represented at the 2004 annual conference) to pursue the refinement and implementation of the approach.

Most of the time, the approach is used in a comparative way, as in the *Human Development Reports*: capabilities are recommended as the best space within which to make comparisons of welfare or quality of life. But it also seems to have implications for thinking about social justice in a modern constitutional democracy, as it appears that a decent society will secure to all citizens a certain level of some key human capabilities. In this chapter, I suggest that there is indeed a further role for the capabilities approach to play in working out a theory of social justice, and one that supplies definite and useful guidance to law and public policy. Capabilities, I argue, provide us with a very helpful way of thinking about entitlements based on justice that a just constitutional democracy ought to secure to all its citizens, entitlements that can be formulated in fundamental constitutional guarantees.[2] Capabilities thus provide the basis for a partial account of social justice. I shall develop this role for the capabilities approach, using examples from a variety of constitutional traditions to illustrate my argument, and showing how a legislative and judicial tradition can further articulate entitlements that are rightly stated at the outset in a rather general and abstract way.

Next, I argue that the capabilities approach provides a better starting point for thinking about fundamental constitutional entitlements, in several ways, than do rights-based approaches, although there is also considerable complementarity between the language of capabilities and the language of rights. I then argue that an approach to constitutional entitlements that focuses on capabilities as a political goal is also superior to the perspective on social justice that derives from the social contract tradition, because it can deal much better with issues of caregiving and the need for care that have rightly become very prominent in recent political and economic debates.[3]

Commending the capabilities approach over its rivals, I then return to Sen's current theory. I shall argue that if capabilities are to play the role I have in mind for them, we will need to depart from Sen's agnosticism concerning which capabilities should be seen as most central for political purposes. We need to take a stand—not, I would argue, grounded in ultimate metaphysics, but rather a stand for political purposes—on a working list of capabilities that can then get further articulated and also supplemented in the course of a legal and political tradition. I argue that Sen's recent tendency to speak of freedom as a general goal to be promoted across the board is not helpful in thinking well about the role for capabilities in such a partial theory of social justice. Some freedoms are central for political purposes and others are not. If we do not make such distinctions, we run a risk both of incoherence (some freedoms limit others) and also of giving support to neoliberal objections that would ultimately be fatal to the project of social justice as I (and I believe Sen) understand it. Moreover, specifying a distinct and relatively limited list of capabilities as constitutionally central is important for another reason as well: It helps us preserve respect for pluralism, in the sense that many citizens in a pluralistic society may not endorse freedom as an across-the-board goal in social life, although they may be happy to endorse specific types of freedom as appropriate political ends.

II. Sen on Social Justice

Sen often suggests that capabilities have a bearing on issues of social justice, and it is useful to begin by drawing the threads of these discussions together so that subsequent comparative remarks have a clear focus. In *Development as Freedom*, as in earlier work, Sen pursues one line of thought, arguing that capabilities provide the best basis for thinking about the goals of development. Both when nations are compared by international measures of welfare and when each nation strives internally to achieve a higher level of development for its people, capabilities provide us with an attractive way of understanding the normative content of the idea of development. Sen has effectively argued that two traditional conceptions of the goals of development are inferior to the framework provided by capabilities. Thinking of development's goal as an increase in GNP per capita occluded distributional inequalities. It also failed to dissaggregate and separately consider important aspects of development, such as health and education, that are demonstrably not very well correlated with GNP, even when we take distribution into account. Thinking of development's goal in terms of utility at least has the merit of looking at what processes do for people. But utility, Sen argues, is inadequate to capture the heterogeneity and noncommensurability of the diverse aspects of development. It also fails to take into account the fact of adaptive preferences, and thus, used as a normative target, it biases the development process in favor of the status quo. Finally, it suggests that the goal of development is a state or condition of persons (e.g., a state of satisfaction), and thus understates the importance of agency and freedom in the development process.

Not surprisingly, I endorse these arguments. But I think that they do not take us very far in thinking about social justice. They give us a general sense of what societies ought to be striving to achieve, but because of Sen's reluctance to make commitments about substance (which capabilities a society should most centrally pursue), even that guidance remains but an outline. And they give us no sense of what a minimum level of capability for a just society might be. The use of capabilities in development is typically comparative merely, as in the *Human Development Reports* of the United Nations Development Programme (UNDP). Thus, 174 nations are compared in areas such as health and educational attainment. But concerning what level of health service, or what level of educational provision, a just society would deliver as a fundamental entitlement of all its citizens, the view is suggestive, but basically silent.

Another famous line of argument pursued by Sen in works from "Equality of What?" to *Inequality Reexamined* seems more closely related to concerns of social justice. This argument begins from the idea of equality as a central political value. Most states consider equality important, Sen argues, and yet they often do not ask perspicuously enough what the right space is within which to make the relevant comparisons. With arguments closely related to his arguments about the goals of development, Sen argues that the space of capabilities provides the most fruitful and ethically satisfactory way of looking at equality as a political goal. Equality of utility or welfare falls short for the reasons I have already summarized. Equality of resources falls short because it fails to take into account the fact that individuals have differing needs for resources if they are to come up to the same level of capability to function. They also have differing abilities to convert resources into actual functioning.

Some of these differences are straightforwardly physical: a child needs more protein than an adult to achieve a similar level of healthy functioning, and a pregnant woman more nutrients than a nonpregnant woman. But the differences that most interest Sen are social and are connected with entrenched discrimination of various types. Thus, in a nation where women are traditionally discouraged from pursuing an education, it will usually take more resources to produce female literacy than male literacy. Or, to cite Sen's famous example, a person in a wheelchair will require more resources connected with mobility than will the person with "normal" mobility, if the two are to attain a similar level of ability to get around. (Although Sen tends to treat this example as one of straightforward physical difference, I believe that we should not treat it so, as the reasons that the wheelchair-bound person is not able to get around are thoroughly social. We know that in a marathon the wheelchair contestants always finish more quickly than those who use their own limbs. What impedes their mobility in life generally is the lack of social provisions: ramps, wheelchair access, lifts on buses, and so on. The social world is made for people with an average set of abilities and disabilities, and not for the person whose condition is nonaverage.[4])

Sen's arguments about equality seem to have the following bearing on issues of social justice and on public policy: to the extent that a society values the equality of persons and pursues that as among its social goals, equality of capabilities looks like the most relevant sort of equality to aim at. But Sen never says to what extent equality of capability *ought* to be a social goal,[5] or how it ought to be combined with other political values in the pursuit of social justice. Thus, the connection of his equality arguments with a theory of justice remains as yet unclear.

III. Fundamental Constitutional Principles

When liberal democracies make constitutions, they typically base their work on a small core of intuitive ideas to which specific constitutional entitlements are referred. Prominent in many modern constitutions is the idea of human dignity, or of a life that is worthy of the dignity of the human being.[6] The basic idea of my version of the capabilities approach, in *Women and Human Development*, is that we begin with a conception of the dignity of the human being, and of a life that is worthy of that dignity—a life that has available in it "truly human functioning," in the sense described by Marx in his 1844 *Economic and Philosophical Manuscripts*. With this basic idea as a starting point, I then attempt to justify a list of ten capabilities as central requirements of a life with dignity:

The Central Human Capabilities

1. Life. Being able to live to the end of a human life of normal length; not dying prematurely or before one's life is so reduced as to be not worth living.
2. Bodily health. Being able to have good health, including reproductive health; to be adequately nourished; to have adequate shelter.
3. Bodily integrity. Being able to move freely from place to place; to be secure against violent assault, including sexual assault and domestic violence; having opportunities for sexual satisfaction and for choice in matters of reproduction.
4. Senses, imagination, and thought. Being able to use the senses, to imagine, think, and reason—and to do these things in a "truly human" way, a way informed and cultivated by an adequate education, including, but by no means limited to, literacy and basic mathematical and scientific training. Being able to use imagination and thought in connection with experiencing and producing works and events of one's own choice, religious,

literary, musical, and so forth. Being able to use one's mind in ways protected by guarantees of freedom of expression with respect to both political and artistic speech, and freedom of religious exercise. Being able to have pleasurable experiences and to avoid nonbeneficial pain.

5. Emotions. Being able to have attachments to things and people outside ourselves; to love those who love and care for us, to grieve at their absence; in general, to love, to grieve, to experience longing, gratitude, and justified anger. Not having one's emotional development blighted by fear and anxiety. (Supporting this capability means supporting forms of human association that can be shown to be crucial in their development.)

6. Practical reason. Being able to form a conception of the good and to engage in critical reflection about the planning of one's life. (This entails protection for the liberty of conscience and religious observance.)

7. Affiliation. (a) Being able to live with and toward others, to recognize and show concern for other human beings, to engage in various forms of social interaction; to be able to imagine the situation of another. (Protecting this capability means protecting institutions that constitute and nourish such forms of affiliation, and also protecting the freedom of assembly and political speech.) (b) Having the social bases of self-respect and nonhumiliation; being able to be treated as a dignified being whose worth is equal to that of others. This entails provisions of nondiscrimination on the basis of race, sex, sexual orientation, ethnicity, caste, religion, and national origin.

8. Other species. Being able to live with concern for and in relation to animals, plants, and the natural world.

9. Play. Being able to laugh, play, and enjoy recreational activities.

10. Control over one's environment. (a) Political. Being able to participate effectively in political choices that govern one's life; having the right of political participation, protections of free speech, and association. (b) Material. Being able to hold property (both land and movable goods), and having property rights on an equal basis with others; having the right to seek employment on an equal basis with others; having the freedom from unwarranted search and seizure. In work, being able to work as a human being, exercising practical reason and entering into meaningful relationships of mutual recognition with other workers.

The idea of capability is combined with the idea of a threshold: It is a minimum obligation of a just society to provide all citizens with every one of these capabilities up to some appropriate threshold level. (I say "minimum obligation" because this use of capabilities is intended as only a partial theory of social justice, not a full such theory. In particular, I do not comment on inequalities above the threshold, not because I think the issue unimportant, but rather because I believe that it is possible to get a robust cross-cultural agreement on a robust list of basic minimum entitlements of all citizens and to turn to that difficult issue afterward.[7])

The proposal is that a typical constitution, in a liberal democratic society, would be based on fundamental political principles that would include all ten of these capabilities, in some form, as fundamental entitlements of all citizens. In one way or another, it would be made clear that these are entitlements based on justice that all citizens have a right to claim, not just things that it is nice to have. A violation of any one of them, or a failure to deliver any one of them, is thus an especially grave type of moral failure on the part of the nation in question, a failure involving matters of basic justice. Typically, this would be done most straightforwardly by enumerating the entitlements, in some suitable form, in a section of the constitutional document dealing with fundamental rights. (There may at times be reasons why nations may prefer to take a different path, either not using a written constitution at all, or not enumerating all these rights in an explicit form; but the idea is that their fundamental political principles, public and available to all, would nonetheless make clear that these are fundamental entitlements based on justice.)

Thus, the Indian Constitution contains a section entitled Fundamental Rights, which are fully justiciable: If a citizen is denied any one of these, that denial immediately becomes a matter for the courts to deal with. It also contains another section, the "Directive Principles of State Policy," which is purely aspirational, stating things that it would be good for the state to try to achieve. My capabilities list is intended to provide a basis for the former, not the latter. Once we supply the threshold level in some appropriate way, the goal is an urgent requirement of justice. Thus, at times, India has considered moving one of the aspirational principles into the Fundamental Rights section. This is now being proposed with the right to free primary and secondary education. What proponents of that switch intend by this is that education, up to the threshold level specified, would be seen not simply as something that is nice to strive for, but as a fundamental entitlement of all citizens based on justice. States that do not deliver it can be taken to court. This is the sort of thing I have in mind.

Another way of putting the core idea is that when a central capability is denied to any citizen, there is always a serious moral violation. Thus, central capabilities are not subject to cost-benefit analysis in the usual way, along with other sources of social advantage. The cost involved in denying a central capability to a citizen is not just a large cost—it is a cost *of a distinctive kind*, one that involves denying someone something to which they have an entitlement based on justice. That means that should we be in the unpleasant predicament

of having to deny some citizens one capability in order to give them another
(let's say we have to deny poor children an education in order to preserve their
parents' lives, which currently depend on child labor), we should view that not
just as a situation where a large cost is incurred, but an especially tragic situation that involves violation of a fundamental entitlement. Seeing the situation that way puts us all on notice that the current status quo, which has
forced this tragic choice, is unacceptable: We must get to work and make a situation in which all fundamental entitlements of citizens can be fulfilled.[8]

Capabilities play another related role in constitutions. They supply limits to
what the state is entitled to permit in the name of cultural and religious pluralism. Thus, a well-known U.S. doctrine (now temporarily defunct[9]) holds
that the state may not impose a "substantial burden" on an individual's free
exercise of religion without a "compelling state interest." In other words, people get to act as they like in religious matters, even to some extent when that
involves violating laws of general applicability (such as drug laws), unless the
state can show that it has a "compelling interest" in the restriction in question.
The notion of "compelling interest" is notoriously vague and squishy in U.S.
constitutional law and has been interpreted rather capriciously in cases involving religion and education, religion and drugs, and so on. My proposal is
that protection of any one of the central capabilities is a sufficient (though not
a necessary[10]) condition for a compelling state interest. Thus, parents who
wish, in the name of religion, to deprive their children of the education that is
specified as their fundamental entitlement under the capabilities list would
not be permitted to do so, though they might control their children's education in matters that do not touch on a central capability.

Of course, the all-important question, with any proposal of this type, is
how to set the threshold level of each capability. The list is very general, and
deliberately so. So too are most constitutions in the modern world. The idea
is that constitutions are to endure over time, but one cannot always foresee the
specific issues that will emerge as central in any particular time. The way modern states typically handle this problem seems to me just right: namely,
through a combination of legislative and judicial action. The thin specification becomes thicker through a jurisprudential tradition, combined with appropriate legislation and the judicial review of that.

Let me give just two examples of how entitlements that might at first seem
hopelessly vague acquire definite outlines over time. The U.S. Constitution
specifies a right of free speech: "Congress shall make no law . . . abridging the
freedom of speech, or of the press." This right is not further specified in the
Constitution itself. Initially, the "free speech" right was understood to be primarily aimed against prior restraint of publication. Many forms of speech, including much political speech, were thought to be unprotected by the Consti-

tution. As recently as 1918, when Eugene Debs went to jail for urging people to resist service in World War I, the political speech of dissenters during wartime could be banned by the Sedition Act, and only the German–American (Jewish) law professor Ernst Freund of the University of Chicago defended the view that this was constitutionally protected speech.[11] By now, Freund's view is universally accepted: The political speech of dissenters is taken to be at the core of what the First Amendment protects. Now, doubts about the threshold focus primarily on artistic speech and commercial speech. Some theories of the First Amendment, such as that of Cass Sunstein, hold that political speech is at the core, and that other forms of speech, while receiving some protection, may not receive the same level of protection that political speech receives.[12] Joshua Cohen's theory is more multifaceted. It identifies a number of distinct interests in speech that citizens may have, and these interests must be carefully balanced against competing interests.[13] The case law has become enormously complex, and it would require a separate chapter to say anything helpful about it. But my point is that we see here how a vaguely specified right can acquire definite contours over time. Even if much remains disputed, there is much about which we have become clear.

Notice that consideration of a nation's particular history and traditions plays a valuable role here in demarcating the precise shape of a given entitlement. The U.S. free speech right extends very widely, protecting political speech of a type that many nations believe it important not to protect. Thus, the Nazi demonstrators were permitted to march in Skokie, Illinois, a Jewish neighborhood: Interpretation of the free speech clause of the U.S. Constitution's First Amendment held that this was protected speech. A similar demonstration in Germany would not be protected by the analogous German free speech right. Germany has decided to demarcate the free speech protection differently, in accordance with its own history and understandings. It seems plausible that both are correct, and that the range of permissible articulations of free speech includes both solutions. In this way, an element of pluralism enters the universalism of the capabilities approach. (I discuss this issue further in Section VI.)

One might suppose that the item "life" on the capabilities list would be so vague as to be utterly unhelpful in a constitutional tradition. That this is not so is shown by the history of the Twenty-first Amendment to the Indian Constitution, which provides that "no person shall be deprived of his life or personal liberty except according to procedure established by law." The words "life and liberty" have been the object of a very interesting jurisprudential tradition, which has interpreted them to entail not mere life, but life with dignity. In *Gopalan v. State of Madras* (AIR 1950 SC 27), a case involving allegedly unlawful police detention, two dissenting justices already argued that preventive detention was inconsistent with the meaning of "life and liberty," as well as with the right to movement guaranteed in Article 19. In 1978, this idea was recognized by the majority in *Maneka Gandhi v. Union of India and Anr* (AIR 1978 SC 597), a case in which Mrs. Gandhi's daughter-in-law moved the court against the impounding of her passport. The Court held that the rights of Articles 19 and 21 involve the right to travel abroad. (Meanwhile, during the Emergency, the Court also held that the right to life can never be suspended, not even when the Constitution itself is suspended: *ADM, Jahalpur v. Shivakant Shukla*, AIR 1976 SC 1207.)

In 1981, in *Francis Coralie Mullin v. Administrator, Union Territory of Delhi* (AIR 1981 SC 746), a case involving a female prisoner who had been denied the right to see her family and her lawyer, the Supreme Court held that the right to life involves "the right to basic necessities of life and also the right to carry on such functions and activities as constitute the bare minimum expression of the human self." They linked "life" to the idea of human dignity. In *Olga Tellis v. Bombay Municipal Corporation* (AIR 1986 SC 180), a case involving the eviction of poor pavement dwellers, the Court extended this doctrine, stating: "'Life' means something more than mere animal existence. It does not mean merely that life cannot be extinguished or taken away, except according to procedure established by law. That is but one aspect of the right to life. An equally important aspect of that right is the right to livelihood because no person can live without the means of living."

During this same period, the Court also held that a right to privacy, modeled on the right recognized in U.S. Constitutional law, was inherent in Article 21. This right seemed to many Indian jurists an important one for Indian constitutional law to recognize, both because of its role in protecting women's bodily autonomy and integrity and because of its other potential uses, especially in plugging a gap created by the fact that the Indian Constitution has no equivalent of the U.S. Fourth Amendment, and police surveillance was proceeding unchecked by any constitutional procedure. The first cases to recognize a right to privacy in connection with Article 21 were cases involving police surveillance. In the first of these, *Kharak Singh v. State of Uttar Pradesh* (AIR 1963 SC 1295), the dissenters recognized such a right, and in the second, *Govind v. State of Madhya Pradesh* (AIR 1975 SC 1378), the majority recognized the right, citing American privacy cases from a variety of distinct areas, including search and seizure, but also including the Fourteenth Amendment privacy right cases *Griswold* and *Roe*.

At issue was a state police regulation, framed in accordance with directives provided by a national Police Act, according to which people who had a criminal record or were in other ways suspected of "a determination to lead a life of crime" could be subject to unannounced domiciliary visits, often in the middle of the night, and could also be followed and spied on when outside the house. Justices Mathew, Iyer, and Goswami, citing the 1877 U.S. case *Munn v. Illinois*, opine that "liberty" in Article 21 should be given an expansive interpretation, as incompatible with "an invasion on the part of the police of the sanctity of a man's home and an intrusion into his personal security and his right to sleep, which is the normal comfort and a dire necessity for human existence even as an animal." The Justices then bring in the notion of privacy, holding that a right to privacy in one's home is implicated in the meaning of liberty. Citing the dissent in *Kharak Singh*, they hold that "in the last resort a person's house, where he lives with his family, is his 'castle,' that nothing is more deleterious to a man's physical happiness and health than a calculated interference with his privacy."

There are some things that one might criticize in this tradition, in particular the quick adoption of a U.S.-style privacy right, which has had some unfortunate consequences, especially in matters of sex equality.[14] But one can see that two very abstract words have been, by and large, helpfully and appropriately elucidated, with reference to a nation's specific history, and with reference to the particular obstacles (intolerance of the homeless, excessive police surveillance) that stand between the citizens of India and the full life with human dignity mentioned in their constitution's preamble. Although the term "capabilities" is nowhere used in the Indian Constitution, these jurisprudential traditions make it very clear that the basic approach to human dignity and empowerment used in the interpretation of Fundamental Rights is already a capabilities approach.

When a constitutional tradition sets a threshold level of a capability, should it proceed conservatively, deferring to current possibilities, or should it proceed aspirationally, giving an incentive for future planning? This difficult question must to some extent be answered by each nation as it grapples with its own history and current possibilities. Obviously, it is a mistake to set the threshold level so high as to make the entire account look utopian and undeliverable. On the other hand, the case of the fundamental right to education in India indicates that one should not simply record what is already in practice.[15] Literacy rates in India stand around 50 percent for women and 67 percent for men. Obviously enough, delivering to all children a primary and secondary education is beyond the reach of current arrangements, and it cannot happen any time soon. On the other hand, the excellent record of some relatively poor states, especially Kerala, in virtually eradicating illiteracy—99 percent adolescent literacy for both boys and girls—indicates that the failure is not "in nature," but rather the result of corruption, laziness, and bad planning. Setting a relatively high threshold, in such a way that states that do not follow Kerala's example can be taken to court by their citizens, seems to be not utopian, in this case, but a tough and also prudent course.

IV. Capabilities and Rights

My list of capabilities includes many of the liberties that are also stressed in the human rights movement. And capabilities, like human rights, supply a moral and humanly rich set of goals for development, in place of "the wealth and poverty of the economists," as Marx so nicely put it. Thus, capabilities have a very close relationship to human rights, as understood in contemporary international discussions. In effect, they cover the terrain covered by both the so-called first-generation rights (political and civil liberties) and the so-called second-generation rights (economic and social rights). And they play a similar role, providing both a basis for cross-cultural comparison and the philosophical underpinning for basic constitutional principles.

Both Sen and I connect the capabilities approach closely to the idea of human rights, and in *Women and Human Development* I have described the relationship between the two ideas at some length.[16] I view my approach as a species of a human rights approach, but it still seems worthwhile to make these connections again in this context. Constitutions are typically presented as protecting a core group of fundamental rights, so one might wonder why I feel the need to analyze these entitlements in terms of the concept of capabilities.

In my view, capabilities are very closely linked to rights, but the language of capabilities gives important precision and supplementation to the language of rights. The idea of human rights is by no means a crystal clear idea. Rights have been understood in many different ways, and difficult theoretical questions are frequently obscured by the use of rights language, which can give the illusion of agreement where there is deep philosophical disagreement. People differ about what the *basis* of a rights claim is: rationality, sentience, and mere life have all had their defenders. They differ, too, about whether rights are pre-political or artifacts of laws and institutions. (Kant held the latter view, although the dominant human rights tradition has held the former.) They differ about whether rights belong only to individual persons, or also to groups. They differ about whether rights are to be regarded as side constraints on goal-promoting action, or rather as one part of the social goal that is being promoted. They differ, again, about the relationship between rights and duties: If *A* has a right to *S*, then does this mean that there is always someone who has a duty to provide *S*, and how shall we decide who that someone is? They differ, finally, about what rights are to be understood as rights *to*. Are human rights primarily rights to be treated in certain ways? Rights to a certain level of achieved well-being? Rights to resources with which one may pursue one's life plan? Rights to certain opportunities and capacities with which one may make choices about one's life plan?

The account of central capabilities has the advantage of taking clear positions on these disputed issues,[17] while stating clearly what the motivating concerns are and what the goal is. The relationship between the two notions, however, needs further clarification.

In some areas, I would argue, the best way of thinking about what rights are is to see them as capabilities. The right to political participation, the right to religious free exercise, the right of free speech—these and others are all best thought of as capacities to function. In other words, to secure a right to a citizen in these areas is to put them in a position of capability to function in that area. (Of course there is another sense of "right" that refers to an undeveloped basis for acquiring the mature capability: People have a right to religious freedom just in virtue of being human, even if the state they live in has not guaranteed them this freedom.) By defining rights in terms of capabilities, we make it clear that a people in country *C* don't really have the right to political participation just because this language exists on paper. They really have this right only if there are effective measures to make people truly capable of political exercise. Women in many nations have a nominal right of political participation without having this right in the sense of capability. For example, they may be threatened with violence should they leave the home. In short, thinking in terms of capability gives us a benchmark as we think about what it is really to secure a right to someone. It makes clear that this involves affirmative material and institutional support, not simply a failure to impede.

There is another set of rights, largely those in the area of property and economic advantage, which seem analytically different in their relationship to capabilities. Take, for example, the right to shelter and housing. These are rights (entitlements based on justice) that can be analyzed in a number of distinct ways: in terms of resources, or utility (satisfaction), or capabilities. (Once again, we must distinguish between the claim that "*A* has a right to shelter"— which frequently refers to *A*'s moral claim in virtue of being human—from the statement that "Country *C* gives its citizens the right to shelter." It is the second sentence whose analysis I am discussing here.) Here again, however, it seems valuable to understand these rights in terms of capabilities. If we think of the right to shelter as a right to a certain amount of resources, then we get into difficulty. Giving resources to people does not always bring differently situated people up to the same level of capability to function. A utility-based analysis also encounters a problem: Traditionally deprived people may be satisfied with a very low living standard, believing that this is all they have any hope of getting. A capabilities analysis, by contrast, looks at how people are *actually enabled* to live. Analyzing economic and material rights in terms of capabilities thus enables us to set forth clearly a rationale we have for spending unequal amounts of money on the disadvantaged, or creating special programs to assist their transition to full capability.

But the language of rights is not simply underspecific. It also has a specific historical problem: It is strongly linked to the idea of "negative liberty" and to the idea that what the state must above all do is stay out of people's lives. Indeed, if one reads the U.S. Constitution, one sees this conception directly. Negative phrasing concerning state action predominates, as in the First Amendment: "Congress shall make no law respecting an establishment of religion, or prohibiting the free exercise thereof; or abridging the freedom of speech, or of the press; or the right of the people peaceably to assemble, and petition the Government for a redress of grievances." Similarly, the Fourteenth Amendment's all-important guarantees are also stated in terms of what the state may not do: "No State shall make or enforce any law which shall abridge the privileges or immunities of citizens of the United States; nor shall any State deprive any person of life, liberty, or property, without due process of law; nor deny to any person within its jurisdiction the equal protection of the laws." This phraseology, deriving from the Enlightenment tradition of negative liberty, leaves things notoriously indeterminate as to whether impediments supplied by the market, or private actors, are to be considered violations of fundamental rights of citizens.

The Indian Constitution typically specifies rights affirmatively.[18] Thus, "All citizens shall have the right to freedom of speech and expression; to assemble peaceably and without arms; to form associations or unions" (Article 19). "There shall be equality of opportunity for all citizens in matters relating to employment or appointment to any office under the state" (Article 16). "No citizen shall, on ground only of religion, race, caste, sex, place of birth or any of them, be subject to any disability, liability, restriction or condition with regard to" (Article 15). "No person shall be deprived of his life or personal liberty except according to procedure established by law" (Article 21).[19] These locutions have usually been understood to imply that impediments supplied by nonstate actors may also be deemed violative of constitutional rights. Moreover, the Indian Constitution is quite explicit that affirmative action programs to aid the lower castes and women are not only compatible with constitutional guarantees, but are actually in their spirit.

The capabilities approach, we may now say, sides with the Indian Constitution and against the (neoliberal interpretation of) the U.S. Constitution.[20] It makes it clear that securing a right to someone requires more than the absence of negative state action.

By insisting in this way on the fact that all capabilities require affirmative institutional and material support, the approach calls into question the facile distinction between "first-generation rights" (political and civil rights) and "second-generation rights" (economic and social rights). Political and civil rights cannot be secured without definite economic arrangements: All rights in this way cost money. Moreover, some depend for their implementation on rights that are supposed to be in the other area. Thus, the full securing of the freedom of speech requires state provision of education. The distinction thus begins to look misleading and confusing, once we see how closely all the capabilities are bound up with one another.

The language of capabilities has one further advantage over the language of rights. It is not strongly linked to one particular cultural and historical tradition, as the language of rights is believed to be. This belief is not very accurate. Although the term "rights" is associated with the European Enlightenment, its component ideas have deep roots in many traditions.[21] Nonetheless, the language of capabilities enables us to bypass this troublesome debate. When we speak simply of what people are actually able to do and to be, we do not even give the appearance of privileging a Western idea. Ideas of activity and ability are everywhere, and there is no culture in which people do not ask themselves what they are able to do, what opportunities they have for functioning.

If we have the language of capabilities, do we also need the language of rights? The language of rights still plays, I believe, four important roles in public discourse, despite its unsatisfactory features. First, when used in the first way, as in the sentence "*A* has a right to have the basic political liberties secured to her by her government," we are reminded that people have justified and urgent claims to certain types of urgent treatment, no matter what the world around them has done about that. It imports the idea of an urgent claim based on justice. However, in constitution making, this idea is already typically made clear in other ways. Thus, writing "all citizens shall have capability *C*" in a section of the constitution dealing with the fundamental entitlements of citizens already conveys that we are talking about a justified claim and an element of basic justice.

Rights language also has value because of the emphasis it places on people's choice and autonomy. The language of capabilities, as I have said, was designed to leave room for choice, and to communicate the idea that there is a big difference between pushing people into functioning in ways you consider valuable and leaving the choice up to them. Sen makes this point very effectively in *Development as Freedom*. But we make this emphasis clear if we combine the capabilities analysis with the language of rights, as my list of capabilities does at several points, and as the Indian Constitution typically does.

On one issue concerning the relationship between capabilities and rights, I differ to some extent with Sen, and I can only briefly describe that difference here.[22] Both earlier and in *Development as Freedom*, Sen takes issue with the idea that rights should be regarded as side constraints on the pursuit of social well-being. He uses Robert Nozick's version of this claim as his target, and he makes the very plausible claim that Nozick is wrong to hold that property rights, construed in Nozickian fashion, are side constraints on the pursuit of social well-being, always to be respected no matter what disasters befall. But there are two ways of making this objection. I think that Sen should have said that Nozick has the wrong account of what fundamental rights people have, including property rights. But if he makes this criticism, he need not object to Nozick's contention that rights are side-constraints. They may still be so— only Nozick has got ahold of the wrong account of rights. Nozick's account of property rights is implausible in all sorts of ways. But if we really have correctly identified the fundamental entitlements of all citizens, then it does seem right to say that those entitlements (in my account, the central capabilities) function as side constraints on the pursuit of overall well-being—that is, we should not pursue greater well-being by taking away any citizen's freedom of religion, freedom of speech, and so on. Now, of course, there may be emergencies in which some of the fundamental entitlements have to be suspended (although Mrs. Indira Gandhi has done a great deal to discredit this idea). But in general, it seems just right that we cannot pursue the good by violating one of these basic requirements of justice.

Another feature of the Indian Constitution helps us here. As a reaction against the suspension of fundamental civil rights during the Emergency (1975–1977), the Indian Supreme Court has evolved a doctrine of the "essential features" of the constitution: features that represent the most fundamental entitlements, such that they cannot be removed even by a constitutional amendment (of the sort that Mrs. Gandhi's large parliamentary majority so easily passed, removing crucial civil liberties).[23] To say that the fundamental entitlements of citizens are like side constraints is to say something like they are essential features of the political structure, such that even a constitutional amendment passed in parliament cannot abrogate them, for the sake of greater prosperity or even security, absent a constitutional crisis in which the very existence of the regime is in jeopardy.[24]

V. Capabilities and the Social Contract Tradition[25]

I have said that the capabilities approach yields an account of basic political principles that can serve as the basis for an account of fundamental constitutional entitlements, and thus provide us with a partial theory of social justice. My use of the approach thus brings capabilities into an intimate relationship with liberal theories of social justice, and in particular with the theory of John Rawls. Sen has long emphasized that capabilities may be seen as an alternative way of construing the Rawlsian notion of primary goods. My account of capabilities in *WHD* makes the intimate relationship to Rawlsian political liberalism very clear, comparing capabilities to Rawlsian primary goods at several points and endorsing the idea of an overlapping consensus. I have long endorsed Sen's contention that Rawls's theory would be better able to give an account of the relevant social equalities and inequalities if the list of primary goods were formulated as a list of capabilities rather than as a list of things.[26]

But there is another problem that ought to trouble us as we ponder the social contract tradition as a source of basic principles of justice. Philosophical views deriving from the classical social contract tradition imagine society as a contract for mutual advantage. They therefore imagine the contracting parties as rough equals, none able to dominate the others, and none asymmetrically dependent on the others. Whatever differences there are among the different founders of that tradition, all accept the basic Lockean conception of a contract among parties who, in the state of nature, are "free, equal, and independent."[27] Thus, for Kant, persons are characterized by both freedom and equality, and the social contract is defined as an agreement among persons so characterized. Contemporary contractarians explicitly adopt this hypothesis. For David Gauthier, people of unusual need are "not party to the moral relationships grounded by a contractarian theory."[28] Similarly, the citizens in Rawls's Well-Ordered Society are "fully cooperating members of society over a complete life."[29]

Life, of course, is not like that. Real people begin their lives as helpless infants and remain in a state of extreme, asymmetrical dependency, both physical and mental, for anywhere from ten to twenty years. At the other end of life, those who are lucky enough to live on into old age are likely to encounter another period of extreme dependency, either physical, mental, or both, which may itself continue in some form for as much as twenty years. During the middle years of life, many of us encounter periods of extreme dependency, some of which involve our mental powers and some our bodily powers only, but all of which may put us in need of daily, even hourly, care by others. Finally, and centrally, there are many citizens who never have the physical and/or mental powers requisite for independence. These citizens are dependent in different ways. Some have high intellectual capabilities but are unable to give and receive love and friendship; some are capable of love, but unable to learn basic intellectual skills. Some have substantial emotional and intellectual capabilities, but in a form or at a level that requires special care. These lifelong states of asymmetrical dependency are in many respects isomorphic to the states of infants and the elderly.

In short, any real society is a care-giving and care-receiving society and must therefore discover ways of coping with these facts of human neediness and dependency that are compatible with the self-respect of the recipients and do not exploit the caregivers. This is a central issue for feminism since, in every part of the world, women do a large part of this work, usually without pay, and often without recognition that it is work. They are often thereby handicapped in other functions of life.[30]

It must be said at the outset that in this particular area a Kantian starting point is likely to give bad guidance. For Kant, human dignity and our moral capacity, dignity's source, are radically separate from the natural world. Morality certainly has the task of providing for human neediness, but the idea that we are at bottom split beings, both rational persons and animal dwellers in the world of nature, never ceases to influence Kant's way of thinking about how these deliberations about our needs will go.

What's wrong with the split? Quite a lot. First, it ignores the fact that our dignity is just the dignity of a certain sort of animal. It is the animal sort of dignity, and that very sort of dignity could not be possessed by a being who was not mortal and vulnerable, just as the beauty of a cherry tree in bloom could not be possessed by a diamond. Second, the split wrongly denies that animality can itself have a dignity; thus, it leads us to slight aspects of our own lives that have worth, and to distort our relation to the other animals.[31] Third, it makes us think of the core of ourselves as self-sufficient, not in need of the gifts of fortune; in so thinking, we greatly distort the nature of our own morality and rationality, which are thoroughly material and animal themselves. We learn to ignore the fact that disease, old age, and accident can impede the moral and rational functions, just as much as the other animal functions. Fourth, it makes us think of ourselves as atemporal. We forget that the usual human lifecycle brings with it periods of extreme dependency, in which our functioning is very similar to that enjoyed by the mentally or physically handicapped throughout their lives.

It is important to notice that the split goes wrong in both directions. It suggests, as I have said, that our rationality is independent of our vulnerable animality, and it also suggests that animality, and nonhuman animals, lack intelligence, are just brutish and "dumb." Both implications of the split should, of course, be called into question. In nature, we find a rich continuum of types of intelligence and of practical capacities of many types; we cannot understand ourselves well without situating ourselves within that continuum.[32]

Political thought in the Kantian social contract tradition (to stick with the part of the tradition I find deepest and most appealing) suffers from the conception of the person with which it begins. Rawls's contracting parties are fully aware of their need for material goods. Here Rawls diverges from Kant, building need into the foundations of the theory.[33] But he does so only to a degree, as the parties are imagined throughout as competent contracting adults, roughly similar in need and capable of a level of social cooperation that makes them able to make a contract with others. Such a hypothesis seems required by the very idea of a contract for mutual advantage.[34]

In so conceiving of persons, Rawls explicitly omits from the situation of basic political choice the more extreme forms of need and dependency human beings may experience. His very concept of social cooperation is based on the idea of reciprocity between rough equals and has no explicit place for relations of extreme dependency. Thus, for example, Rawls refuses to grant that we have any duties of justice to animals on the grounds that they are not capable of reciprocity (*TJ* 17, 504–5); they are owed "compassion and humanity," but "they are outside the scope of the theory of justice, and it does not seem possible to extend the contract doctrine so as to include them in a natural way" (*TJ*, 512). This makes a big difference to his theory of political distribution, as his account of the primary goods (introduced, as it is) as an account of the needs of citizens who are characterized by the two moral powers and by the capacity to be "fully cooperating" has no place for the need of many real people for the kind of care we give to people who are not independent.[35]

Now, of course Rawls is perfectly aware that his theory focuses on some cases and leaves others to the side. He insists that, although the need for care for people who are not independent is "a pressing practical question," it may reasonably be postponed to the legislative stage after basic political institutions are designed:

> So let's add that all citizens are fully cooperating members of society over the course of a complete life. This means that everyone has sufficient intellectual powers to play a normal part in society, and no one suffers from unusual needs that are especially difficult to fulfill, for example, unusual and costly medical requirements. Of course, care for those with such requirements is a pressing practical question. But at this initial stage, the fundamental problem of social justice arises between those who are full and active and morally conscientious participants in society, and directly or indirectly associated together throughout a complete life. Therefore, it is sensible to lay aside certain difficult complications. If we can work out a theory that covers the fundamental case, we can try to extend it to other cases later. (*DL* 546)

This reply seems inadequate. Care for children, the elderly, and the mentally and physically handicapped is a major part of the work that needs to be done in any society, and in most societies it is a source of great injustice. Any theory of justice needs to think about the problem from the beginning, in the design of the most basic level of institutions, and particularly in its theory of the primary goods.[36]

What, then, can be done to give the problem of care and dependency sufficient prominence in a theory of justice? The first thing we might try, which
has been suggested by Eva Kittay in her fine book, is to add the need for care
during periods of extreme and asymmetrical dependency to the Rawlsian list
of primary goods, thinking of care as among the basic needs of citizens.[37]

This suggestion, if we adopt it, would lead us to make another modifica-
tion, for care is hardly a commodity, like income and wealth, to be measured
by the sheer amount of it that citizens have. As Sen has long suggested (see
section II above), we would do well to understand the entire list of primary
goods as a list not of things, but of central capabilities. This change would not
only enable us to deal better with people's needs for various types of love and
care as elements of the list, but would also answer the point that Sen has repeatedly made all along about the unreliability of income and wealth as in-
dices of well-being. The well-being of citizens will now be measured not by
the sheer amount of income and wealth they have, but by the degree to which
they have the various capabilities on the list. One may be well off in terms of
income and wealth and yet be unable to function well in the workplace because of burdens of caregiving at home.[38]

If we accepted these two changes, we would surely add a third, highly relevant to our thoughts about infancy and old age. We would add other capabilitylike items to the list of basic goods. For example, the social basis of health,
imagination, and emotional well-being are items that figure on my list.[39]

Suppose, then, that we make these three changes in the list of primary goods:
We add care in times of extreme dependency to the list of primary goods; we
reconfigure the list as a list of capabilities; and we add other pertinent items to
the list as well. Have we done enough to salvage the contract doctrine as a way
of generating basic political principles? I believe that there is still room for
doubt. Consider the role of primary goods in Rawls's theory. The account of
primary goods is introduced in connection with the Kantian political conception of the person, as an account of what citizens characterized by the two
moral powers need.[40] Thus, we have attributed basic importance to care only
from the point of view of our own current independence. It is good to be cared
for only because care subserves moral personality, understood in a Kantian way
as conceptually quite distinct from need and animality. This seems like another
more subtle way of making our animality subserve our humanity, where humanity is understood to exclude animality. The idea is that because we are dignified beings capable of political reciprocity, we had better provide for times
when we are not that, so we can get back to being that as quickly as possible. I
think that this is a dubious enough way to think about illnesses in the prime of
life; but it surely leads us in the direction of a contemptuous attitude toward
infancy and childhood and, a particular danger in our society, toward elderly

disability. Finally, it leads us strongly in the direction of not fully and equally valuing those with lifelong mental disabilities: Somehow or other, care for them is supposed to be valuable only for the sake of what it does for the "fully cooperating." They are, it would seem, being used as means for someone else's ends, and their full humanity is still being denied.

So I believe that we need to delve deeper, redesigning the elements of the classical social contract tradition that cause the difficulty. This is a complicated matter, as it is also complicated to say what forms of contractarianism would survive this redesign. My book *Frontiers of Justice* takes up this challenge. One part of a good response to the challenge will surely be to design a political conception of the person that brings the rational and the animal into a more intimate relation with one another, and to acknowledge that there are many types of dignity in the world, including the dignity of children and adults with mental disabilities, the dignity of people with senile dementia, and the dignity of babies at the breast. We want the picture of the parties who design political institutions to build these facts in from the start. The kind of reciprocity in which we humanly engage has its periods of symmetry, but also, of necessity, its periods of more or less extreme asymmetry—and this is part of our lives that we bring into our situation as parties who design just institutions.

I believe, then, that we need to adopt a political conception of the person that is more Aristotelian than Kantian,[41] one that sees the person from the start as both capable and needy—"in need of a rich plurality of life-activities," to use Marx's phrase, whose availability will be the measure of well-being. Such a conception of the person, which builds growth and decline into the trajectory of human life, will put us on the road to thinking well about what society should design. We don't have to contract for what we need by producing; we have a claim to support in the dignity of our human need itself. Since this is not just an Aristotelian idea, but one that corresponds to human experience, there is good reason to think that it can command a political consensus in a pluralistic society. If we begin with this conception of the person and with a suitable list of the central capabilities as primary goods, we can begin designing institutions by asking what it would take to get citizens up to an acceptable level on all these capabilities. Although Sen refrains from specifying a political conception of the person, I believe that this suggestion is squarely in line with his ideas.

In *Women and Human Development* and *Frontiers of Justice*, I propose that the idea of central human capabilities be used as the analogue of Rawlsian primary goods, and that the guiding political conception of the person should be an Aristotelian/Marxian conception of the human being as in need of a rich plurality of life activities, to be shaped by both practical reason and affiliation. I argue that these interlocking conceptions can form the core of a political conception that is a form of political liberalism, close to Rawls's in many ways. The core of the political conception is endorsed for political purposes only, giving citizens a great deal of space to pursue their own comprehensive conceptions of value, whether secular or religious. Yet more room for a reasonable pluralism in conceptions of the good is secured by insisting that the appropriate political goal is capability only. Citizens should be given the option, in each area, of functioning in accordance with a given capability or not so functioning. To secure a capability to a citizen it is not enough to create a sphere of noninterference; the public conception must design the material and institutional environment so that it provides the requisite affirmative support for all the relevant capabilities.[42] Thus, care for physical and mental dependency needs will enter into the conception at many points, as part of what is required to secure to citizens one of the capabilities on the list.

My solution to these problems, then, lies squarely within the liberal tradition. But Kittay suggests that we should go further, departing from that tradition altogether. She holds that Western political theory must be radically reconfigured to put the fact of dependency at its heart. The fact, she says, that we are all "some mother's child," existing in intertwined relations of dependency, should be the guiding image for political thought.[43] Such a care-based theory, she thinks, will be likely to be very different from any liberal theory, since the liberal tradition is deeply committed to goals of independence and liberty. Although Kittay supplies few details to clarify the practical meaning of the difference, I think her idea is that the care-based theory would support a type of politics that provides comprehensive support for need throughout all citizens' lives, as in some familiar ideals of the welfare state—one in which liberty is far less important than security and well-being.

Kittay is not altogether consistent on this point. At times, she uses classic liberal arguments, saying that we need to remember that caregivers have their own lives to lead and to support policies that give them more choices.[44] But on the whole, she rejects, in the abstract, solutions that emphasize freedom as a central political goal. The concrete measures she favors do not seem to have such sweeping antiliberal implications. The restoration and expansion of Aid to Families with Dependent Children, expansion of the Family and Medical Leave Act of 1993, various educational measures promoting the dignity of the disabled through a judicious combination of "mainstreaming" and separate education[45]—all these are familiar liberal policies, which can be combined with an emphasis on choice and liberty as important social goals. Kittay's most controversial proposal—that of a direct non-means-tested payment to those who care for family dependents at home—clearly has, or could have, a liberal rationale: that of ensuring that these people are seen as active, dignified workers rather than passive noncontributors.

Indeed, if we adopt all the changes I have proposed, we will still have a theory that is basically liberal. Theories that take their start from an idea of human capability and functioning emphasize the importance of giving all citizens the chance to develop the full range of human powers, at whatever level their condition allows, and to enjoy the sort of liberty and independence their condition allows. Would we do better to reject this theory in favor of Kittay's idea, rejecting independence as a major social goal and conceiving of the state as a universal mother? To be sure, nobody is ever self-sufficient; the independence we enjoy is always both temporary and partial, and it is good to be reminded of that fact by a theory that also stresses the importance of care in times of dependency. But is being "some mother's child" a sufficient image for the citizen in a just society? I think we need a lot more: liberty and opportunity, the chance to form a plan of life, the chance to learn and imagine on one's own. These goals are as important for the mentally handicapped as they are for others, although they are much more difficult to achieve.

Once again, although Sen has not commented explicitly on issues of mental disability and senility, I believe that the view I have just mapped out is squarely in line with his emphasis on freedom as a goal. We see, then, here again, that the capabilities approach solves some problems central to a theory of social justice that other liberal theories seem unable to solve well; the capability-based solution seems to be an attractive way of thinking about basic constitutional principles.

VI. Endorsing a List

One obvious difference between Sen's writings and my own is that for some time I have endorsed a specific list of the Central Human Capabilities as a focus both for comparative quality-of-life measurement and for the formulation of basic political principles of the sort that can play a role in fundamental constitutional guarantees. Because considerations of pluralism have been on my mind since the beginning, I have worked sensitivity to cultural difference into my understanding of the list in several ways.

First, I consider the list open-ended and subject to ongoing revision and rethinking, in the way that any set of constitutional guarantees is always subject to supplementation (or deletion).

Second, I also insist that the items on the list ought to be specified in a somewhat abstract and general way, precisely in order to leave room for the activities of specifying and deliberating by citizens and their legislatures and courts that I have outlined in the section "Sen on Social Justice." As I said there, I believe that within certain parameters it is perfectly appropriate that different nations should do this somewhat differently, taking their histories and special circumstances into account. Thus, a free speech right that suits Germany well might be too restrictive in the different climate of the United States.

Third, I consider the list to be a freestanding "partial moral conception," to use John Rawls's phrase—that is, it is explicitly introduced for political purposes only, and without any grounding in metaphysical ideas of the sort that divide people along lines of culture and religion.[46] As Rawls says, we can view this list as a "module" that can be endorsed by people who otherwise have very different conceptions of the ultimate meaning and purpose of life; they will connect it to their religious or secular comprehensive doctrines in many ways.

Fourth, if we insist that the appropriate political target is capability and not functioning, we protect pluralism here again.[47] Many people who are willing to support a capability as a fundamental constitutional entitlement would feel violated were the associated functioning made constitutionally basic. Thus, the right to vote can be endorsed by believing citizens who would feel deeply violated by mandatory voting because it goes against their religious conception. (The American Amish are in this category, as they believe that it is wrong to participate in political life, but they endorse the right of citizens to vote.) The free expression of religion can be endorsed by people who would totally object to any establishment of religion that would involve dragooning all citizens into some type of religious functioning.

Fifth, the major liberties that protect pluralism are central items on the list: the freedom of speech, the freedom of association, the freedom of conscience.[48] By placing them on the list, we give them a central and nonnegotiable place in the future of any nation that builds a constitution around them. I shall return to that point.

Sixth, I insist on a rather strong separation between issues of justification and issues of implementation. I believe that we can justify this list as a good basis for political principles all round the world, but this does not mean that we thereby license intervention with the affairs of a state that does not recognize them. It is a basis for persuasion, but I hold that military and economic sanctions are justified only in certain very grave circumstances involving traditionally recognized crimes against humanity.[49] So it seems less objectionable to recommend something to everyone, once we point out that it is part of the view that state sovereignty, grounded in the consent of the people, is a very important part of the whole package.[50]

Where does Sen stand on these questions? I find a puzzling tension in his writings at this point. On the one hand, he speaks as if certain specific capabilities are absolutely central and nonnegotiable. One cannot read his discussions of health, education, political and civil liberties, and the free choice of occupation without feeling that he agrees totally with my view that these human capabilities should enjoy a strong priority and should be made central by states the world over, as fundamental entitlements of each and every citizen (although he says little about how a threshold level of each capability would be constructed). In the case of liberty, he actually endorses giving liberty a considerable priority, although without giving an exhaustive enumeration of the liberties that would fall under this principle. His role in the formulation of the measures that go into the *Human Development Reports*, moreover, clearly shows him endorsing a group of health- and education-related capabilities as the appropriate way to measure quality of life across nations.

On the other hand, Sen has conspicuously refused to endorse any account of the central capabilities, apparently connecting this reluctance with issues of pluralism. Thus, the examples mentioned above remain in limbo: Clearly, they are examples of some things he thinks very important, but it is not clear to what extent he is prepared to recommend them as important goals for all the world's people. It is equally unclear whether there are other capabilities not mentioned so frequently that might be equally important, and, if so, what those capabilities might be.

In *Development as Freedom* things become, I believe, even more problematic. Throughout the work, Sen speaks of "the perspective of freedom" and uses language, again and again, suggesting that freedom is a general all-purpose social good, and that capabilities are to be seen as instances of this more general good of human freedom. Such a view is not incompatible with ranking some freedoms ahead of others for political purposes, of course. But it does seem to go in a problematic direction.

First of all, it is unclear whether the idea of promoting freedom is even a coherent political project. Some freedoms limit others. The freedom of rich people to make large donations to political campaigns limits the equal worth of the right to vote. The freedom of businesses to pollute the environment limits the freedom of citizens to enjoy an unpolluted environment. The freedom of landowners to keep their land limits projects of land reform that might be argued to be central to many freedoms for the poor. And so on.

Furthermore, even if there were a coherent project that viewed all freedoms as desirable social goals, it is not at all clear that this is the sort of project someone with Sen's political and ethical views ought to endorse. The examples I have just given show us that any political project that is going to protect the equal worth of certain basic liberties for the poor, and to improve their living conditions, needs to say forthrightly that some freedoms are central for political purposes and some are distinctly not. Some freedoms involve basic social entitlements and others do not. Some lie at the heart of a view of political justice and others do not. Among the ones that do not lie at the core, some are simply less important, but others may be positively bad.

For example, the freedom of rich people to make large campaign contributions, although defended by many Americans in the name of the general good of freedom, seems to me not among those freedoms that lie at the heart of a set of basic constitutional entitlements to which a just society should commit itself. In many circumstances, it is actually a bad thing, and constraint on it is a very good thing. Similarly, the freedom of industry to pollute the environment, though cherished by many Americans in the name of the general good of freedom, seems to me not among those freedoms that should enjoy constitutional protection; beyond a certain point, the freedom to pollute is bad and should be constrained by law. And while property rights are certainly a good thing up to a point, the freedom of large landowners in India to hold onto their property under gender-discriminatory ceiling laws (a freedom that some early Supreme Court decisions held to enjoy constitutional protection) is not part of the account of property rights as central human entitlements that a just society would want to endorse. To define property capabilities in a gender-discriminatory way is actually a bad thing.

In short, no society that pursues equality or even an ample social minimum can avoid curtailing freedom in very many ways, and what it ought to say is: Those freedoms are not good, they are not part of a core group of entitlements based on justice that we think all citizens have. Of other freedoms, for example, the freedom of motorcyclists to drive without helmets, they can say these freedoms are not very important; they are neither very bad nor very good. We do not take a stand for core constitutional purposes on them, and we will allow local bodies to extend or restrict them as they like. In other words, all societies that pursue a reasonably just political conception have to evaluate human freedoms, saying that some are central and some trivial, some good and some actively bad.

This evaluation typically takes a particular form when constitutions are made. Certain freedoms are taken to be entitlements of citizens based on justice. When any one of these is abridged, that is an especially grave failure of the political system. As I have argued in section II, the abridgment is not just a cost to be borne; it is a cost of a distinctive kind, involving a violation of basic justice. When some freedom outside the core is abridged, that may be a small cost or a large cost, but it is not a cost of exactly that same kind, one that in justice no citizen should be asked to bear. This qualitative difference is independent of the amount of cost, at least as figured in terms of standard subjective willingness-to-pay models. Thus, motorcyclists may mind greatly a law that tells them to put on a helmet, and they may feel that it wrecks their lives. In terms of standard willingness-to-pay models, they might be willing to pay quite a lot for the right to drive without a helmet. On the other hand, many citizens probably would not think that not being able to vote was a big cost. In terms of standard willingness-to-pay models, at least, they would not pay much for the right to vote, and some might have to be paid for voting. And yet, I would want to say (as do most constitutions of the world) that the right to vote is a fundamental entitlement based on justice, whereas the right to drive without a helmet is not.[51]

I would argue that Sen cannot avoid committing himself to a core list of fundamental capabilities once he faces such questions. And even for more pragmatic reasons, if capabilities are to serve the purposes I have sketched in this chapter, providing the basis for constitutional guarantees, they will obviously have to be specified, if only in the open-ended and humble way I have outlined. One cannot have a constitution that says, under the heading of Fundamental Rights, "All citizens are entitled to freedom understood as capability." Besides being wrong and misleading in the ways I have already argued, such a blanket endorsement of freedom/capability as a goal would be hopelessly vague and could not be interpreted in the requisite way by a legislative/judicial tradition.

Someone may now say, sure, there has to be a definite list in the case of each nation that is making a constitution, but why not leave the list-making to them? Of course, as I've already said, in the sense of *implementation*, and also in the sense of *more precise* specification, I do. The question, to be a real objection to my proposal, must be, why should we hold out to all nations a set of norms that we believe justified by a good philosophical argument, rather than letting each one justify its own set of norms? The answer, it seems to me, is given in all of Sen's work: Some human matters are too important to be left to whim and caprice, or even to the dictates of a cultural tradition. To say that education for women, or adequate health care, is not justified just in case some nation believes that it is not justified seems like a capitulation to subjective preferences of the sort that Sen has opposed throughout his career. As he has repeatedly stated, capabilities have intrinsic importance. If we believe that, we also believe that it is right to say to nations that don't sufficiently recognize one of them: You know, you too should endorse equal education for girls, and understand it as a fundamental constitutional entitlement. You too should provide a certain level of health care to all citizens, and view this as among their fundamental constitutional entitlements. Just because the United States does not choose to recognize a fundamental right to health care, that doesn't make the United States right or morally justified.

Some people interested in capabilities might be reluctant to endorse a list because of concerns about pluralism. (Sen says that this is not his concern.) But here, we may make two points that pertain specifically to the norm of respect for pluralism. First, the value of respect for pluralism itself requires a commitment to some cross-cultural principles as fundamental entitlements. Real respect for pluralism means strong and unwavering protection for religious freedom, for the freedom of association, and for the freedom of speech. If we say that we are for pluralism, and yet refuse to commit ourselves to the nonnegotiability of these items as fundamental building blocks of a just political order, we show that we are really half-hearted about pluralism.

I am sure that Sen would agree with this. I am sure, too, that he would say the same about other items on my list, such as health and education: If a nation says that they are for human capabilities, but refuses to give these special protections for all citizens, citing reasons of cultural or religious pluralism, Sen will surely say that they are not making a good argument, or giving genuine protection to pluralism. Instead, they are, very often, denying people (often women in particular) the chance to figure out what culture and form of life they actually want. So they are actually curtailing the most meaningful kind of pluralism, which requires having a life of one's own and some choices regarding it. And that goal surely requires a certain level of basic health and education. But then we are both, in effect, making a list of such entitlements, and the only question then must be what shall go on the list and how long it will be.

The second argument is one that derives from the Rawlsian idea of political liberalism, and I am not certain that Sen would endorse it. The argument says that classical liberalism erred by endorsing freedom or autonomy as a general good in human life. Both earlier liberals such as Mill and modern comprehensive liberals such as Joseph Raz hold that autonomy and freedom of choice are essential ingredients in valuable human lives, and that society is entitled to promote freedom across the board. Rawls and I hold that this general endorsement of freedom shows deficient respect for citizens whose comprehensive conceptions of the good human life do not make freedom and autonomy central human values. People who belong to an authoritarian religion cannot agree with Raz or Mill that autonomy is a generally good thing. Mill responds, in chapter 3 of *On Liberty*, by denigrating such people (he understands Calvinists to be such people). Presumably, the Millean state would denigrate them too, and would design education and other institutions to disfavor them, although their civil liberties would not be restricted. Rawls and I agree that this strategy shows deficient respect for a reasonable pluralism of different comprehensive conceptions of the good life. We should respect people who prefer a life within an authoritarian religion (or personal relationship), so long as certain basic opportunities and exit options are firmly guaranteed.

I hold that this respect for pluralism is fostered both by making capability and not functioning the appropriate political goal and also by endorsing a relatively small list of core capabilities for political purposes. Thus, we say two things to religious citizens. First, that endorsing the capabilities list does not require them to endorse the associated functioning as a good in their own lives, a point I have stressed earlier in this section. Second, we say that the very fact that it is a short list shows that we are leaving them lots of room to value other things in mapping out their plan of life. We do not ask them to endorse freedom as a general good—as we might seem to do if we talk a lot about freedom but fail to make a list. Instead, we just ask them to endorse this short list of freedoms (as capabilities) for political purposes and as applicable to all citizens. They may then get on with the lives they prefer.

The expectation is that a Roman Catholic citizen, say, can endorse this short list of fundamental liberties for political purposes without feeling that her view of Church authority and its decisive role in her life is thereby being denigrated. Even an Amish citizen, who believes that all participation in public life is simply wrong, can still feel that it's all right to endorse the capabilities list for political purposes because no general endorsement of autonomy as an end tells her that her life is less worthwhile than other lives. And, as I argued in *WHD*, even a woman who believes that the seclusion of women is right may endorse this small menu of liberties and opportunities for all women, although she herself will use few of them—and she will feel that the conception is one that respects her because it does not announce that only autonomous lives are worthwhile.

I am not certain whether Sen is in this sense a comprehensive liberal like Raz, or a political liberal like Rawls and me. But to the extent that he finds Rawls's arguments on this score persuasive, he has yet a further reason to endorse a definite and relatively circumscribed list of capabilities as political goals, rather than to praise freedom as a general social good.

It should be emphasized that there is up until now no deep difference between Sen's position and my own because we are asking different questions. I am using capabilities (together with other ideas, such as the idea of a threshold, the idea of human dignity, and the idea of overlapping consensus) to map out a minimal theory of social justice that can be the basis for constitution making. Sen is asking different, comparative questions. My argument is simply that if he does want to map out a theory of social justice, as he at times suggests he will do, he will then need to commit himself to some definite content.

The question of how to frame such a list and what to put on it is surely a difficult one in many ways. But I have argued that there is no way to take the capabilities approach forward, making it really productive for political thought about basic social justice, without facing this question and giving it the best answer one can.

Notes

1. This chapter is a close relative of "Capabilities as Fundamental Entitlements: Sen and Social Justice," *Feminist Economics* 9 (2003): 33–59. This chapter has a greater focus on legal and constitutional questions.

2. I make this case at greater length in *Women and Human Development: The Capabilities Approach* (hereafter *WHD*) (Cambridge, UK: Cambridge University Press, 2000). The present chapter focuses more on specifically legal and constitutional matters than does the book, which simply presents capabilities as a source of basic political principles that can serve as the basis for an account of constitutional entitlements. My approach is further developed in *Frontiers of Justice: Disability, Nationality, Species Membership* (Cambridge, MA: Harvard University Press, 2005).

3. See especially Eva Kittay, *Love's Labor: Essays on Women, Equality, and Dependency* (New York: Routledge, 1999); Nancy Folbre, "Care and the Global Economy," background paper prepared for the *Human Development Report 1999*, United Nations Development Programme (New York: Oxford University Press, 1999), and, based largely on Folbre, chap. 3 of *Human Development Report 1999*; Joan Williams, *Unbending Gender: Why Family and Work Conflict and What to Do about It* (New York: Oxford University Press, 2000); Mona Harrington, *Care and Equality* (New York: Knopf, 1999). Earlier influential work in this area includes Martha A. Fineman, *The Illusion of Equality* (Chicago: University of Chicago Press, 1991), and *The Neutered Mother: The Sexual Family and Other Twentieth-Century Tragedies* (New York: Routledge, 1995); Sarah Ruddick, *Maternal Thinking* (New York: Beacon Press, 1989); Joan Tronto, *Moral Boundaries: A Political Argument for an Ethic of Care* (New York: Routledge, 1993); Virginia Held, *Feminist Morality: Transforming Culture, Society, and Politics* (Chicago: University of Chicago Press, 1993); Robin West, *Caring for Justice* (New York: New York University Press, 1997); Nancy Folbre, *The Invisible Heart: Economics and Family Values* (New York: New Press, 2001). For an excellent collection of articles from diverse feminist perspectives, see *Justice and Care: Essential Readings in Feminist Ethics*, ed. Virginia Held (Boulder, CO: Westview Press, 1995). See also my "The Future of Feminist Liberalism," *Proceedings and Addresses of the American Philosophical Association* 74 (2000): 47–79. And, finally, see *Human Development Report 1999* (New York: Oxford University Press, 1999).

4. See my "Disabled Lives: Who Cares?" *New York Review of Books*, January 11, 2001, 34–37. See also *Hiding from Humanity: Disgust, Shame, and the Law* (Princeton, NJ: Princeton University Press, 2004), chap. 6, and *Frontiers of Justice*, chaps. 2 and 3. All societies cater to the disabilities of the average person. Thus, we do not have staircases with steps so high that only giants can climb them, or orchestras tuned to play at pitches inaudible to human ears and audible only to dogs.

A further problem not mentioned by Sen, but relevant to his critique of Rawls: Even if the person in the wheelchair were equally well off with regard to economic well-being, there is a separate issue of dignity and self-respect. By measuring relative social positions by income and wealth alone, Rawls ignores the possibility that a group may be reasonably well-off economically, but suffer grave disabilities with regard to the social bases of self-respect. One might argue that gays and lesbians in our society are in precisely that position. Certainly, the physically and mentally handicapped will be in that position, as their economic fortunes rise—unless society makes a major and fundamental commitment to inclusion and respect.

5. Obviously, the case for this depends very much both on what capability we are considering and on how we describe it. Thus, equality of capability seems to be important when we consider the right to vote, the freedom of religion, and so on; but if we consider the capability to play basketball, it seems ludicrous to suppose that society should be very much concerned about even a minimum threshold level of it, much less complete equality. With something like health, much hangs on whether we define the relevant capability as "access to the social bases of health" or "the ability to be healthy." The former seems like something that a just society should distribute on a basis of equality; the latter contains an element of chance that no just society could, or should, altogether eliminate. So the question whether equality of capability is a good social goal cannot be well answered without specifying a list of the relevant capabilities, another point in favor of the argument I advance below. On all of this, see *Frontiers of Justice*, chap. 5, sect. IV.

6. For just two examples, see the Constitution of India, Preamble, which announces as central ideas justice, liberty, equality, and fraternity, and defines the last as involving "assuring the dignity of the individual"; and the Constitution of Germany, Article 1: "Human dignity is inviolable. To protect it is the duty of all state authority."

7. In *Frontiers of Justice* (chap. 5, sect. IV), I argue, however, that some capabilities have not been *adequately* secured unless they are *equally* secured; the list already makes this clear, in the way in which it describes the political rights and liberties, but I argue that the same analysis extends to religious freedom, educational opportunity, and several other cases.

8. See my "The Costs of Tragedy: Some Moral Limits of Cost-Benefit Analysis," in *Cost-Benefit Analysis: Legal, Economic, and Philosophical Perspectives*, eds. Eric A. Posner and Matthew D. Adler (Chicago: University of Chicago Press, 2001), 169–200.

9. See the history of this in *WHD*, chap. 3.

10. Because other considerations (e.g., of stability) might also supply the state with a compelling interest: see *WHD*, chap. 3.

11. Ernst Freund, "The *Debs* Case and Freedom of Speech," *The New Republic*, May 3, 1919. For the text of Freund's article and a discussion of the controversy in which it played a formative role, see Harry Kalven, Jr., "Ernst Freund and the First Amendment Tradition," *University of Chicago Law Review* 40 (1973), 235–47.

12. Cass R. Sunstein, *Democracy and the Problem of Free Speech* (New York: Basic Books, 1993); Sunstein, however, holds that many artworks contain political speech.

13. Joshua Cohen, "Freedom of Expression," *Philosophy and Public Affairs* 22 (1993), 207–63.

14. See my "Sex Equality, Liberty, and Privacy: A Comparative Approach to the Feminist Critique," in eds. E. Sridharan, R. Sudarshan, and Z. Hasan, *Fifty Years of the Republic*, forthcoming from Oxford University Press, Delhi. For a more general treatment of related constitutional issues, see my "India, Sex Equality, and Constitutional Law," in eds. Beverley Baines and Ruth Rubio-Marin, *The Gender of Constitutional Jurisprudence* (Cambridge, UK: Cambridge University Press, 2005), 174–204.

15. See the longer discussion of this case in "The Costs of Tragedy."

16. See also my "Capabilities and Rights," *Fordham Law Review* 66 (1997): 273–300.

17. In the philosophical arguments of *WHD* and *Frontiers of Justice*.

18. Not invariably: Article 14, closely modeled on the equal protection clause of the U.S. Fourteenth Amendment, reads: "The State shall not deny to any person equality before the law or the equal protection of the laws within the territory of India."

19. For further discussion of all these rights, see my "India: Implementing Sex Equality through Law," *Chicago Journal of International Law* 2 (2001): 35–58, and "India, Sex Equality, and Constitutional Law," forthcoming in *Constitutions of the World and Women*, ed. Beverley Baines (Cambridge, UK: Cambridge University Press).

20. Of course, this account of both is in many ways too simple; I refer primarily to the wording of the documents here, not to the complicated jurisprudential traditions stemming from them.

21. See Sen's "Human Rights and Asian Values," *The New Republic*, July 10/17, 1997, and my *WHD*, chap. 1.

22. The full version of my argument is given in "Capabilities and Rights."

23. See my discussion in "India, Sex Equality, and Constitutional Law."

24. See Rawls, *Political Liberalism*, for a similar position about the freedom of speech.

25. The argument of this section is a somewhat shorter version of the argument of the relevant section of "The Future of Feminist Liberalism." I still leave in quite a lot of detail, given that the nonphilosophers in the group are unlikely to have seen that publication. All these issues are treated in much greater detail in *Frontiers of Justice*, whose primary theme is the relationship between the capabilities approach and the social contract tradition.

26. The list is actually heterogeneous, including liberties, opportunities, and powers alongside income and wealth; recently, Rawls has added still other capabilitylike items to the list, such as access to health care and the availability of leisure time.

27. J. Locke, *Second Treatise on Government* (1690), chap. 8.

28. David Gauthier, *Morals by Agreement* (New York: Oxford University Press, 1986), 18, speaking of all "persons who decrease th[e] average level" of well-being in a society.

29. In the subsequent discussion, I shall refer to the following works of Rawls: *A Theory of Justice* (Cambridge, MA: Harvard University Press, 1971), hereafter *TJ*; *Political Liberalism*, expanded paperback edition (New York: Columbia University Press, 1996), hereafter *PL*; the Dewey Lectures (*DL*), *Kantian Constructivism in Moral Theory*, *Journal of Philosophy* 77 (1980), 515–71. References to citizens as "fully cooperating" occur frequently in *DL* and *PL*, for example, *DL* 546, *PL* 183.

30. This is a major theme in recent feminist work: see articles cited in note 3 above.

31. For one particularly valuable treatment of this theme, see James Rachels, *Created from Animals: The Moral Implications of Darwinism* (New York: Oxford University Press, 1990). Two wonderful pictures of the animal sort of dignity: Barbara Smuts, untitled reply to J. M. Coetzee, in *The Lives of Animals*, ed. Amy Gutmann (Princeton, NJ: Princeton University Press, 1999), and, my favorite, George Pitcher, *The Dogs Who Came to Stay* (New York: G. Putnam, 1995). I discuss the implications of recognizing the dignity of nonhuman animals in a review article about Steven M. Wise's *Rattling the*

Cage: Toward Legal Rights for Animals (Cambridge, MA: Perseus Books, 2000), forthcoming in *The Harvard Law Review.* See also Alasdair MacIntyre, *Dependent Rational Animals: Why Human Beings Need the Virtues* (Peru, IL: Open Court Publishing, 1999).

32. See especially Rachels and MacIntyre.

33. I do not mean to deny that Kant gives need an important role in his theory. For just one good treatment of this aspect of Kant's thought, see Allen Wood, *Kant's Ethical Theory* (Cambridge, UK: Cambridge University Press, 1999). What I mean is that whereas for Kant personality and animality are conceptually independent, and personality is not itself understood in terms of need, for Rawls these two elements are more thoroughly integrated, and the person is understood from the first as in need of material and other goods.

34. I defend these claims in *Frontiers of Justice* with reference to a close analysis of the text of Rawls, which is obviously lacking here.

35. As Eva Kittay has argued in an excellent discussion (*Love's Labor*, 88–99, and see also "Human Dependency and Rawlsian Equality," in *Feminists Rethink the Self*, ed. Diana T. Meyers (Boulder, CO: Westview, 1997), 219–66, there are five places in Rawls's theory where he fails to confront facts of asymmetrical neediness that might naturally have been confronted. (1) His account of the "circumstances of justice" assumes a rough equality between persons, such that none could dominate all the others; thus, we are not invited to consider relations of justice that might obtain between an adult and her infants, or her senile demented parents. (2) Rawls's idealization of citizens as "fully cooperating" and the like puts to one side the large facts about extreme neediness I have just mentioned. (3) His conception of social cooperation, again, is based on the idea of reciprocity between equals and has no explicit place for relations of extreme dependency. (4) His account of the primary goods, introduced, as it is, as an account of the needs of citizens who are characterized by the two moral powers and by the capacity to be "fully cooperating," has no place for the need of many real people for the kind of care we give to people who are not independent. And (5) his account of citizens' freedom as involving the concept of being a self-authenticating source of valid claims (e.g., *PL*, 32) fails to make a place for any freedom that might be enjoyed by someone who is not independent in that sense.

36. See Kittay, *Love's Labor*, 77: "Dependency must be faced from the beginning of any project in egalitarian theory that hopes to include all persons within its scope." For a remarkable narrative of a particular life that shows exactly how many social structures play a part in the life of a mentally handicapped child from the very beginning, see Michael Bérubé, *Life as We Know It: A Father, A Family, and An Exceptional Child* (New York: Vintage, 1996).

37. Kittay, *Love's Labor*, 102–3.

38. On this point, see especially Joan Williams, *Unbending Gender: Why Family and Work Conflict and What To Do About It* (Oxford: Oxford University Press, 2000).

39. See my discussion of this point in *WHD*, chap. 1.

40. In *TJ*, primary goods were characterized as an all-purpose means to the pursuit of one's own conception of the good, whatever it is; in *DL* and *PL*, the interpretation shifts, and Rawls acknowledges that they are means with regard to the Kantian political conception of the person: see *PL*, 187–90.

41. As the late Peter Cicchino eloquently put this point, Aristotle's conception is not deductive or a priori: It respects widely held views about human reality, but takes experience as its source and guide. Second, it takes seriously the materiality of human beings—their need for food, shelter, friendship, care, what might be called their basic dependency. Third, it is epistemologically modest—it does not claim to have the exactitude of mathematics, but rather is content to look for "such precision as accords with the subject-matter" (Cicchino, "Building on Foundational Myths: Feminism and the Recovery of 'Human Nature': A Response to Martha Fineman," *Journal of Gender, Social Policy, and Law* 8 (2000): 73–84.

42. In that way, my view is close to the type of liberalism defended (against Lockean contractarianism) by T. H. Green, though my form is not perfectionistic, but is, rather, a form of political liberalism. I have found very illuminating the discussion of the liberal tradition in John Deigh, "Liberalism and Freedom," in *Social and Political Philosophy: Contemporary Perspectives*, ed. James Sterba (London: Routledge, 2001).

43. Kittay, *Love's Labor*, chap. 1, part III, on political strategies, is entitled "Some Mother's Child."

44. For passages that focus on the need of the individual for choice and independence, see, for example, 34–35, 53, 98, 192, and note 32.

45. Kittay, *Love's Labor*, chap. 5.

46. For the relation of this idea to objectivity, see my "Political Objectivity," *New Literary History* 32 (2001), 883–906.

47. See my discussion of this issue in *WHD*, chap. 1; and for a rejoinder to perfectionist critics, see "Aristotle, Politics, and Human Capabilities: A Response to Antony, Arneson, Charlesworth, and Mulgan," in a symposium on my political thought in *Ethics* 111 (2000), 102–40.

48. I am very skeptical of attempts to add group cultural rights to the list because every group contains hierarchy; thus, to give a group rights *qua* group is often to give the powerful members a license to continue subordinating the less powerful. Moreover, ethnic and cultural groups are likely in this way to be promoted above other groups around which many people define the meaning of their lives: the women's movement, for example, or groups formed around occupation or sexual orientation. For an elaboration of these points, see my "The Complexity of Groups," *Philosophy and Social Research* 29 (2003): 502–20.

49. See my "Women and the Law of Peoples," *Politics, Philosophy, and Economics* 1 (2002): 283–38; "Women and Theories of Global Justice: Our Need for New Paradigms," *The Ethics of Assistance: Morality and the Distant Needy*, ed. Deen K. Chatterjee (Cambridge, UK: Cambridge University Press, 2004), 147–76; and *Frontiers of Justice*, chap. 4.

50. This issue is discussed in detail, with reference to international relations, in *Frontiers of Justice*, chap. 4.

51. See my further discussion of these qualitative differences in "The Costs of Tragedy."

III

DEMOCRACY, NATIONALISM, AND POLITICAL GLOBALIZATION

5

The Varieties of Nationalism

Andrew Oldenquist

THE FAILURE OF GOVERNMENTS TO UNDERSTAND ethnic nationalism and how fiercely minorities will fight for independence or, at least, cultural autonomy, leads to one tragedy after another. Chechenya, Kosovo, Turkish and Iraqi Kurdistan, and Aceh will not be the last. The Western intelligentsia do nothing to counter this failure of understanding when they claim nationalism is a temporary effect of capitalism and the Industrial Revolution and only two hundred years old. At the same time and not very consistently, they identify nationalism with xenophobic tribalism and chauvinism, which have been around as long as humans have been social animals. Benjamin Barber, for example, describes ethnic nationalism as "people who define themselves by the slaughter of tribal neighbors living next door."[1] There is also a widespread sense that the related sentiments of group loyalty, nationalism, and patriotism are all immoral because they do not consider the good of everyone equally, but are partial and put one's own group first, thereby implying "my country, right or wrong." This in turn is claimed to imply that nationalism necessarily clashes both with democracy and with steps toward political globalization, such as the European Union. I argue that these implications are mistakes: Democracy, while distinct from nationalism, is perfectly consistent with it, and globalization is in fact an expansion of the group loyalty that is at the heart of nationalism.

From 1990 through 2004, twenty-one ethnic countries have come into being (or reemerged) from the breakup of the USSR, Yugoslavia, Czechoslovakia, and the secession of Eritrea from Ethiopia. Given this, a negative or at least nervous reaction to the startling growth of ethnic separatism should not be a complete surprise. Yet, since the end of the Cold War, criticism of and even hostility toward emerging ethnic nations has increased more than seems reasonable; self-determination itself has come to be treated with a certain contempt and associated more with tribalism than with struggles for freedom. The breakup of Yugoslavia, in particular, has been treated as a tragedy. The widespread, condescending characterization of ethnic separatist conflict as ethnic "rivalry" and "feuding" would not be thought by Iraqi Kurds and Kosovar Albanians or, earlier in the past century, by Irish or Algerians, to accurately describe their struggles. While I hope to show that criticisms of nationalism often are canards and confusions, neither opponents nor defenders own the moral high ground. The tribal nature of humans presents us with a dilemma comprised, on the one hand, of the inability of people to live without group loyalties and social identities, and, on the other hand, by the war and suffering insider–outsider conflicts cause. In this context, the obvious appeal of political globalization—the ideal of world unity—is that specieswide loyalty and social identity eliminate outsiders—human ones, at least—without killing anybody.

Three kinds of nationalism are confused and conflated by its critics, if ever distinguished in the first place: unifying or assimilative nationalism, which created Italy; ethnic separatist nationalism, which created Ireland; and ongoing patriotic nationalism or national consciousness, found in all countries. Each may, but usually does not, take forms that are xenophobic and murderous. In the light of its three varieties, I will give varying degrees of attention to six criticisms of nationalism:

1. It is a product of capitalism and the Industrial Revolution, hence much more recent, and less essential, than is usually supposed (Ernest Gellner, Eric Hobsbawm).
2. Separatist nationalism can be acceptable only if its underlying goal is to achieve democracy.
3. Patriotism can be separated from blind loyalty and be made principled and universal (Jürgen Habermas).
4. If we encourage separatists, the world will split into "5,000 countries" (Warren Christopher).
5. Supporting existing borders is simply a better safeguard against war (William Pfaff).
6. Nationalism makes the interests of the state supreme and those of the individual negligible, racializes ethnic difference, and leads to intolerance and genocide (William Pfaff, Isaiah Berlin).[2]

By an "ethnic group," I mean a people defined by a distinct culture, almost always by a homeland, and usually by language or religion. I use the term "ethnic country" such that most countries are ethnic ones, Sweden the land of Swedish-speaking Swedes, and so on, notwithstanding that all countries have ethnic minorities. When no group is an overwhelming majority and the various ethnic groups live in historical homelands, we have multiethnic countries such as India and the former USSR. Every currently existing European country except Switzerland and Belgium is an ethnic country, identified by a predominant group and language, whereas India and Indonesia, along with the former USSR, Yugoslavia, and Czechoslovakia, were always multiethnic. There is no logic or facts that can settle borderline cases of an ethnic country. Do the Swedes in Finland make that country multiethnic, or instead an ethnic country with a minority? In the realm of human society, everything shades off into what it is not and the taxonomy is usually determined by one's politics or ideology, an example being the boundary between ethnicity and race.

"Nationalism" may well be unsalvageable as a neutral term and even people sympathetic to unifying nationalism, ethnic nationalism, or ordinary patriotism tend to call it "nationality," "separatism," or "national consciousness"—anything but nationalism. Those on the other side of the issue who think nationalism—almost never separated into its kinds—more dangerous than its suppression are happy to call it nationalism, and they may go on to define it in terms of its excesses so that its very definition condemns it. Yet, small countries that have only recently won their independence and ethnic groups that seek it rightly think of themselves as nationalists. For them, a neutral meaning would be useful and I suggest including among one's paramount values a commitment to seek and preserve the sovereignty of one's nation and to defend its honor, people, and territory. Czeslaw Milosz said

> Liberal thought of our time has often treated nationalism as a relic of an unenlightened tribal past. No wonder that many are now bewildered by the passions aroused by the question of national identity in Eastern Europe and the former Soviet Union.... Nationalism was undoubtedly the cement keeping each of these countries together. It would have been better had a less compromised term been available; but if an ethnic group with the same language and common past is regarded as the creator and rightful owner of the State, that is nationalism.[3]

In unifying nationalism, contiguous regions come together with some pretense to a voluntary uniting of similar peoples. Prior to the mid-nineteenth century, the "unified" peoples were not very similar and the unifying was not voluntary. As it becomes less voluntary and the groups less similar, unifying nationalism shades off into imperialism. Tsarist Russia unified parts of Europe and Asia and, after World War I, Yugoslavia unified Balkan Slavs. While Chechens and Tajiks are not by any stretch of the imagination types of Russians—Bavarians, Saxons, and Prussians, however unique each is, are still types of Germans and, therefore, they more readily relinquish separate sovereignty. Once it is distinguished from imperialism and from the national boundary drawing of conquerors and colonialists, of the three varieties it is easiest to claim that unifying nationalism is a recent phenomenon. Yet, the incorporation of closely related tribes into England occurred before Hobsbawm and Gellner claim nationalism was invented, and I suspect historians know of other early examples. In our own time, the emerging European Community can be viewed as a new, although relatively attenuated, case of unifying nationalism. New unifying identities do not necessarily conflict with narrower ones: Social identities and their concomitant loyalties usually are nested; one can, for example, simultaneously value one's identities as English, British, and European.

The suggestion that nationalism is a brief mad dance in the march of history ignores thousands of years of separatist nationalism, not to mention tens of thousands of years of clan and tribal loyalty. It rejects similarities between modern ethnic separatism and the striving of ethnic groups for their land and independence since before the Hebrews sought to be free of Egyptians, Babylonians, Macedonians, Romans, Turks, and the British. If nationalism were no older than the Napoleonic era, we would have to wonder what the Irish were excited about for the past eight hundred years. This narrowed and parochial view of nationalism as a recent phenomenon is itself recent, tailored to what led to Mussolini and Hitler. It ignores the age-old story of tribe, loyalty, fear of outsiders, and desire to be ruled by one's own. Separatist and unifying nationalism need to be appraised independently, not merely because the one is old and the other newer, but also because the two have different, indeed opposite, goals. Yet they are both tribal ideas, the one the idea of seizing political independence for one's ethnic group, the other a willingness to subsume one's ethnic identity under a broader identity and loyalty. The idea of Burgundians joining Italy is not completely unlike that of Italy joining Europe.

The third kind of nationalism is the ongoing patriotism and national consciousness felt by citizens in every country. It is not a desire to unify or separate, but a politicized loyalty felt in ethnic countries such as Italy, multiethnic ones such as Indonesia, and ethnically mixed, immigrant countries such as Canada and the United States. National loyalty is as old as clans and tribes and, after the family, defines the primary domain of group loyalty. It takes different forms depending on a country's relation to ethnicity: In ethnic countries such as Hungary, national loyalty overlays and politicizes ethnic national identity, in this way allowing someone to be a Hungarian (politically) who is not a Hungarian (ethnically). In multiethnic countries such as India, it creates a political national consciousness that overlays regional ethnic loyalties, thus drawing together diverse peoples into a common political identity. And in immigrant countries such as the United States, and with the exception of Native Americans, political national identity substitutes for ethnic identity and is the only basis for national identity and patriotism.

The only way to make the nationalism of established states recent is to argue, as Eric Hobsbawm does, that the nation-state that is a precondition of nationalism is itself recent, and that earlier there were only tribes and empires, to which the idea of nationalism does not apply. This prompts the question why the modern nation-state is a precondition of nationalism. Countries, lands, empires, kingdoms, principalities, states, city-states, nations, nation-states, federations, republics, tribes, and clans all generate feelings of group loyalty, patriotism, and willingness to risk one's life when the group is attacked. The difference between nationalist and tribal or imperial loyalty is negligible. The loyalty to Rome of a non-Italian imperial Roman is not ethnic, but political, but so is a Canadian's loyalty. What should we call the loyalties of Prussians and Athenians before Germany and Greece existed? Someone who, three hundred years ago, was a Prussian first and a German second seems no less a nationalist than a contemporary German. Someone who, twenty-four hundred years ago, was an Athenian first and a Greek second seems no less a nationalist than someone today who is a Greek first, a European second, and an Athenian third.

If, as some thinkers maintain, civilization is tending toward global unity, nineteenth century unifying nationalism was at least a step in the direction of political (as distinct from merely economic) globalization, whereas, this thinking goes, separatist nationalism is tribal and divisive—an attempt to make history run backward. From this standpoint, one might retain a kind thought or two for the USSR for rising above the tribal and the ethnic as part of the halting march of history toward true globalization, except for the fact that the unity of the USSR was no more voluntary, and therefore no more democratic, than that of the Russian Empire it succeeded, and thus falls on the latter side of the distinction between unification and imperialism. Democracy is not part of this supposed march of history because democratic thinking favors people's desires to be ruled by themselves instead of foreigners. Hence, democratic principles often but not always are more consonant with small countries—that is, with the parts more than with the whole. The idea of a historical evolution toward political globalization, or simply the idea that big, multiethnic countries are better than lots of little ethnic ones, is an ideal that, currently, seldom coincides with what people actually want, hence political globalization can be democratic only when we suppose a corresponding change in the objects of people's loyalties and in their felt social identities. A global perspective in the political sense depends on the philosophical ideal that unity is better than multiplicity, but its moral acceptability depends on the assumption that people will be satisfied when unified—or, more sinisterly, would be satisfied were they to understand things properly (whether or not they ever do).

While democracy tends to support self-determination or separatist nationalism, self-determination is not pursued to obtain democracy, contrary to what is sometimes claimed. Neither do separatists get aroused only when the central government is undemocratic. A totalitarian central government may provide separatists with an additional motive as well as win them international sympathy, and democracy may lighten their burden, but what they seek is independence, whether or not the mother country is democratic and whether or not they themselves are committed to democracy. The idea that democracy and not nationalism is what really motivates separatists is wishful thinking by those opposed to nationalism—it is not as though, if only they were ruled democratically and equitably, Latvia wouldn't mind being part of the USSR, Algeria wouldn't mind being part of France, and Ireland wouldn't mind remaining part of the British Empire.

One might argue that only democratic aspirations can justify secession, even if it isn't what motivates the separatists. Separatists themselves appeal to democratic ideals, making an analogy with the political liberty of citizens. For example, they maintain fairness requires that Kurds, living in their historical homeland and speaking their own language, should have an independent, effective voice in the global community, just as individual citizens seek, and believe fairness requires, independent, effective voices in their national community. It would seem inconsistent were Slovenia to demand a voice in the global community by appeal to democratic principles and then deny its own citizens a voice in their government. But it is hard to see how that kind of failing defeats a group's claim to self-determination, as nearly half of the world's countries are not democratic and are not thought for that reason to forfeit their sovereignty. There is an inconsistent moralism to saying we will support independence (or earlier, decolonization) only if we are reasonably sure the new state will be democratic. Independence and democracy are separate goods and it doesn't follow from the likelihood of a separatist group failing to establish democracy that others have a right to deny them independence.

Ethnic nationalism becomes militant when a people is made to feel threatened, or when treaties put large numbers of people on the wrong side of the border, as in the case of the award of Transylvania, with its two million Hungarians, to Romania in 1921 for fighting on the allied side in World War I. Unlike Eastern Europe and the Balkans, Western Europe sorted out its boundaries along roughly ethnic lines over the past few centuries. In Eastern Europe separatist movements were boxed up until much more recently by the Russian

Empire and the Soviet Union, and in the Balkans by the Ottoman Turks, Austria–Hungary, and Yugoslavia; it is not surprising that when the box is opened they jump out, giving us greater disorder in Eastern Europe and the Balkans than in the West.

It is especially difficult for Americans to understand ethnic nationalist movements because the United States never fought in the name of ethnic nationalism and American national identity is not grounded in ethnicity. Neither is America a true multiethnic country. The immigrant Irish, Ukrainians, Chinese, and other groups, including imported African slaves, never had historical homelands in America on which to stake territorial claims that competed with their American national identity. This contrasts sharply with the situation in Russia, Indonesia, and India, where Chechens, East Timorese, and Kashmiris have historical homelands—turf they have lived on for centuries— to render their claims concrete as well as solve the problem of whether they would be independent or autonomous. Hence, to criticize the ethnic nationalism of Chechens or Kurds as "tribal" and ask why they cannot live peacefully with their neighbors like the different ethnic groups in America is to criticize a kind of national striving Americans cannot feel. It makes no sense to assume that nationalist claims of ethnic groups in Europe, Asia, or Africa have no greater legitimate force than would demands for independence by Irish Americans or Ohioans.

While American national loyalty is political and not ethnic, neither is it only the intellectual appreciation of a constitution or moral regard for rights and freedoms; it is national consciousness, a shared sense of possession and social identity, felt through the country's geography, history, customs, achievements, and tribulations, as well as its democratic principles. A shared history is essential to the construction of group loyalty, whether it is to an ethnic, multiethnic, or immigrant country.

Jürgen Habermas maintains that the tribal nation is prepolitical and particularistic, an object of blind loyalty, whereas the modern political state is based on constitutional principles. "Constitutional patriotism" (*Verfassungspatriotismus*) is the natural successor to patriotism and ethnic nationalism; it must eventually supersede them.[4] The distinction between the state as tribe and as constitutionally grounded civil society is an important one that I will consider shortly; Habermas, however, makes these two dimensions of the state mutually exclusive because he sees them as developmental, unidirectional, historical stages. This historicism rules out complementary roles for loyalty-based and constitutionally based conceptions of the state. Presumably, as patriotism evolves beyond particularized loyalty to one's own ethnic group or country, and onward to constitutional patriotism, nationalist passions will abate and countries will be more tolerant and democratic.

As we see in the case of the United States, people need not live in an ethnic homeland to develop a sense of loyalty and patriotism that is more than merely the moral appreciation of constitutional principles. What Habermas rejects is the very idea of loyalty or group egoistic regard—that is, the idea that one is specially obligated to one's country because it is one's own, and he substitutes for loyalty universal moral principles incorporated in a constitution. It is understandable why a German philosopher does this, as group loyalty found its most lethal and destructive manifestation in Nazi Germany. Yet for Habermas, constitutional patriotism is a spectacular oxymoron. For him, constitutional principles regarding rights (as distinct from rules setting up legislative machinery) are universal and global, and they have equal merit regardless what country's constitution they are in. Thus, we can see constitutional patriotism as a kind of philosophical globalization, the rejection of particularism in morality.

Patriotism is group egoism; it is a kind of loyalty whose object is one's own country, regardless how similar one's country may be to another country that is not one's own. Principles judge the repeatable features of things and do not accept as relevant to my obligations the fact that a country is mine.[5] Suppose Habermas discovers that the principles he prizes are best exemplified in Mexico's constitution. Is Mexico then the object of his "patriotism"? Habermas wants us to base obligations only on principles, but wants to retain the word "patriotism" regardless of the violence this does to its meaning. The ethnic state and the constitutional state are not mutually exclusive stages of historical development, but may coexist as complementary aspects of a country, even though loyalty and moral principles are conceptually distinct and neither can be reduced to the other.

An objection to revealing sympathy for ethnic independence movements is that they will be encouraged, and then there will be no end to them, resulting in many new wars. Former American Secretary of State Warren Christopher said on television in 1995 that if we encouraged separatism, we would end up with five thousand countries; about the same time, Senator Daniel Patrick Moynihan said we should "get ready for fifty new countries in the next fifty years." Since he spoke, Macedonia and Eritrea became independent. This rate of increase should not be disturbing; between 1946 and 1994, United Nations membership increased from 52 to 183, which is more than two-and-one-half times the rate Senator Moynihan says is in store for us.

We should not assume most ethnic groups will demand independence even if the Great Powers and the United Nations express sympathy because, quite apart from their belief that they might be punished if they tried, most ethnic groups have good reasons not to seek national sovereignty. These reasons include

1. They are reasonably content as they are (for example, French, German, and Italian speakers in Switzerland and, for the moment, Puerto Ricans).
2. National loyalties successfully overlay regional ones and they don't feel especially oppressed (for example, the Balinese, Sundanese, Bataks, Minangkabau, and most but not all of the other groups in Indonesia).
3. They are linguistically similar and geographically contiguous (the provinces of Italy, the German Länder, the clans of Scotland).
4. They consider themselves already independent (tribes in Amazonia and New Guinea).
5. They don't think they could make it economically, even if they feel oppressed (Nagas in India, Native American tribes, most small landlocked groups).

Even in Russia, where there is fear the Chechen revolt will be copied elsewhere, the majority of the twenty-two ethnic republics and ten autonomous ethnic districts know they would not do well economically if they had full independence. Most of the world's ethnic groups do not want independence, which means the principle of self-determination does not imply a state for every tribe and we do not have to think of ethnic nationalism as a genie that must be kept in its bottle.

William Pfaff argues that peace is better served by supporting existing borders, however much this may frustrate secession-minded minorities. He says

> An international guarantee of existing frontiers in the Balkans and Eastern Europe, so as to deprive transnational ethnic rivalry of its political and military explosiveness, could provide one substantial form of defense against the spread of violence and disorder. Such a guarantee would undoubtedly have to be implemented by NATO.[6]

One counterconsideration is that countries whose borders follow ethnic lines have one less source of conflict with their neighbors, and when they do not follow ethnic lines, the suppressed minorities are unpredictable and permanent sources of worry, rather like old iron boilers. The more fundamental question is whether the avoidance of violence and disorder is always the most important consideration. Writing before NATO intervened in Kosovo in 1998, Pfaff's words imply NATO should have supported Serbian suppression of the Albanian majority so as to guarantee that Kosovo would not change the existing frontiers by seceding. Yet, suppression is itself an evil, to be subtracted from whatever good it achieves. The forty-seven-year Soviet rule in Latvia might by itself be as bad as a short spasm of violence, although I am not suggesting anyone knows how to calculate such a result.

Pfaff also maintains that the ethnic state is an illusion; it is, he says, "A product of the political imagination; it does not exist in reality. Ethnic nationalism is the product of a certain idea of the nation that originated in German romanticism. . . . Romanticism glorified native earth, instinct, the priority of emotion over abstraction and thought, and hence the unity of race and state."[7] It does not exist in reality, Pfaff says, because all so-called ethnic states contain ethnic minorities.

This is a fine example of a kind of verbal magic that allows us to make large objects disappear: We decide what we want to disappear, such as the ethnic state, democracy, or communism, and then we say that what an ethnic state (or democracy or communism) really is can be found in such-and-such a theory in, for example, German or Marxist philosophy. Then we open our eyes, look about, and find there are no countries or political systems that satisfy the definition. Hence, there aren't any communist countries, or democratic ones, or ethnic states, or at least there aren't any genuine ones. But we shouldn't worry less about ethnic countries merely because they do not exist. If we stipulate that a country isn't an ethnic one if it has minorities, of course there aren't any ethnic countries. The idea that a "genuine" ethnic country has no minorities also helps critics associate ethnic nationalism with nineteenth-century theories about the "unity of race and state." This association then supports the further claim that ethnic nationalists really do want a "pure" country, without minorities, as do some of those writers of books in German romanticism, even at the cost of ethnic cleansing or genocide. Thus, the idea of an ethnic country is changed from a familiar reality to a sinister ideal.

For Isaiah Berlin, nationalism is an ideology that derives from a xenophobic version of community along with the organic theory of society; it is, he says, "the elevation of the interests of the unity and self-determination of the nation to the status of the supreme value before which all other considerations must, if need be, yield at times, an ideology to which German and Italian thinkers seemed particularly prone."[8]

I believe it is true that I complete my humanity by acquiring the social identities and, initially at least, the goals and values of our social groups, including nations. I've called such allegiances loyalties and group egoism.[9] But what interests Sir Isaiah is nationalism as the expression of dreadful excesses of group loyalty and social identity—fanatic nationalism and the right of one's nation to trample what stands in its path. He goes on to say, "these goals are supreme," and the "essential human unit . . . is . . . the nation,"[10] to which all other human groups are subordinated. Thus, his description of human social nature as it relates to national loyalty is that narrowed and hypertrophied version of it found in Fichte and Hegel. "This," he says, "is the ideology of organicism, loyalty, the Volk as the true carrier of the national values."[11] Any rebuttal of Sir Isaiah's intended reductio has to show that this isn't the version of nationalism most nationalists find reasonable, that his version is not implied by more innocent versions, and that there is no causal or logical conveyor that takes one from innocent to fanatic nationalism.

Contemplate, if you will, Chechen, Eritrean, and Slovene patriots, whom we inform have succumbed to nationalism, a German theory that places the state above morality, makes the individual expendable like a leaf on a tree, and justifies the slaughter of neighboring ethnic groups. The bewildered Chechens, Eritreans, and Slovenes will look puzzled and say, "Who, me?" Ethnic separatists really are nationalists, but they neither necessarily believe those things, nor are they somehow being irresistibly pushed (by logic or "history") toward believing them. When critics consulting nineteenth-century theories say nationalism (in those theories) is essentially chauvinistic and xenophobic, it is unwarranted to draw the same conclusion about actual national independence movements, such as Chechens and Kurds, and suggest to policy makers that what they really want is what those theories say.

A modern ethnic country is at once a civil-constitutional state whose members are citizens, and an ethnic, linguistic state, most of whose members are ethnic brethren. The former is a political creation, concerned with citizens and potential citizens as individuals and with their mutual rights and obligations. The latter is tribal in the sense that, almost always, an identifiable people predates and created the political state. I say almost always because, while it may at first seem strange, the "tribal" side of this distinction is not necessarily based on ethnicity but can, in a country such as the United States, be a sense of national consciousness and loyalty created by the shared history of people of mixed ethnicity. The focus is on one's country as an object of loyalty or group egoism, hence more a sentiment than a judgment. People of most countries are both ethnic brethren and citizens, but not in the United States and Canada where what is tribal is only metaphorically so because the state as an object of group loyalty has no ethnic origin or identity.

A realm of values corresponds to each of these social roles. The realm of loyalties is group egoist and partial: I support my country, my family, my neighborhood because they are mine. This realm is boundary conscious and often outward looking in being concerned with special obligations to one's group as well as with external threats and intergroup competition. It is animated by issues of immigration, refugees, repatriation, and perceived threats to sovereignty. The civil realm is inward looking and sees fellow citizens as tokens of a national instead of an ethnic type. This is the realm of law and constitution, designed not to protect citizens from outsiders but from each other; here, among the insiders, laws apply universally and loyalties and ethnicity in principle have no place. From this perspective, one's moral universe is one's fellow citizens.[12]

In ethnic countries, it is common for potential immigrants to be filtered on ethnic criteria. However, the logic of the situation tells us that once immigrants of whatever ethnicity are legally in the country, it is too late for ethnic considerations; now they are insiders and the guiding idea is the constitution, not insider–outsider distinctions. Just letting them in to live under the laws changes their status, for they are now potential citizens under laws made for a single civil society, and ethnic grounds for decisions about citizenship and other matters no longer make sense. The time to treat people as outsiders is when they are outsiders, looking in, and not treat them as second-class insiders after they are admitted. One national community implies one set of national rules that applies to everyone in it.

An immigrant in a country is very much like an adopted child. A family has no obligation to adopt anyone, and if it does adopt it can (and families commonly do) filter candidates by race and gender. Once adopted, the child becomes an insider, equal with the rest of the family before the rules governing the family polity and possessing rights nonfamily members lack. Notoriously, some adopted children are not treated as well as the family's biological children. But the point is that no one even tries to justify such treatment. The logic of families and their obligations to members as distinct from nonmembers is very similar to that of countries and the different obligations of citizens to one another and to foreigners.

The claims of nationalism are prima facie and sometimes compete with wider objects of loyalty such as humanity, as well as with narrower ones such as family; as though this were not problem enough, they also compete with overlapping loyalties such as religion and, of course, with moral principles. Thus, we all confront a complex ethics of parts and wholes. That is, unless we are fanatics, for some people place no limits on their country's self-interested actions and acknowledge no possible counterweight to their national loyalty. These nationalists are single-tribe fanatics, as are religious fanatics, racial fanatics, and most fanatics. They are group egoists who countenance no countervailing considerations, just as "pure" egoists admit no intrinsic merit to the interests of other people. All one can say is that some people are fanatics and most are not.

I am not defending tribalizing the world. "Natural" ethnic borders everywhere—a state for every ethnic group—is unreasonable and unrealizable, and its advocates may come to believe there is something wrong with the very idea of a conglomerate country such as India. Then they may, "on principle," support small, unrepresentative, separatist factions, or believe that the United Nations should encourage nascent liberation movements. They may stress the easier democracy of smaller, more homogeneous countries. Equally unreasonable and unrealizable, at least in any foreseeable future, is political globalization. Smaller-scale loves and loyalties and small-scale bases for emotional security lie very deep in human beings.

There is no logic or reasoning by which we may prove that small objects of loyalty are better than large ones, or vice versa, but perhaps one argument should be mentioned briefly. It is said, mainly by utilitarians, that because the world contains more people than does a country or family, these smaller units count for less when there is a conflict with the good of humanity. But this begs the question. There are (hopefully) more future people than living ones, more primates—"my fellow primates"—than people, more vertebrates than primates, and so on, and it is clear that the mere relative numerousness of a group doesn't make it count for more than a smaller group differently characterized. Moreover, and distinct from the weight consequent on how we characterize a group, loyalties tend to attenuate and weaken as their objects become broader and individuals within them are farther away. This may have something to do with the smallish groups within which early humans evolved into social animals.

The same general sense that people should, as much as possible, manage their own fates—that governments and the global community should let them have what they want instead of what is good for them—has hastened the breakup of colonial empires, created sympathy for self-determination, and spurred the recent growth in the number of democracies. If the United Nations and the Great Powers came to look more favorably on voluntary plebiscite, partition, and migration, it would make the position of irredentists more difficult and constitute a morally feasible long-term solution when groups of people cannot live together or forgive one another. Is this "giving in to nationalism"? Certainly it is. There is ample evidence that asking people to set aside nationalist feelings is asking too much. Blanket condemnation of nationalism—in any of its three varieties—is as irrational as the Victorians' blanket condemnation of sex, and pointing to atrocities, saying, "See what nationalism leads to?" is rather like saying, "See what sex leads to?" when someone is raped.

A general reprobation of ethnic nationalism has the moral edge if tilting toward ethnic boundaries leads to more suffering than does continued suppression. But this, especially if we consider the long term, is dubious. In the absence of evidence that peace or democracy requires it, there is nothing particularly attractive about political globalization, only a philosophical desire for unity. There is, however, a moral edge to letting people have what they want, including, for example, what Scots, Chechens, and Kurds may want, when it can be done with minimal frustration of the legitimate desires of other groups and countries. The idea is not to cheer for secession or autonomy, but to accept it when it is politically achievable and ethnic groups loudly demand it. And there is nothing inconsistent about having small new countries along with European and world communities. Acknowledging nested multiple loyalties is something people do all the time.

Notes

1. Benjamin Barber, "Global Multiculturalism and the American Experiment," *World Policy Journal* 10 (1) 1993.

2. Ernest Gellner, *Nations and Nationalism* (Ithaca, NY: Cornell University Press, 1983); Eric J. Hobsbawm, *Nations and Nationalism Since 1780* (Cambridge, UK: Cambridge University Press, 1990); Isaiah Berlin, "Nationalism: Past Neglect and Present Power," *The Partisan Review*, 46 (3) 337–58, 1979; William Pfaff, "Invitation to War," *Foreign Affairs* 72 (3) 97–109, 1993; former United States Secretary of State Warren Christopher in a 1995 television news interview.

3. Czeslaw Milosz, "Swing Shift in the Baltics," *The New York Review of Books,* November 4, 1993.

4. Habermas discusses *Verfassungspatriotismus* (constitutional patriotism) in his essay "Citizenship and National Identity, Reflections on the Future of Europe" ("Staatsbürgerschaft und Nationale Identität, Überlegungen zur Europäischen Zukunft") (St. Gallen, Switzerland: Erker-Verlag, 1991).

5. By acknowledging that everyone should have special regard for their own countries, sometimes it is claimed that obligations of loyalty actually are universalizable. This misses the point and is like saying that an egoist's judgment is universalizable and therefore isn't biased, if this egoist agrees that everybody may make egoistic judgments—that is, everyone may be biased.

6. Pfaff, "Invitation to War."

7. Pfaff, "Invitation to War."

8. Isaiah Berlin, "Nationalism: Past Neglect and Present Power."

9. See *The Non-Suicidal Society* (Indiana University Press, 1986) and "Loyalties," (*Journal of Philosophy*, 79, 173–93, 1982), where these ideas are explored at length.

10. Berlin, "Nationalism: Past Neglect and Present Power."

11. Berlin, "Nationalism: Past Neglect and Present Power."

12. I am grateful to my students at the University of Leipzig, summer semester 1994, for helping me with these distinctions, and which I discuss in "Einwanderungsland Deutschland?" ("Is Germany an Immigrant State?") in the anthology *Der Neue Nationalstaat* (*The New National State*), ed. Rüdiger Voigt (Baden-Baden, Germany: Nomos, 1998).

6

Global Democracy:
International, Not Cosmopolitan[1]

Kok-Chor Tan

A KEY IDEA OF LIBERAL NATIONALISM is that the nation-state is the primary site
of deliberative democratic politics. Deliberative democracy is "a conception of democratic politics in which decisions and policies are justified in a
process of discussion among free and equal citizens or their accountable representatives" (Gutmann and Thompson 2000, 161). Fundamentally, this
means that a democratically arrived at public policy is one in which individuals affected by the policy could reasonably consent to. According to liberal
nationalists, this ideal of democracy requires, foremost, that individuals share
a common language, a vernacular with which to effectively debate and to collectively decide on matters that affect them (Kymlicka 2001, 213, 226–27).
Moreover, democratic politics require a sufficient level of trust and mutual respect among citizens so as to motivate them to honor democratic decisions
that are not in their favor, on the understanding that should decisions be in
their favor next time, these would likewise be respected (Kymlicka 2001).
Most democrats agree that democratic politics are possible only if citizens adequately trust and respect each other; but nationalists make the additional
claim that a shared national identity best provides the sense of solidarity, the
"fellow-feeling" necessary for generating and sustaining this mutual respect
and trust among persons who are practically strangers to each other, as citizens generally are.

   This nationalist-democratic thesis, or nationalist thesis for short, may be
challenged by some liberal democrats, even though it is arguably implicit in
much of the liberal democratic tradition.[2] J. S. Mill, perhaps, was more explicit
than most liberal democrats when he wrote that "free institutions are next to

impossible in a country made up of different nationalities. Among a people without fellow-feeling, especially if they read and speak different languages, the united public opinion, necessary to the working of representative government, cannot exist" (Mill 1991, 428).

It is not my aim in this chapter to argue for or against the basic premises of the nationalist thesis. What I wish to explore is whether and how the nationalist thesis, that the nation is the primary locus of democratic politics, can meet the new challenges brought about by globalization. As national boundaries become more permeable with respect to the decisions and practices of actors and forces outside the borders of nations, keeping democracy located at the national level appears to be insufficient for ensuring that individuals who would be affected by these decisions and practices have a decision in the matter. And this is plainly contrary to the deliberative democratic ideal that collective decisions ought to be those decisions that individuals affected could reasonably consent to. To counter this global democratic deficit that has been rendered more salient by the forces of globalization, some theorists argue that we need to develop an account of democracy that can transcend the limits of the nation-centric idea of democracy.

But what are the prospects for globalizing democracy if the "common sympathies" necessary for democratic deliberation exist between fellow members of a nation but "do not exist between them and any others" (Mill 1991, 427)? If the nationalist thesis is correct, how can we conceive of and achieve global democracy?

I proceed by recounting the nationalist thesis, pointing out why nationalists think that the nation is the basic site of deliberative democracy. In the second part of this chapter, I recall some of the familiar arguments as to why a nation-bound concept of democracy is thought to be inadequate in the face of increasing economic globalization. Next, I look at cosmopolitan democracy as a proposed solution to the challenge of globalization, and I clarify and identify the ways in which the cosmopolitan idea of democracy is at odds with the nationalist thesis. Then, in the fourth section, I examine an alternative to cosmopolitan democracy that does not contradict (but indeed builds on) the nationalist thesis. I will argue that global democracy conceived literally as an inter*national* democracy—that is, as a democracy of "democracies rooted in nation-states" (Holden 2000, 214)—can go some way toward correcting the global democratic deficit. Indeed, building on existing democratic institutions at the national level provides a more realistic and practical way of achieving global democracy than the cosmopolitan democratic approach. If the nationalist thesis is a necessity, this necessity can be turned into a virtue. Finally, in the fifth and last section, I clarify why the nationalist obstacle to cosmopolitan *democracy* does not undermine cosmopolitanism understood as an ideal about *justice*.

I. Nationality and Democracy

Will Kymlicka writes that "democratic politics is politics in the vernacular" (2001, 213), meaning by this that democratic deliberation is possible only among individuals who share a common language. One reason for this is that ordinary people feel "comfortable debating political issues in their own tongue," and that, as a general rule, only elites can acquire fluency in more than one language. So to require people to deliberate in a language foreign to them is to defend a form of elitism at best, and at worst to exclude them from deliberative politics—a violation of the democratic ideal either way. Also, "political communication has a large ritualistic component" that a mere technical competence in a language may not be sensitive to (2001, 213). For example, Yael Tamir notes how the Israeli parliament, the Knesset, follows after the "Great Knesset," which was a central religious and political institution during the period of the Second Temple (Tamir 1993, 148). The Knesset's proceedings and procedures thus reflect a particular culture and background history that a merely technical understanding of Hebrew may not suffice to render comprehensible and familiar. Thus, Kymlicka concludes that "the more political debate is conducted in the vernacular, the more participatory it will be" (2001, 214).

In addition to the common language that shared nationality provides, another crucial role nationality plays in servicing democratic politics is that it provides a sense of solidarity and unity that is necessary for generating the requisite level of mutual respect and trust among individuals. Democracy requires individuals to respect the reasonable views of their fellow citizens even if they are in deep disagreement with each other, and conversely that they are to forward arguments and views that each can "reasonably be expected reasonably to endorse" (Rawls 1999, 140). It also requires a certain degree of trust so that the losers in a given democratic process can be motivated to honor the result, because they are confident that should the results be in their favor next time, their opponents would likewise honor these results (Kymlicka 2001, 226; also Miller 1995, 90).

Fellow nationals are, of course, not intimate with each other as, say, friends or kin are. But fellow feelings, nationalists argue, need not be restricted only to people who are closely related to one another. Co-nationals see themselves as part of a collective with a common past and a shared future, and even if they are not actually acquainted with each other, "in the minds of each lives the image of their communion" (Anderson 1993, 6). It is for this reason that Benedict Anderson famously refers to the nation as "an imagined community," meaning by this not that the nation is a fictitious association that is unworthy of people's allegiances, but that it is a significant allegiance-generating association that is premised on a people's image or collective consciousness of its historic and communal distinctness.

Thus, David Miller writes that democratic politics "are likely to function most effectively when they embrace just a single national community" (Miller 1995, 90). This is because the virtues of mutual trust and respect, moderation and self-restraint, and, one might add, the idea of public reason (Rawls 1993, 1999), are crucial for a functioning democratic political community, and common nationality provides the "cement" for engendering and nurturing these virtues (see Canovan 1996).[3]

In sum, "national political forums with a single common language form the primary locus of democratic participation in the modern world, and are more genuinely participatory than political forums at higher levels that cut across language-lines" (Kymlicka 2001, 227). Nationality provides the cultural linguistic basis for democratic deliberation and the source of democratic trust and respect among citizens.[4]

II. Globalization and the Democratic Deficit

The nation-centric account of democracy is commonly said to be outmoded in an era of economic globalization. Economic globalization, or globalization for short, refers to the process of increasing integration and interdependency of national economies, the increasing mobility of capital and labor across national boundaries, the creation of new global markets and products (e.g., financial markets and their "products" such as investment schemes), and the creation of international organs and regulations to facilitate and govern these new interactions (e.g., the World Trade Organizaton). Globalization is the progression toward a boundless global economy (or at least the approximation of) in which national ties and membership are becoming less and less relevant with respect to economic practices and decisions.

Yet the burdens and benefits of the increasingly globalized economy are far from being equally shared among the world's population. In spite of this newly shared global economic space (or because of it, some say), global income disparity has risen rather than fallen. One basic reason for this increasing inequality against the backdrop of globalization is the so-called democratic deficit in the global sphere. Economic decisions are global in the scope of their effects and implications, and are often even made by institutions and organizations, such as the World Bank, the International Monetary Fund (IMF), multinational corporations (MNCs), and so on, that transcend national affiliation in the traditional sense. Yet these decisions are not regulated by procedures that reflect the will and views of individuals who are affected significantly by them. As John Dryzek points out, "globalization means that important issues increasingly elude the control of nation-states" (1999, 30). This lack of democratic control, especially on the part of individuals most vulnerable to the globalizing economy, over the terms and processes of globalization results in the unequal allocation of benefits and burdens among individuals globally.

As the scope of our economic interaction widens, so too should the scope of our democratic procedure in order to regulate this interaction on terms that all can accept. Normative considerations, in short, ought to be globalized as our economic decisions and practices take on a more global scope. Something like this is underscored by Hume when he wrote that if "several distinct societies maintain a kind of intercourse for mutual convenience and advantage, the boundary of justice still grows larger, in proportion to the largeness of men's view, and the force of their mutual connexions" (Hume 1777, 153). As members of nations, especially those in the developing world, become increasingly vulnerable to decisions of other countries as a result of increased enmeshment of national economies, limiting any democratic control they may exercise within their borders does not go far enough to ensure that decisions that have grave impact on them are decisions they could reasonably consent to.

III. Cosmopolitan Democracy, World State, and World Citizenship

But how can the current global democratic deficit be best corrected? How best to "globalize" democracy, so to speak? Some theorists argue that to counter the democratic deficit, we need to reconceptualize democracy, to rethink democracy as a global rather than a nationally rooted ideal. As one commentator puts it, "Democracy at the national level has become meaningless as real decisions are made at a higher level, and these higher-level institutions are largely exempt from democratic oversight or accountability" (Lynch 2000, 96). The overlapping "networks of interaction" between states, acerbated by a globalizing economy, do not coincide with the bounded territories within which democratic deliberation takes place. Thus, as David Held has put it, "the idea of a democratic order can no longer be simply defended as an idea suitable to a particular closed political community or state" (Held 2000, 19, 28; also Held 1995).

Some theorists have, therefore, proposed a cosmopolitan conception of democracy as a response to what they believe to be the increasing redundancy of
the national ideal of the democratic ideal. As the primary arena of human social and economic life is no longer confined to the borders of the nation-state,
so no longer should the primary arena of democratic politics be similarly confined. Keeping democracy nation-centered is anachronistic in light of the increasingly shared social and economic space of our world. The traditional pre-
supposition of democracy—that it is a nationally bounded concept—has to
be replaced by an unbounded concept of democracy to meet the new realities
of globalization. Held thus recommends:

> Against this background [of globalization], democracy must be thought of as a
> "double-sided process". . . [meaning] not just the deepening of democracy within
> a national community, but also the extension of democratic processes across ter-
> ritorial borders. Democracy for the new millennium must involve cosmopolitan
> citizens able to gain access to, and mediate between, and render accountable, the
> social, economic and political processes and flows which cuts across and trans-
> form their traditional community boundaries. (2000, 30)

Instead of continuing to regard democracy as primarily an ideal that must be
anchored in the idea of a nation, cosmopolitan democrats propose that democracy be seen as primarily a transnational ideal that is directly applicable
to individuals of the world taken as a single social scheme.

Cosmopolitan democrats do not deny that the nation is an important democratic site, but they hold that it is not necessarily the most important, and
certainly not the only site to be governed by democratic principles. Individuals ought to engage in democratic deliberations with other individuals across
national lines, as members of transnational or even global associations, which
will enable them to better influence and regulate global decisions that have
great effects on their lives. Cosmopolitan democrats may point to the fact of
new and multiple transnational allegiances individuals are able to form and
have as evidence of the possibility of transnational identity necessary for
grounding cosmopolitan democracy.

Thus, basic to the idea of cosmopolitan democracy is that there ought to be
overlapping transnational institutions and associations in which individuals
have a direct deliberative role. People are not just democratic citizens of their
state, but they are also members of the global community through their membership and participation in various associations and activities within and
without their own countries. Some cosmopolitans propose the formation of a
world parliament of a sort, in the form of democratically elected people's assembly—a world assembly of individuals elected directly by individuals independent of their nationalities to complement the United Nations General As-

sembly in which countries rather than individuals as such are represented (Archibugi et al. 2000).

Before exploring the cosmopolitan democratic idea more fully, it is useful to be clear on what the cosmopolitan democratic ideal entails. The term "cosmopolitan democracy" is potentially misleading because cosmopolitanism is commonly associated with a world state, a *cosmos polis,* and cosmopolitan democracy correspondingly is commonly thought to mean a democracy situated within this world state. But the idea of a world state is itself highly contentious for the reasons Kant has pointed out—namely, that a world state is likely to be a despotic state, if at all attainable or sustainable, given the vast expanse of geographical space and diversity of views it would have to contain. Indeed, the association of cosmopolitanism with world statism is one central reason why critics of cosmopolitanism are quick to reject it (cf. Zolo 1997)

But, in fact, few cosmopolitan democrats themselves actually advocate a world state. Held, for instance, stresses that his cosmopolitan theory proposes not a world state, but a network of transnational institutions and organizations, and individual commitments and interests that cut across national and territorial boundaries. So this misunderstanding with respect to the political context of cosmopolitan democracy is one that cosmopolitans can clear up. The notion of a world state is not one that cosmopolitans must commit themselves to.

But while the commitment to world statism is (often wrongly) attributed to cosmopolitan democrats rather than actually affirmed by them, cosmopolitan democrats often speak approvingly of a cosmopolitan or world citizenship. For instance, Held writes that "each person of a state must learn to become a cosmopolitan citizen—a person capable of mediating between national traditions, communities, and alternative forms of life" (Held 2000, 29; also Linklater 1999 and Heater 1990).

Concerning the idea of world citizenship, critics of cosmopolitanism charge that the idea of a world citizen absent a world state seems incoherent. Citizenship, properly understood, is a "bounded" concept that expresses a membership in a distinct polity that comes with certain obligations in addition to rights (Miller 1999). Citizenship is, in other words, a political-legal concept, and so world *citizenship* properly understood must entail a world state and a legal order within which the idea of world citizenship can be situated. But because cosmopolitans rarely call for a world state themselves, it is "misleading" to describe cosmopolitan democracy in terms of the "creation of democratic citizenship on the transnational level" (Kymlicka 2001, 325). Cosmopolitan democracy does not "create any form of collective deliberation and decision making that connects and binds individuals across national boundaries" with a common political identity (Kymlicka 2001, 325).

Thus, because cosmopolitans rarely affirm the idea of a world state, they can only mean by cosmopolitan citizenship something quite distinct from how we ordinarily conceive of citizenship. The fundamental inspiration behind Martha Nussbaum's call for world citizenship is not that of extending our ordinary conception of citizenship to a world polity as such, but to "make all human beings part of our community of dialogue and concern, base our political deliberations on interlocking commonality, and give the circle that defines our humanity special attention and respect" (Nussbaum 1996, 9). This is a moral aspiration rather than a legal-political reality. The world citizenship cosmopolitans aspire toward is a moral rather than legal category. Cosmopolitans are not bent on creating a world state as such, but the creation of a common moral world and the recognition of the membership of all humans in this moral world. Cosmopolitans, in short, intend their call for world citizens to be understood metaphorically, rather than literally.

Some commentators feel that this metaphorical use of "citizenship" may present more trouble than it is worth. Stephen Neff, for instance, says that it is, in the end, unfortunate that cosmopolitans speak freely of world citizenship given the distractions and confusion this poses, when they mean rather generally the attractive idea of a shared humanity (1999, 118). Indeed, the normative goals of cosmopolitanism, that of global justice, protecting human rights, and a more democratic global arena "can be brought about in ways," argues Neff, "which do not require a distinct concept of cosmopolitan citizenship" (119).

These are legitimate concerns. But perhaps too much has been made of the cosmopolitan invocation of world citizenship. Once it is clear how cosmopolitans are in fact using the term "citizenship," the idea of a world citizenship need not be objectionable, but can, on the contrary, be a useful counterforce to the tendencies of people to think *exclusively* in nationalistic terms. At any rate, once these utopian ideas—that of world government and world citizenship in the literal sense—are disentangled from the cosmopolitan ideal, seemingly serious contradictions between cosmopolitan democracy and the national-democratic thesis are circumvented.

Still, in spite of these clarifications, cosmopolitan democracy remains at odds with the nationalist thesis in a real and fundamental way. Basic to the cosmopolitan democratic view is that the nation-state cannot remain the primary locus of democratic decision making. Although cosmopolitan democrats need not go all the way and seek to replace nation-states with a world state, they advocate the creation of overlapping transnational and regional institutions that cut across national boundaries and in which individuals can have a direct participatory democratic role. The proposal of a people's assembly, as mentioned above, is one such example; in fact, the directly elected European Parliament is often seen as a prototype of such a world assembly (Held 2000, 29). Democratic citizenship in nation-states is only one among different democratic forms of memberships that individuals ought to have, and is certainly not necessarily the most basic or significant.

But, as mentioned above, nationalist theorists point out that nationhood provides the solidarity and common language necessary for democratic politics; yet "the cosmopolitan governance proposed by Held is for the most part silent on" this crucial point (Kymlicka 2001, 239). What would serve as the basis of solidarity and common understanding at the global level among people of diverse nationalities? If individuals are to be directly represented at global decision making irrespective of nationality, it is not clear if linguistic diversity can be overcome and if the diversity in worldviews and affinities can properly support a democratic deliberative order based on mutual trust and respect across national lines. Hypothetically, if we actually do establish a directly elected world parliament, how likely would it be for, say, a Canadian to seriously consider voting for, and to do so in an informed manner, an Indonesian candidate given the linguistic and cultural barriers between them? Indeed, as Bellamy and Jones point out, the European experience has shown this to be quite unlikely. In spite of the success of the European Union (EU) in bringing together democratic nations under a single formal/legal organization, the creation of a unified European demos remains elusive (2000, 211). Indeed, the diversity of national identification remains in spite of economic and monetary integration at the level of Europe. Polls show that most Europeans tend to see themselves as members of particular nations, rather than as members of a European polity (cited in Bellamy and Jones 2000, 211).[5]

Extending direct democratic participation beyond national boundaries may also undermine democratic accountability. Dennis Thompson observes that "when we look at the experience of extending governmental authority beyond national boundaries, we cannot be encouraged by what we see. As the EU has gained more power and become more effective, it has also drawn more criticism for its lack of democratic accountability" (1986, 115). As we increase the number of decision-making authorities that are directly accountable to individuals, as the cosmopolitan idea calls for, the more difficult it will be to actually hold these authorities accountable (Thompson 1986, 115–16). "By its very nature, such a network [of regional and international agencies and authorities] does not give those citizens outside particular agencies or assemblies any significant control, and does not provide any way for citizens within them to deal with the effects of the uncoordinated decisions of other agencies and assemblies" (Thompson 1986, 115–16). As we multiply democratic authorities, the more we undermine the democratic ideals of effective control and accountability. Thompson has aptly labeled this "the problem of many hands."

To be sure, the problem of many hands is not uniquely a problem for cosmopolitan democracy; it confounds domestic democrats as well to the extent that there are multiple democratically accountable decision-making entities within a society (Thompson 1986). But it is a problem that is compounded when attempting to extend deliberative democracy globally.

There is also the problem of fostering and securing a global civil society that can underpin a functioning democracy of individuals in the global arena. Democrats take as one important precondition for a flourishing democracy the presence of a flourishing civil society. Yet, it is not clear how a global civil society could be engendered. Richard Falk holds out hope, cautiously, that a global civil society may emerge as a result of globalization, in that "as the global village becomes more an experienced, daily reality" (Falk 2000, 176), individuals can come to see themselves as members of a shared community of fate. This optimism presupposes that the sense of solidarity and common sympathies and fellow-feelings that are the preconditions of civil society can be engendered globally because of people's common experiences and realities as a result of increased globalization. Yet shared experience and reality alone may not be sufficient. A prior sense of identity may be necessary before individuals can come to appreciate and perceive certain experiences and realities as *shared*. Why, for example, would Americans attempt to understand the effects of globalization on foreigners and to share in their worldview? The felt impact of free trade and economic liberalization for Americans and the Chinese workers are quite different; unless there is first a prior sense of affinity and mutual feeling between the two peoples, experiences need not be seen as shared and held in common.

One might propose that shared values and causes could provide the glue to bind individuals from different nations together, thus creating the global civil society needed to ground cosmopolitan democracy. Held points to the "new voices" motivated by shared principles in events such as the Rio Conference and the Beijing Conference on Women's Rights as hopeful signs of strengthening global ties and the founding of a global civil society. While Held acknowledges that these attempts to create "new forms of public life and new ways of debating regional and global issues" are still very nascent, and so it is too early to say whether these attempts to foster a global civil society will eventually succeed, he nonetheless thinks that "they point in the direction" of such possibilities (2000, 29).

But in reply to Held, nationalists would urge that we should not be too hasty to conflate transnational activism motivated by shared goals and interests with transnational democratic deliberation. The former kind of coalition is unraveled once goals and interests diverge; democratic associations, on the other hand, ought to be able to withstand such value disagreements. Indeed, democratic associations presuppose divergent goals among its members, and hence the need for democratic deliberation to fairly and reasonably adjudicate divergent claims. The ties that bind a democratic order together cannot be secured by shared interests or principles, for these are not robust and permanent enough to generate the kinds of shared sympathies, and mutual respect and trust, necessary for actual deliberative democracy (Kymlicka 2001, 325).

VI. A Democracy of National Democracies

For the above reasons, nationalist theorists remain skeptical about the prospects for cosmopolitan democracy. Defenders of cosmopolitan democracy have, of course, challenged the claims of the nationalists. They argue that, contra the nationalist thesis, deliberative democratic associations larger than the nation, and that cut across national and other boundaries, can be formed, fostered, and sustained, the lack of shared nationality and language notwithstanding (e.g., Weinstock 2001). Indeed, they may point out that nationalists are guilty of a certain double standard by holding cosmopolitans to a higher standard of deliberative ideal than is expected of deliberative democrats in the national context. After all, the ideal of deliberation *within* multicultural countries faces the same issues of linguistic and cultural diversity that nationalists say cosmopolitans must surmount; also, deliberative democracy in modern nation-states, which are certainly not intimate associations, does not require *direct* individual involvement in all matters, but that individuals may be represented indirectly at different levels through different constituencies and other subnational associations. So cosmopolitans are not alone guilty of assuming a higher degree of direct individual involvement than is realistically possible. Perhaps the most challenging of the nationalist objections against the cosmopolitan concerns the basis of solidarity and affinity for democratic politics. Yet, as some cosmopolitans have countered, it is important not to underestimate the malleability of people's sense of solidarity and fellow-feeling with others. Indeed, if nationalism is properly seen as a morally expansionist project—that is, a project that seeks to compel people to overcome their parochial ties of kinship and tribalism in order to include strangers (i.e., their co-nationals) within their arc of moral concern, rather than as a morally limiting project—then there is no immediate reason to think that this expansion of human moral motivation cannot be developed beyond the bounds of the nation (Jones 1999)

Be that as it may, I leave this dispute over the nationalist thesis aside, and I want to examine the possibility of global democracy on the assumption that the thesis is correct. What are the prospects for global democracy if the nation is indeed the basic and exclusive site of genuine democratic deliberation? Are there alternative ways of conceptualizing global democracy other than on cosmopolitan terms?

The obvious alternative to cosmopolitan democracy is to conceive of global democracy as a democracy of nation-states. The nationalist thesis does not force one to the dismal conclusion that the forces of globalization are beyond democratic control, that the democratic deficit is an inevitable aspect of a world made up of distinct nationalities. Nationalists, in particular liberal nationalists, hold out the possibility that greater democracy both within and between democratic nation-states can serve as a solution to the democratic deficit. On this view, we do not need so much as a cosmopolitan democracy—that is, a democracy of individuals across national boundaries—but an international democracy—a democracy of democratic nations.

The important difference between this account of global democracy and that of cosmopolitan democracy is that instead of taking individuals to be *directly* represented in the international arena through their direct membership in various transnational associations, the nationalist takes individuals to have only an *indirect* role at the international level. The global democracy strictly speaking is not between individuals as such, but between nations, or more correctly, between representatives of nations.

Conceiving global democracy literally as an inter*national* democracy rather than cosmopolitan democracy conforms to the nationalist thesis that the nation is the primary site of real deliberative democracy among individuals. Individuals will democratically elect representatives to represent them in the global deliberations, democratically decide on the sorts of issues that would be their concern, and their representatives can in turn democratically deliberate these matters with other democratically elected representatives from other nations. Thus, the nationalist thesis does not preclude the possibility of democratic deliberation between nations (represented by democratically elected representatives democratically accountable to their own nationals), and they certainly concur with cosmopolitans that we need more democracy at the global level—and that this may require reforming existing institutions as well as establishing new ones. But in the view of national democrats, the current global deficit is not due to the lack of *direct* individual participation in global institutions, but rather, the fact that some nations are not democratically represented at important global institutions on the one side and the lack of democracy at the national level on the other. The decision-making procedures of important institutions like the World Bank and the IMF are cases in point. Should global institutions be reformed and democratized by having a fairer and more proportionate representation of nations, and by restructuring their decision-making procedures along more democratic lines, much of the democratic deficit may be corrected without the need to envisage a global democracy in which individuals are represented directly regardless of nationality.

Democratic nations can also regulate the conduct of nonnational institutions like MNCs without necessarily adopting the cosmopolitan approach of direct individual involvement. What this requires is the democratization of these institutions to allow for better representation by countries. There is no reason why the democratic deficit has to be corrected by allowing individuals direct participation in these organizations. To be sure, no cosmopolitan democrats would recommend that individuals be directly consulted when decisions are being made by highly specialized institutions. But they would expect that the decision makers in these institutions be directly accountable to individuals. More importantly, they require the downplaying of national-level democracy in some respects; indeed, they take national democracy to be one of the reasons for the global democratic deficit. International democracy, on the other hand, takes greater national-level democracy to provide a solution to the global democratic deficit.

If the above is right, global democracy can be achieved in a two-stage procedure as an alternative to the single-stage procedure envisioned by cosmopolitan democrats. The first stage concerns fostering and improving democracy within nations, and the second stage concerns democratizing existing international institutions, or even establishing new ones to regulate international activities not yet regulated. This requires democratization at both national and international levels, but the premises of the nationalist thesis are preserved. Genuine deliberation between individuals is still at the national level, and greater democratization of international institutions allows representatives of all nations to present their constituents' concerns and decisions to others in a democratic global setting.

This, of course, means that global democracy can be attained only if national democracy is first achieved, that representatives at the global level are indeed democratic representatives. A global democratic forum represented by undemocratically appointed national delegates would not fix the global democratic deficit. A democracy of tyrants by definition cannot be, strictly speaking, a global democracy, even if tyrants deliberate democratically among themselves at the international level. Global democracy needs foremost national democracy. To be sure, not many countries in our world would qualify as democratic, and so we are a long way from even satisfying the first stage of the two-level approach to global democracy. But unlike the case of cosmopolitan democracy, nationalists would argue that on this two-stage approach, the basic sites to be democratized are already present, and the potential for democratizing them are real. Indeed, the first task is to further democratize these

existing sites, not to erode the political relevance of these sites, as the cosmopolitan democratic ideal might imply.

One concern cosmopolitans might have with the two-stage approach to
global democracy is that not all nation-states are democratic states, and so a
global democracy among states cannot sufficiently ensure that *individuals* are
empowered to have control over decisions that have implications for them.
But this points out a challenge for the democratic nationalist approach, not its
refutation. It only means that the nationalist democrats need to further the
process of democratization within countries and not neglect their importance. Ensuring greater democracy within countries is a goal toward greater
global democracy and not an obstacle to it. Nationalism provides the building
blocks, therefore, for global democracy, not its obstacles.

Another cosmopolitan concern is that democracies within nations need not
necessarily entail democracy between nations. What is to prevent a democratic
society from dealing with other societies on undemocratic terms? Is there not
the fear that a society of democratic citizens might want their representatives
to narrowly pursue and protect their democratically arrived at interests in the
global arena, even if this means not deliberating with representatives of other
countries on fair terms? Democratic politics within states could be consistent
with power politics between states, one might allege. It is for this reason,
among others, that cosmopolitans worry that keeping democracy limited to
the nation-state cannot fully motivate the development of a genuine global democracy. Thus, the nationalist's concentration on inculcating deliberative democracy on the national level may be an impediment to democracy at the
global level, rather than serving as its entry point.

But this objection underestimates the moral character and scope of democratic citizenship. Democratic citizens are motivated not just to deliberate
about their own national interests to the exclusion of the interests of foreigners. The nationalist thesis, as described above, is not incompatible with what
Amy Gutmann has called democratic humanism. "Democratic humanism
supports an education that encourages citizens to deliberate about justice as
part of their political culture—justice for their fellow citizens as well as for
their fellow human beings, who are citizens of other societies" (1996, 70).
Truly democratic citizens would be interested in dealing justly and fairly with
other nations, and this would involve minimally the requirement that their
representatives deal with other representatives on fair and democratic terms
in the global plane. As Frederick Engels puts it, a nation cannot be truly free
if it continues to oppress other nations (Cunningham 1994, 104). Democratic
citizens, therefore, are not so limited in their moral sight as to hold the ideal
of democratic respect to be exclusive to compatriots and not applicable to
nonnationals. It is just that on the nationalistic view, they will not be deliber-

ating *directly* with other individuals from different nations; the main deliberations between individuals are situated at the national level, but individuals are still able to deal democratically with other citizens through their national representatives. Democratic citizens are thus able to transcend their limited national interests to take into account the interests of others. The ideal "statesman," to borrow from Rawls, will take one of the crucial aims of democratic development to be that of extending her people's scope of moral concern beyond their political boundaries, so that they can learn to relate to other peoples on terms other than narrowly defined self-interested ones (1999, 112–13).

The crucial role of democratic citizenship for global justice makes the nationalist thesis even more poignant. We must take education for democratic *citizenship* at the national level seriously if this is necessary for greater global democracy, and if the nation is the place where individuals can best act effectively to promote justice both at home and abroad. With respect to the last point, Gutmann writes: "Democratic citizens have institutional means at their disposal that solidarity individuals, or citizens of the world only, do not" (1996, 71). Global democracy, in short, begins with the education of democratic *citizens.*

This last point is especially useful, for it highlights the strategic role of nationalizing democracy for the end of global democracy. Unlike the cosmopolitan democratic approach, which will call for the creation of new forms of governance, the nationalist approach calls on democrats to improve on existing global institutions and structures, and, importantly, to strengthen democratic national governments. The latter is thus not only more realistic, but it also more clearly shows the way. It points out that one crucial way toward achieving global democracy is to strengthen domestic democracy.

The above suggests that a democracy of national democracies is not only more likely, but also more attractive in terms of clearly identifying a site that needs to be rendered democratic. Indeed, the ethical significance of democratic nation building should not be overlooked. Michael Ignatieff, referring to the Balkans, Somalia, and most notably Afghanistan, points out that the anarchy that results from failed or collapsed states "is the chief cause" of human rights abuses today. In a sense then, "state sovereignty, instead of being the enemy of human rights, has to be seen as their basic condition" (Ignatieff 2002). Similarly, Bellamy and Jones point out that in the absence of a world authority, weakening democracy at the national level (as one might risk doing by striving for unrooted forms of democracy) could result in what they call a "regulatory hole" that could be filled by undemocratic elements of power (2000, 212; also Hirst and Thompson 2000a, 2000b), thus compromising not only democratic ideals, but also world security and very basic human rights.

The second stage of achieving a democracy between democracies—namely, the democratization of international institutions and the creation of new ones where required—is crucial, of course, and nationalists do not deny this point. A world of democratic nations would be of no effect against the global democratic deficit if these democracies do not deal with each other democratically. Where the nationalists differ importantly from cosmopolitans is that they do not think that these democratic international institutions must represent individuals directly in a way that transcend their nationalities. The fact that the IMF, World Bank, and World Trade Organization ought to be more democratic, as commonly called for, does not mean that individuals of the world are now to directly elect representatives to these organizations, but that these organizations become more widely representative and be held more accountable to countries affected by their decisions. The reform called for is thus not the reconceptualization of these institutions as cosmopolitan bodies in which individuals are directly represented, but the more modest one of allowing greater representation of countries within existing institutional structures.

That democracy is limited by nationalist constraints need not, therefore, rule out the possibility of a global democratic order if that is conceived as a democracy between democratic nations. The global democratic deficit can be overcome by strengthening democracies within nations and by improving on our existing international structures to make them more democratic. The cosmopolitan democratic idea of a democracy beyond nations is not the only available response to the global democratic deficit. And if the nationalist thesis is right, it cannot be a successful option. Reaffirming the importance of the nation as the site of democracy thus does not contradict the aspiration for global democracy.

I do not want to overstate the difference between the internationalist democratic approach and the idea of cosmopolitan democracy. Both are concerned with the global democratic deficit; and the cosmopolitan democrat need not reject the importance of democracy at the national level. But cosmopolitan democrats want to deny that the nation should be the *fundamental* site of democracy if global democracy is to be achieved, and thus argue that the traditional association between democracy and nationality be transcended and that new sites of democratic deliberation that cut across national boundaries be created. By contrast, nationalists do not think that nationality and democratic deliberation can be separated in this way. But this need not spell doom for global democracy. For nationalists who are also concerned about global democracy, democratic institutions at the national level provide citizens with the levers for promoting global democracy. Rather than seeing the nation as an obstacle to global democratization, and hence whose privileged association with deliberative democracy is to be challenged, nationalists would treat the nation as the necessary starting point of global democracy and argue that global democracy is achievable only by strengthening, not weakening, national democracy. If the nationalist thesis is a necessity in the sense that it aptly describes a basic fact of the world, democratic internationalists turn this necessity into a virtue.

V. Nationalism and Cosmopolitan Justice

If the nationalist thesis is right, global democracy can nonetheless be achieved if conceived as a democracy of "democracies rooted in nation-states" (Holden 2000, 214), rather than as a democracy of individuals in the world taken as a single scheme as called for by cosmopolitan democracy. As we saw, this means that global democracy is best seen as a two-level procedure—first as a democracy of individuals within nations, and then as a democracy between (representatives of) nations.

This approach to global democracy seems to closely follow Rawls's global theory of justice in *The Law of Peoples* where the principles of international justice are determined by representatives of peoples rather than by individuals as such (Rawls 1999). One might think then that this rejection of cosmopolitan democracy entails a rejection of cosmopolitan justice, namely, the idea that the basic principles of justice ought to be determined from a point of view that is impartial to individuals' nationality. But this need not follow. First, the ideal of democratic deliberation operates at a different conceptual level from that of deliberation about *justice*. Consequently, and secondly, the nationalist worries against cosmopolitan democracy do not apply to deliberations about justice. That is, the nationalist limitations against deliberative democracy do not impose on deliberations about justice.

Let me explain these points in order. Unlike deliberations about justice, which operate at the abstract level of determining general principles by which to regulate the basic institutions of society, the ideal of deliberative democracy operates in what Gutmann and Thompson have called "the middle range of abstraction, between foundational principles and institutional rules" (Gutmann and Thompson 1996, 5). To make this point on Rawlsian terms, deliberative democracy is concerned with the legislative stage of justice, whereas deliberations about justice concern the basic principles that would regulate the social setting within which such legislative deliberations take place. More importantly, while deliberative democracy concerns actual deliberation between actually socially situated persons about how best to realize the requirements of justice, deliberation about justice is seen as a hypothetical deliberation, indeed as a deliberation that may be undertaken by a single person herself "here and now" (Rawls 1971). As Samuel Freeman neatly puts it, deliberative democracy is a normative "model of deliberation that legislative and other decision-making bodies are to emulate. . . . As a model of decision-making, it is to be distinguished from the theoretical construct of hypothetical agreement that typifies contractarian theory [of justice]" (Freeman 2000, 379). The ideal conditions for democratic deliberation and deliberation about justice are quite different then, as are their aims. To put it differently, deliberation about justice aims to provide principles to regulate institutions; deliberative democracy aims to clarify laws and the rules of institutions in light of these principles.

My claim above has been that when it comes to deciding on specific institutional rules and procedures to regulate decisions that affect global society, we adopt a two-stage democratic procedure as opposed to a single-stage (cosmopolitan) approach in which individuals are directly represented in global democratic deliberations. Specific issues need to be actually deliberated, and here genuine deliberation would have to meet the test of comprehensibility and mutual trust and respect. But if deliberation about justice is a different form of deliberation, if it is a hypothetical deliberation about abstract principles, then it need not necessarily be wedded to this two-stage procedure, but can instead take on a cosmopolitan form in which individuals abstracted from nations, rather than representatives of nations, can individually reflect on, and draw conclusions about, the terms of global justice.

The reason, and this takes us to the second point, why one can expect a single global procedure when deliberating about justice but not in the case of democratic deliberation about legislation and institutional specifics is that in the former, the deliberation is hypothetical, whereas in the latter, it is actual (e.g., Freeman 2000, 380; also Gutmann and Thompson 2000). The original position is one famous hypothetical device of representation any person, "here and now," may invoke in deciding what justice demands.[6] The original position construction presents a deliberative model that is thus not constrained by considerations of language, national affinity, and so on because it operates at a level of abstraction that is independent of such real limitations. "Hypothetical agreements (such as the original position . . .) contain conditions that are not realizable in the world," as Freeman writes (Freeman 2000, 379); but being hypothetical, it need not be bound by real constraints. Thus, the construct of hypothetical agreements, like Rawls's original position for determining principles of justice, is not necessary to deliberative democracy (Freeman 2000). Conversely, and more to my point, the conditions for deliberative democracy, such as shared language, mutual feelings, and the like, do not apply to the construction of hypothetical agreements about justice. These are different kinds of deliberation for which different idealized conditions are required, and in the case of deliberations about justice, differences in nationality may be put to one side. Indeed, they must be put to one side.

The nationalistic worries that plague cosmopolitan democracy, therefore, need not plague cosmopolitan justice—any individual here and now may reflect on what cosmopolitan justice requires; no actual deliberation is required, so the linguistic and cultural solidarity problems do not even arise. Just as it is possible for a single citizen to conceive behind the veil of ignorance principles of justice for her entire society, so it is possible, by extension, for a single person to conceive of principles for the world. Deliberations about justice are hypothetical deliberations rather than actual, and so unlike the actual deliberation of democracy, are not confounded by the real problems and limitations of language and solidarity identified by the nationalist thesis.

I have not given any arguments why principles of justice ought to be conceived on cosmopolitan terms; my aim in this section has been to show the nationalist objections against cosmopolitan democracy do not affect arguments for cosmopolitan justice because the nationalist claims affect only the conditions for democratic deliberation (which is a real-world deliberation), but not the hypothetical deliberation about justice that can take place in the mind of a single individual.[7] The realization of cosmopolitan democracy requires certain conditions that the nationalist thesis preempts; cosmopolitan justice, on the contrary, requires different kinds of idealized conditions that are not precluded by the nationalist thesis. One could endorse the cosmopolitan view about justice, yet be skeptical that the specific policy issues that arise within the framework of cosmopolitan justice could be resolved by individuals *directly* in a way that cut across the diverse linguistic and cultural ties of nationality.[8]

In summary, even if the nationalist thesis that the nation is the primary site of democracy is correct, the prospects for global democracy need not be hopeless. Nationalists recognize the need for greater democratization of international institutions and associations, but they also see the need to emphasize greater democracy at the national level, and indeed see this to be a necessary condition for genuine global democracy. The nation is not seen as an obstacle to global democracy, and so whose demise is to be encouraged, but as its basic starting point. On this view, democratic nations are the seeds of global democracy. Unlike cosmopolitan democrats who would wish to disperse the locus of democratic politics away from the nation upward toward transnational institutions, the nationalists argue that the global context does not provide the basic preconditions for deliberative democracy, and that attempts to diminish the importance of the nation as a site of democracy might have the contrary effect of undermining the only available conditions for genuine deliberation. A democracy of nationally rooted democracies provides the best available approach to global democracy that builds on rather than disrupts these conditions of democracy, and provides a realistic solution to the global democratic deficit.

Notes

1. This chapter was initially drafted in spring 2001 when I was on a Social Sciences and Humanities Research Council of Canada (SSHRCC) Postdoctoral Fellowship at Queen's University. I am grateful to SSHRCC for support, and I am especially grateful to Will Kymlicka for many discussions on the topic of nationalism and global justice. I thank Michael Krausz for his comments on an early draft, and especially Deen Chatterjee for inviting me to write this chapter and for his suggestions and questions on earlier drafts. Finally, thanks to Carrie Obry for her help with copy editing.

2. See, for example, Kymlicka (1995) and Tamir (1993) who point out the ways in which the nationalist ideal is assumed in much of contemporary liberal theory.

3. Some nationalists go on to point out that the ideal of distributive justice must also presuppose a community in which "members recognize such obligations of justice to one another" (Miller 1995, 93). Thus, shared nationality is basic to an egalitarian democratic state. "Where citizens of a state are also compatriots [i.e., co-nationals], the mutual trust that this engenders makes it more likely that they will be able to solve collective action problems, to support redistributive principles of justice, and to practice deliberative forms of democracy" (Miller 1995, 98).

4. Indeed, some may argue that attempts to transplant the nation as the basic site of democratic politics risk undermining the conditions—the shared sympathies and common understandings—that make democratic politics possible in the first place by overstraining and taxing these sympathies and commitments.

5. The noticeable conservative shift in attitudes toward non-European immigration among Europeans can be seen as a response to the threat of Europeanization on national identity.

6. Rawls's original position procedure, to recall, conceives of parties to the deliberation about justice as free and equal. This condition of equality and freedom is ensured by means of the "veil of ignorance" behind which parties to the deliberation are to imagine that they do not know contingent and specific facts about themselves, such as their social class, the talents they have, their own conception of the good, and so on.

7. Rawls has given reasons for rejecting the cosmopolitan account of justice (Rawls 1999); see also Freeman's creative construction and defense of Rawls's international theory (2006). But my aim, as said, is only to show that cosmopolitan democracy and cosmopolitan justice are two different demands, and arguments against cosmopolitan democracy need not affect cosmopolitan justice. For my views on cosmopolitan justice and Rawls, see Tan (2000) and (2001).

8. This last point raises questions concerning the relationship between justice and democratic legitimacy. Democratic legitimacy holds that coercive force be exercised only on terms that parties concerned can reasonably accept as reasonable. The worry

then might be that my disengagement of cosmopolitan justice from democratic deliberation will allow some parties (e.g., liberal democratic peoples) to illegitimately impose their vision of a just world order on other (nonliberal) peoples. As I said, this is not the place to defend the legitimacy of liberal cosmopolitan justice. Suffice it to say that the Rawlsian contractarian approach that some cosmopolitans have adopted for the purpose of arriving at principles of cosmopolitan justice is defended as a procedure consistent with the diversity of ends that peoples as corporate units are supposed to have (see, e.g., Beitz [1999]). So understood, cosmopolitan justice does not violate the norms of democratic legitimacy because it presents principles of justice that all reasonable peoples are presumed to find reasonable. I am grateful to Deen Chatterjee for helpful comments here.

Bibliography

Anderson, Benedict. 1993. *Imagined Communities* (London: Verso).

Archibugi, Daniele, S. Balduini, and M. Donati. 2000. "The United Nations as an Agency of Global Democracy." Pp. 125–42 in B. Holden, ed., *Global Democracy: Key Debates* (London: Routledge).

Archibugi, Daniele, D. Held, and M. Kohler, eds. 1998. *Re-imaging Political Community* (Cambridge, UK: Polity Press).

Beitz, Charles. 1999 [1979]. *Political Theory and International Relations* (Princeton, NJ: Princeton University Press).

Bellamy, Richard and J. Barry Jones. 2000. "Globalization and Democracy: An Afterword." In B. Holden, ed., *Global Democracy: Key Debates* (London: Routledge).

Canovan, Margaret. 1996. *Nationhood and Political Theory* (Cheltenham, UK: Edward Elgar).

Cohen, Joshua, ed. 1996. *For Love of Country* (Boston: Beacon Press).

Cunningham, Frank. 1994. *The Real World of Democracy Revisited* (Atlantic Highlands, NJ: Humanities Press).

Dryzek, John. 1999. "Transnational Democracy." *Journal of Political Philosophy* 7: 30–51.

Falk, Richard. 2000. "Global Civil Society and the Democratic Prospect." In B. Holden, ed., *Golden Democracy: Key Debates* (London: Routledge).

Freeman, Samuel. 2000. "Deliberative Democracy: A Sympathetic Comment." *Philosophy and Public Affairs* 29/4: 371–418.

———. 2006. "The Law of Peoples, Social Cooperation, Human Rights, and Distributive Justice." *Social Philosophy and Policy* 23 (1): 29–68.

Golub, Jonathan. 2000. "Globalization, Sovereignty, and Policy-Making: Insights from the European Integration." In B. Holden, ed., *Global Democracy: Key Debates* (London: Routledge).

Gutmann, Amy. 1996. "Democratic Citizenship." In J. Cohen, ed., *For Love of Country* (Boston: Beacon Press).

Gutmann, Amy and Dennis Thompson. 1996. *Democracy and Disagreement* (Cambridge, MA: Harvard University Press).

———. 2000. "Why Deliberative Democracy Is Different," *Social Philosophy and Policy* 17: 161–80.

Heater, Derek. 1990. *Citizenship: The Civic Ideal in World History, Politics, and Education* (London: Longman).

Hirst, Paul and G. Thompson. 2000a. "Global Myths and National Policies." In B. Holden, ed., *Global Democracy: Key Debates* (London: Routledge).

———. 2000b. "The Myth of Globalization." In Frans Buelen, ed., *Globalization and the Nation State* (London: Edward Elgar).

Held, David. 1995. *Democracy and the Global Order* (Cambridge, UK: Polity Press).

———. 2000. "The Changing Contours of Political Community." In B. Holden, ed., *Global Democracy: Key Debates* (London: Routledge).

Holden, Barry, ed. 2000. *Global Democracy: Key Debates* (London: Routledge).

Hutchings, Kimberly and R. Dannreuther. 1999. *Cosmopolitan Citizenship* (New York: St. Martin's Press).

Hume, David. 1777 [1977]. *An Enquiry Concerning the Principles of Morals* (Indianapolis, IN: Hackett Publishing Co.).

Ignatieff, Michael. 2002. "Intervention and State Failure." *Dissent* 49 (1): 115–23.

Jones, Charles. 1999. *Global Justice* (Oxford: Oxford University Press).

Kymlicka, Will. 1995. *Multicultural Citizenship* (Oxford: Oxford University Press).

———. 2001. *Politics in the Vernacular* (Oxford: Oxford University Press).

Linklater, Andrew. 1999. "Cosmopolitan Citizenship." In K. Hutchings and R. Dannreuther, *Cosmopolitan Citizenship* (New York: St. Martin's Press).

Lynch, Marc. 2000. "Globalization and International Democracy." *International Studies Review* 2 (3): 91–101.

Mill, J. S. 1991 [1861]. "Considerations on Representative Government." In *John Stuart Mill: On Liberty and Other Essays* (Oxford: Oxford University Press).

Miller, David. 1995. *On Nationality* (Oxford: Oxford University Press).

———. 1999. "Bounded Citizenship." In K. Hutchings and R. Dannreuther, *Cosmopolitan Citizenship* (New York: St. Martin's Press).

Neff, Stephen C. 1999. "International Law and the Critique of Cosmopolitan Citizenship." In K. Hutchings and R. Dannreuthe, *Cosmopolitan Citizenship* (New York: St. Martin's Press).

Nussbaum, Martha. 1996. *For Love of Country* (Boston: Beacon Press).

———. 1997. *Cultivating Humanity* (Cambridge, MA: Harvard University Press).

Rawls, John. 1971. *A Theory of Justice* (Cambridge, MA: Harvard University Press).

———. 1993. *Political Liberalis* (New York: Columbia University Press).

———. 1999. *The Law of Peoples* (Cambridge, MA: Harvard University Press).

Saskia, Sassen. 1998. *Globalization and Its Discontents* (New York: New Press).

Tamir, Yael. 1993. *Liberal Nationalism* (Princeton, NJ: Princeton University Press).

Tan, Kok-Chor. 2000. *Toleration, Diversity, and Global Justice* (College Park, PA: Penn State Press).

———. 2001. "Critical Notice of Rawls's *The Laws of Peoples.*" *Canadian Journal of Philosophy* 31 (1): 113–32.

Thompson, Dennis. 1986. *Political Ethics and Public Office* (Cambridge, MA: Harvard University Press).

———. 1999. "Democratic Theory and Global Society." *Journal of Political Philosophy* 7/2: 111–25.

Weinstock, Daniel. 2001. "Prospects for Transnational Citizenship and Democracy." *Ethics and International Affairs* 15 (2): 53–66.

Zolo, Danielo. 1997. *Cosmopolis: Prospects for World Government* (Cambridge, UK: Polity Press).

———. 1999. "The Lords of Peace: From the Holy Alliance to the New International Criminal Tribunal." In B. Holden, ed., *Global Democracy: Key Debates* (London: Routledge).

IV

GLOBAL PUBLIC AND
THE NEW WORLD ORDER

7

Rawls's *Law of Peoples* and the New World Order

William McBride

D O THE MOST SALIENT EVENTS of the period beginning on September 11, 2001, and culminating (at least for now) in the U.S.-led attack on Iraq in 2003 amount to a significant detour in the course of history?[1] Does John Rawls's *The Law of Peoples*, published in 1999 and based on a lecture given in 1993, anticipate this detour, if there has been one? And, in light of these events and this book, what are we to say concerning the "political liberalism" with which Rawls identified himself? My answers to these questions, which form the structure of this chapter, are *yes*, *yes*, and *farewell*, respectively.

The Emerging *Zeitgeist*

Sometimes a slow learner, or, in the words of one relative of mine, "a closet optimist," I began the post–World Trade Center annihilation period resisting this often-heard claim: "Everything has changed since September 11." This seemed to me much too facile. I pointed out, repeatedly, that (1) the police-state mentality and reality that were being spread and incarnated in such documents as the "Uniting and Strengthening America by Providing Appropriate Tools Required to Intercept and Obstruct Terrorism Act of 2001" (the "USA PATRIOT Act" to the uninitiated); (2) actions such as the suspension of the rights of prisoners captured in Afghanistan and Iraq by declaring them illegal combatants; (3) the denial of normal due process to increasing numbers of resident aliens and even to a couple of "marginal" U.S. citizens; and (4) the ever-burgeoning American prison population were all developments that had their roots in *pre*-September

11 legislation and policies. This was true, but there comes a point, as the old dialectical thinkers used to assert, at which quantity turns into quality. It may be difficult to pinpoint with precision, more difficult than pushing buttons to launch satellite-guided missiles, but eventually the evidence is there, *res ipsa loquitur*, and one can no longer deny what has become obvious. Thus, it is my contention that the project of the present book, to examine globalization and the future of liberal democracy, must now be understood within a significantly, even vastly, different context from when it was first conceived.

In effect, the present U.S. government is both asserting and actually exercising global hegemony to a far greater extent than at any time past and freely employs the language of open-ended, limitless war and threats of war to reinforce its claims. Comparisons with Imperial Rome, which were relatively original when I first began to introduce them in papers presented in the spring of 2002, have now become commonplace if not banal; moreover, they have come to be embraced, rather than repudiated, by supporters of the current American regime. It has even been reported that the words of an obscure Roman writer, "*oderint dum metuant*" (let them hate [us] as long as they fear [us]), have become a favorite slogan of the more educated among them. (I prefer Tacitus' "*solitudinem faciunt, pacem appellant*"—they create a wasteland and call it peace.) How do all these developments affect the process of "globalization," which was the buzzword par excellence of the pre-September 11, 2001, era?

The key may be found in words attributed to Henry Kissinger in a lecture given two years earlier—important evidence for my earlier view that the current situation is not *entirely* novel—in Dublin: "The basic challenge is that what is called globalization is really another name for the dominant role of the United States."[2] The term "globalization" acquired yet another meaning—one which may or may not have some permanence, depending on the outcome of the rifts created by the attack on Iraq—when in early 2002 Russia accepted a role of partnership in the North Atlantic Treaty Organization (NATO). For if one looks at a globe and focuses on the westernmost part of Alaska and the easternmost part of Siberia, one becomes aware that only a few kilometers of the Bering Strait prevent NATO from complete encirclement of the Earth. Not only the North Atlantic Ocean, but the northern Pacific Ocean as well, are *maria nostra*, our seas. By contrast, the Roman Empire confined the designation, *mare nostrum*, to the Mediterranean Sea alone.

Who, in fact, are the "we" to whom the world's oceans belong? Although a completely accurate answer to this question would require including some reservations and qualifications and adding some codicils, the simple answer at the present moment in time is this: To the U.S. government. The regime currently in power—I am referring here almost exclusively to the Executive

Branch of the government, since both the legislative and the judicial branches have on the whole, again with a few qualifications, deferred to it in all matters having to do with what is called "security"—has made use of the infamous events of September 11 and of the sympathy that was expressed for the United States immediately after those events in order to demand fealty from the rest of the world. The *de facto* president, Mr. Bush, expressed it in his speech to Congress on September 20, 2001: "Every nation in every region now has a decision to make. Either you are with us, or you are with the terrorists. From this day forward, any nation that continues to harbor or support terrorism will be regarded by the United States as a hostile regime." And, it should be added, the second Bush dynasty has arrogated to itself the power to determine what does and what does not constitute "terrorism," and of course to attack preemptively, as it has now begun to do. In short, under "Quincy" (a Bush family joke, alluding to Presidents Adams), we seem to be confronted with a much more genuinely *new* world order than we were under Bush *père*, who invoked that expression at the time of the first Gulf War.

In past articles, I considered the fate of local and regional civil societies in light of the increasing cultural hegemony of a transnational culture that is dominated, above all, by American, and to a lesser extent by Western European, elements.[3] One question that I raised in these essays concerns the extent to which some of the most powerful transnational corporate interests were in fact in a position of dominance *over* political regimes—not just in the case of smaller countries, where it was and is perfectly obvious that they were and are, but even in the case of the "hyperpower." At present, it seems the balance in this matter has tilted in the direction of the dominance of the hyperpower, the U.S. government, over the transnationals, for at least two interrelated reasons. First, because the Bush administration is so completely dedicated to furthering the fundamental interests of the large capitalist firms (the contracts made with administration-connected firms for rebuilding Iraq are an especially blatant example of this) and is so filled with individuals who have held high positions in the corporate world that at present very little gap exists between the two perspectives. Second, because the huge increase in militarization and in police-state apparatus following the events of September 11 and then accompanying the build-up to the attack on Iraq has vastly augmented the government's power, with no comparable increase in independent power on the part of the capitalist corporations, except those that manufacture weapons and so-called security devices.

These ominous developments may well point to a future change in the nature of the hegemonic culture itself, which, in addition to its obvious commitment to maximizing corporate profits, has until now been characterized as a culture of consumerism. But if such a change is occurring, it is not yet entirely obvious.[4] In the same speech from which I quoted earlier, when Bush was asked "What is expected of us?" he answered: "I ask your continued participation and confidence in the American economy." In other words, keep consuming at a high rate.

In any event, the present situation of globalization now needs to be comprehended in a quite different way from which it was understood in even the recent past. The rhetoric of the globalization ideologies of the 1990s was above all that of the "free market," in which in theory, though of course not in practice, all "players" were supposed to be contending "on a level playing field," to coin a phrase. Already at that time, certain practices under new U.S. federal laws, such as those involving confiscation of assets with very little respect for due process under the Rico Act, had been put in place, but only a few relatively isolated voices, such as that of the libertarian Cato Institute, were raised in alarm. Now, however, the confiscation of assets has become a global practice of the hyperpower, undertaken both in the name of combating terrorism and in the name of waging war. (As of press time, the question of who owns the assets of conquered Iraq is being discussed.)

I return to my earlier reference to ownership, when I asked to whom the world's "oceans"—meaning not just the waters, but also the lands contiguous thereto—now belong. When thinking of the ownership of the globe, I hear Marx, in *Capital*, opining that in the future, the ownership of portions of the earth will seem just as preposterous as the ownership of human beings as slaves seemed in his day. But, in fact, the preposterous, the absurd, prevails today: Just as many American citizens actually did own slaves until only a few years before Marx wrote those words, so the current U.S. government really *does* (in a certain sense, if ownership is defined as ultimate control for use) lay claim to ownership of the globe. How else are we to interpret its insistence on being free to attack at will wherever and whenever it deems it fitting to do so, its constant reiteration that the so-called war on terrorism will be open-ended and without foreseeable termination, its rejection of the jurisdiction of international courts, its repudiation of even a very mild and relatively ineffectual treaty on global warming, and on and on? And all these assertions are being made by a government that effectively dominates the world's major financial institutions, including the International Monetary Fund (IMF) and the World Bank, and of which the annual military expenditures will be either more than half or close to half (there are rival sets of statistics on this point) those of total military expenditures worldwide![5]

Where, it may well be asked, does democracy figure into this emerging situation? As a mantra, but little more. Once in a while it is invoked, along with "freedom," as the goal that hyperpower military and diplomatic offensives are designed to promote. It rings very hollow indeed when considered in the current context, in which existing domestic and international institutions that exhibit at least some traces of democratic inspiration are treated with open contempt, as mechanisms to be manipulated when possible, and simply bypassed otherwise. (These words, harsh as they sound, are simply objective descriptions of what happened during the long build-up to the spring 2003 attack on Iraq, descriptions that can readily be supported by citing numerous public statements made by Messieurs Bush, Rumsfeld, Perle, et al.)

Within the global ruling circles, moreover, it is taken for granted that "social democracy" (to say nothing of "democratic socialism"!) is a contradiction in terms, so that "democracy," when it is trotted out for rhetorical purposes as a label for what is supposedly being aimed at, is assumed to mean "capitalist democracy"—that is, a system in which the wealthiest members of society are entitled to unlimited kudos and rewards and the rest of the population is entitled to the assurance that it is not barred in principle from attaining similar wealth. (There are, of course, numerous statistics available to show that, while certain select countries have managed to achieve economic progress relative to their past statuses, on the whole the global gap between wealth and poverty continues to widen. This is a complex matter that other contributors to the present book have addressed more adequately than I can here.) In short, one salient, and still little-noted, effect of the emerging Zeitgeist that I have been depicting is a considerable devaluation, worldwide, of liberal democracy.

For many philosophers and social theorists generally, John Rawls, more than any other single thinker, epitomized triumphant liberal democratic theory marching in the vanguard of liberal democratic practice during the final third of the last century. That is, Rawls's proposals, in *A Theory of Justice*, concerning the optimally just distribution of liberties and resources within a single society, such as that of the United States, seemed to reflect some of the loftier social aspirations of thoughtful members of American and West European societies, while at the same time going beyond the actual states of affairs within those societies in a more equitable direction. The picture that he painted was in some ways abstract—the "Original Position," for example, is an unabashedly hypothetical construct—and in other ways relatively concrete, though imaginary. (For example, Rawls's suggestions concerning a constitutional convention at the beginning of Part Two of the book.) Rawls successfully combined great self-assurance—the vague but powerful allusion to "purity of heart" in the final sentence of *A Theory of Justice* well illustrates this—with an openness concerning the possible economic and other structures that might be utilized to effect his goals. One of his less frequently noted intellectual debts, for instance, was to the British economist J. E. Meade, whose *Efficiency, Equality, and the Ownership of Property* advocated a mixture of some socialization of net property ownership with a more equitable distribution of privately owned property.[6]

Over succeeding years, Rawls seemed to retreat from his earlier sense of confidence and to concern himself increasingly with political arrangements designed to permit societies to cope with large clusters of members who fail to share a liberal worldview. The essay collection that best captures Rawls's middle-period was titled *Political Liberalism*. This work exhibits a certain greater defensiveness about the theory of justice itself, together with a more clearly articulated skepticism, at times bordering on contempt, concerning "comprehensive theories" such as Jürgen Habermas. In a subtle, mostly unspoken way, it reflects the fact that by the time of its publication as a whole book in 1993, the very word, "liberalism," now popularly identified as "the 'L' word," had begun to lose much of its formerly very positive resonance worldwide. Finally, in the most important original work in social philosophy from his last years, *The Law of Peoples*, Rawls attempted to attend to issues of global justice that he had hitherto neglected by articulating an avowedly liberal stance toward a world of peoples and states, of which many are decidedly nonliberal. While this book has, quite rightly as I shall show, occasioned considerable disappointment among philosophers concerned with globalization issues, it may be seen as anticipating, often despite itself and in ways that might well have made the late John Rawls uncomfortable, the emerging Zeitgeist that I have just tried to delineate. Let us now proceed to consider both some of the disappointments and some of the elements of prescience to be found in this slim volume.

The Law of Peoples and the Zeitgeist

Many political theorists who were attracted to Rawls during the waning decades of the last century focused, as *A Theory of Justice* encourages, on his so-called difference principle, the spirit of which was believed conducive to valorizing, morally speaking, a more, though not absolutely, egalitarian society in terms of the distribution of desired social goods. Notoriously, the early Rawls even went so far as to advocate developing mechanisms to compensate for "the natural lottery," whereby some human beings appear to be born more talented than others. So it should have been no surprise that, when Rawls finally turned his attention to justice on an international scale after two decades during which goods distribution in the "real world"—both globally and in many nations including the United States and its erstwhile Cold War antagonists of the old Soviet Bloc—had moved in a dramatically *less* egalitarian direction, many Rawls *afficionados* anticipated an outcome analogical to that of *A Theory of Justice*. That is, they anticipated a theory of *global* justice that would recapitulate the deeply compensatory instincts that had seemed to motivate his *domestic* theory. Instead, they encountered assertions such as the following:

> There are two views about [equality among peoples]. One holds that equality is just, or a good in itself. *The Law of Peoples*, on the other hand, holds that inequalities are not always unjust. . . . In itself, it doesn't matter how great the gap between the rich and poor may be. What matters are the consequences. In a liberal domestic society that gap cannot be wider than the principle of reciprocity allows, so that the least advantaged . . . have sufficient all-purpose means to make intelligent and effective use of their freedoms and to lead reasonable and worthwhile lives. When that situation exists, there is no further need to narrow the gap. Similarly, in the basic structure of the Society of Peoples, once the duty of assistance is satisfied and all peoples have a working liberal or decent government, there is again no reason to narrow the gap between the average wealth of different peoples.[7]

A little further on, Rawls says that any possible feelings of inferiority experienced by one people toward another because of the latter's greater wealth are simply unjustified, as long as the "duty of assistance" (to peoples in catastrophic conditions, notably widespread famine) has been fulfilled by the wealthy one. If the less affluent "people" is dissatisfied with its status, he pontificates, let it either save more or borrow from others! Not only does this section of the text unequivocally reject global egalitarian and "cosmopolitan" impulses (the latter on the rather odd ground that cosmopolitanism is too individualistic and unconcerned with the justice of social structures), but in its zeal to do so it retrospectively puts into question, as in the passage cited above, some common, equality-friendly interpretations of the idea of distributive justice as found in the early Rawls, as well.

If the later Rawls suffered a certain loss of confidence concerning the universalizability, or at least the universal acceptability at the present time, of his basic theory, in *The Law of Peoples* he exhibits a seemingly compensatory access of self-righteousness. One of the most infamous of its passages along these lines is the following:

> I believe that the causes of the wealth of a people and the forms it takes lie in their political culture and in the religious, philosophical, and moral traditions that support the basic structure of their political and social institutions, as well as in the industriousness and cooperative talents of its members, all supported by their political virtues. I would further conjecture that there is no society anywhere in the world—except for marginal cases—with resources so scarce that it could not, were it reasonably and rationally organized and governed, become well-ordered.[8]

In other words, if some societies are, as he puts it, "burdened," it's mostly their own fault: They have poor political cultures, they lack probity, and so on. Above all, they must be unreasonable and irrational—two words that, together with their contraries, recur again and again in Rawls's later work. Throughout this book, he shows virtually no appreciation of the role of concrete historical factors familiar to everyone, such as imperialism, colonization, and capitalism, in shaping the world's societies as they exist today.[9] When he does make an occasional reference to pre-twentieth-century history, his judgments are often, to be charitable, somewhat quirky, as in his assertions that, while Washington and Lincoln were statesmen, Bismarck was not,[10] and that Spain, France, and the Hapsburg Empire were among the "outlaw states" of early modern Europe because they tried to impose their cultures on the rest of the Continent.[11] (Impositions on other continents by other powers, such as Great Britain throughout Africa and Asia and the United States in the Philippines, are not mentioned here.) And he has already declared, prior to passing these judgments, that the leaders of "outlaw states" are "criminals."[12]

The context in which Rawls makes these pronouncements is his extensive, generally favorable discussion of just-war theory. At the outset of the book, he stipulates a fivefold classification scheme: reasonable [*sic*] liberal peoples, decent but nonliberal (and somewhat unreasonable?) peoples, outlaw states, societies burdened by unfavorable conditions, and benevolent absolutisms. By deploying this scheme, he then has no difficulty in identifying "outlaw states" (*not, nota bene,* "peoples"), which he sometimes calls "rogue states," with their "criminal" leaders, as potentially deserving of attack by "decent" peoples, at least for reasons of self-defense or in order to suppress violations of human rights. Although he does suggest a couple of criteria (first, nonaggressivity; second, respect for equal rights and obligations within the framework of a "common good idea of justice") for determining to which peoples certificates of decency are to be awarded and from which states they are to be withheld, the potential for mischief in such demonization procedures should nevertheless seem obvious to most readers: who shall be the judge,[13] the applier of the criteria?

The tone of his discussions makes it clear that Rawls knows, or thinks he knows, what a society that is "nearly just" and therefore worthy (via some unstated mechanism) of passing such judgments—even though its leadership may occasionally err in such cases as, say, the dropping of nuclear bombs on Hiroshima and Nagasaki or the overthrowing of democratic regimes in Chile, Iran, and Guatemala—looks like. It looks most like the reasonable liberal democratic, nonaggressive, rights-respecting "people" known as the United States of America. And so he eventually draws a conclusion that has been adumbrated throughout the book concerning the Political Liberal's historic burden: "One does not find peace by declaring war irrational or wasteful, though indeed it may be so, but by preparing the way for peoples to develop a basic structure that supports a reasonably just or decent regime and makes possible a reasonable Law of Peoples."[14] *Si pacem vis, bellum prepara*, as they used to say.

If, the "L" word aside, much of this language sounds familiar today, that is because it is. A coalition of the decent, or words to that effect, was recently formed under the aegis of the government of the most reasonable and decent people of all, the one just mentioned, to begin demolishing the axis of evil, the imputed coalition of "rogue states." Having declared initial victory, the liberator has indeed begun to work to impose new "basic structures" among the "people" that it has liberated. A decent and reasonable new Iraq, resplendent with a culture of civic virtue, is predicted to emerge. Be that as it may, it is not the philosopher's business to deal with the pettier details. As Rawls presciently declared in the Introduction to *The Law of Peoples*:

> I shall only briefly mention the question of controlling nuclear weapons and other weapons of mass destruction. Among reasonably just liberal and decent peoples the control of such weapons would be relatively easy, since they could be effectively banned. These peoples have no reason for going to war with one another. Yet so long as there are outlaw states—as we suppose—some nuclear weapons need to be retained to keep those states at bay and to make sure they do not use those weapons against liberal or decent peoples. How best to do this belongs to expert knowledge, which philosophy doesn't possess.[15]

Farewell to Political Liberalism

"Expert knowledge, which philosophy doesn't possess." Right. Check. Certainly Rawls's philosophy doesn't possess it. I could proceed to analyze numerous other issues touched on in *The Law of Peoples*—its highly sophistic treatment of emigration/immigration problems, for example—but space is limited, and other philosophers have much more interesting things to say about many of them than Rawls does.[16] Instead, I think it is time to try to take an overview—to recapitulate and put into perspective the paradoxical place, as I see it, that this late Rawlsian incursion into globalization phenomena occupies within the ongoing interaction between a burgeoning theoretical literature concerning them and their actual historical evolution. To put it bluntly, Rawls's theoretical approach, relative to those of contemporaries dealing with similar themes, is both fairly reactionary and fairly unsophisticated. It is reactionary both in its forthright rejection of currently popular resource redistribution schemes, such as those of Beitz and Pogge, which he takes on at the end of the final section of the book, and in its assumption that a highly inegalitarian world of sovereign sociopolitical entities, though somewhat limited in sovereignty by transnational human rights standards, will and should endure as such rather than being gradually replaced, as writers favoring moderate cosmopolitanism typically advocate, by regional and global federations. It is also reactionary, as we have seen, in its frequent recurrence to the notion of just wars that may rightly and reasonably be waged by the more "decent" of these entities.

Rawls's approach is unsophisticated perhaps above all in his extremely naïve assumption that by regarding these entities as "peoples" rather than "states," and offering only a very hasty initial account of what he means by a "*liberal* people" (only the first of the five types that he lists, it should be recalled), he has nevertheless laid the groundwork for achieving adequate conceptual clarity. Given this dense fogginess at the outset of the book, it is then not surprising, for example, that he fails even to *consider* the burning issue of nationalism—or that, in a different context, he can casually refer to a society's "prevailing religious and social values, freely held by its women" (this is a society that he is imagining in which a high birthrate obtains),[17] as if *all* the women of *any* modern society would or ever could freely choose a single given set of values. In short, he appears in this book to have tried to finesse many of the most salient complexities that characterize contemporary societies—perhaps because of his lack of "expert knowledge"?—and the result is, to put it mildly, unsatisfactory.

One interesting paradox, however, is that this relatively reactionary and unsophisticated late Rawlsian theory corresponds in many interesting ways to current historical practice as it has evolved especially since September 2001. The present government of the hegemonic hyperpower that was Rawls's native country has indeed shown itself hostile to global redistributions of resources, and to global treaties and institutions such as world courts that seem even to hint at any reduction in its own sovereignty, while anathematizing "rogue states" and conducting an open-ended "war against terrorism" that it declares to be in the service of justice itself. And the language of its leaders is often very unsophisticated, failing to take account of nuances and niceties, especially with respect to historical background and cultural difference. At the same time, in thorough consistency with what Rawls himself repeats in numerous places, it constantly emphasizes the wish that sociopolitical institutions worldwide may eventually come to resemble "ours"—that is, become what it calls "democratic" (though of course without the qualifier "liberal" in front of "democratic"!).

The current methods employed to implement this announced policy, however, point to a further paradox, the more important of the two. It is that the very atmosphere in which Rawls wrote and his earlier philosophy was discussed and admired—that of a self-confident, tolerant America, generally supportive of rights, freedom, and, yes, democracy—is rapidly becoming a distant memory, replaced as it has been by a defensive, arrogant, and intolerant nascent police state that, while its government does indeed still deploy those ideals as slogans, has in many ways embarked on a process of suppressing their reality. The "nearly just" society of Rawls's youth has become so enamored of concrete "justice" as to boast 25 percent of the world's prison population while constituting less than 5 percent of its population. Its media have become increasingly monolithic and hostile to views not in accord with those of their mostly right-wing owners, as statistics concerning this ownership and the content of the almost universally cheerleader-like coverage of the "battle" against Iraq[18] (just one episode in the larger war, after all!) together attest. Its "image" in public opinion polls, for whatever little that may be worth, has become extremely negative virtually throughout the world, by contrast with a far more positive perception only a few years ago. In short, as defiant Francophones like to say, "*Ce ne sont pas les États-Unis de Papa*" (it's not Dad's United States)—not even the United States of Bush *père*, and certainly not the society envisaged by the early John Rawls.

What has happened to effect such dramatic changes is a whole series of events, of course, among which those of September 11 loom large, but at the basis of which is the rapacious global capitalism that has become almost totally dominant over the world's economies, at least since the dissolution of the Soviet Bloc, if not before.[19] Its ideology of efficiency-for-profit is singularly unaccommodating of early-Rawlsian concerns about justice, except when these create PR problems, or of democracy, which it regards as a nuisance in workplaces and as outrageous when it appears in the form of resistance to full privatization voiced by individuals and/or their governments, whether representative or nonrepresentative governments, in "less developed countries." Thus, international lending agencies routinely offer such governments the choice of either surrendering effective control over their economic policies or being refused admission to the global market. Even water resources are seen as fair game for privatization by transnational corporations. In one footnote (to a two-paragraph discussion of "The Question of Offering Incentives") in *The Law of Peoples*, Rawls blandly and congratulatorily notes that "today's IMF often attaches political conditions to loans, including conditions that do seem to require a move toward more open and liberal democratic institutions,"[20] whereas in another footnote, mentioned in *my* note 8, he makes an out-of-context disparaging reference to "global capitalism." That this colossal reality, currently determining the fates of all of the world's "peoples" in ways that are so often antidemocratic and/or unjust, receives direct attention in a couple of footnotes and virtually nowhere else in a book supposedly dealing with issues of global justice is simply astonishing.

Back in the homeland, as it is now called, "democracy," in the form of voting rituals, and capitalism tend increasingly, in a *certain* sense, to go hand-in-hand, both at the level of government, dominated as it is more than ever by wealthy special interests, and at the popular level, where the percentage of political candidates elected after spending less than their opponents is diminishing toward the vanishing point. In other words, rapacious capitalism is thoroughly trumping democracy, and any claim that the two cohere rings increasingly hollow. Thus, even though there is considerable truth to the historical observation that the rise of political liberalism and that of capitalism coincided and that this was by no means a mere accident, the time is now upon us, capitalism-plagued and democracy-starved denizens of the twenty-first century, to bid farewell to the theory of political liberalism just as our rulers are bidding farewell to its practice, and to look for new, critical intellectual tools to combat the deep evils accompanying what is vaguely known as "globalization." For that purpose, Rawlsian theory is of little or no use.

Notes

1. I am using this word in imitation of Sartre's references, in volume 2 of his *Critique of Dialectical Reason*, to Stalinism as a "*déviation*," detour, on the "road to socialism"—one from which socialism never recovered. In a similar vein, I am making no assumptions about history having a precharted course, or, consequently, about the possibility of our ever recovering.

2. Lecture given at Trinity College, October 12, 1999, as cited by Sam Gindlin, "Social Justice and Globalization: Are They Compatible?" *Monthly Review* 54 (2) (2002): 11.

3. See McBride, *From Yugoslav Praxis to Global Pathos: Anti-Hegemonic Post-Post Marxist Essays* (Lanham, MD: Rowman & Littlefield, 2001), especially chapters 11, 12, and 13.

4. One way in which the two trends, militarism and consumerism, can be blended together along with a powerful admixture of religion is illustrated by a website advertisement, sent to me two weeks into the Iraq invasion, for a cute little soldier figurine enclosed in a glass representation of the Hand of God, sold under the title "Lord Bless This Defender of Freedom."

5. Most of the text of the four preceding paragraphs is taken from a paper entitled "Globalization and Inter-Cultural Dialogue" that I presented at a conference, on the same theme as the title, at the Institute of Philosophy of the Russian Academy of Science in Moscow, in June 2002. It has been published in Russian translation: "Globalizatsiya I mezhkulturnii dialog," tr. D. Lakhuti, *Voprosy Filosofii* (Moscow, 2002), 80–87.

6. This work came to my attention through the award-winning paper on Rawls by Wonsup Jung, submitted to the American Philosophical Association in connection with the 1998 World Congress of Philosophy in Boston, to which I responded. See my

"Reply to Wonsup Jung," *Philosophical Forum* (Seoul National University) 26 (1998): 233–40, especially 235–36. I conclude this reply by suggesting that "we must, while never forgetting to thank Professor Rawls from the bottom of our hearts for his enormous contributions, begin to look toward new paradigms in this area of philosophy."

7. John Rawls, *The Law of Peoples* (Cambridge, MA: Harvard University Press, 1999), 113–14.

8. Rawls, *The Law of Peoples*, 108.

9. As far as I can tell, the word, "capitalism" appears only once in the text, in a footnote on page 39, in which Rawls cites Michael Walzer's highly disparaging reference, echoing Sidgwick, to the allegedly deracinated, wall-less world "of the political economist" and inserts, in brackets, "or of global capitalism, I might add." I shall return to this.

10. Rawls, *The Law of Peoples*, 97. A simple inquiry into President Washington's preemptive campaign to eradicate Native Americans in the territory in which I currently reside, North Central Indiana, or into Lincoln's various suspensions of civil liberties in the interest of Union victory would at least, I would like to think, have raised Rawls's discomfort level about making such assertions.

11. Rawls, *The Law of Peoples*, 105.

12. Rawls, *The Law of Peoples*, 95.

13. This is the question that John Locke thinks it appropriate to raise at the end of his *Second Treatise*, à propos of judging whether the prince or the legislative has acted contrary to his or its trust. Locke, of course, has an answer: God in Heaven is Judge.

14. Rawls, *The Law of Peoples*, 123.

15. Rawls, *The Law of Peoples*, 9.

16. On immigration, for instance, there is Phillip Cole's excellent *Philosophies of Exclusion: Liberal Political Theory and Immigration* (Edinburgh, UK: Edinburgh University Press, 2000), which treats the issue as a reef on which liberal theory appears to have shipwrecked.

17. Cole, *Philosophies of Exclusion*, 118.

18. For one confirmation of this assertion by someone with more stomach than I had to watch the coverage in question, see Michael Massing, "The Unseen War," *New York Review of Books* 9 (May 29, 2003): 16–19.

19. In a sense, this is the conclusion to which Ted Honderich is finally driven, after laying out all of his impressive moral considerations, in the final chapter of *After the Terror* (Edinburgh, UK: Edinburgh University Press, 2002). In his lengthy opening discussion of the "bad lives" of so many of the world's "peoples," to coin a phrase, he is even moved, on page 10, to evoke a word that, I find, figures ever larger in contemporary discussions of these realities: *evil*. He claims, rightly in his own case, to be making "less contentious use of [the] term than some do," but the more contentious uses are, understandably, proliferating at a rapid rate.

20. *The Law of Peoples*, 85.

8

The Global Public and Its Problems[1]

Frank Cunningham

P ROBLEMATIC ENOUGH EACH IN ITS OWN RIGHT, the intersection of globalization and democracy presents an especially daunting challenge. Globalization— that is, the causal interpenetration of major social, economic, political, cultural, and environmental phenomena on a worldwide scale and increasingly independent of nation-state control[2]—is recognized, even by those who believe that it provides exciting opportunities, as posing significant coordination problems. Addressing these problems democratically confronts the additional difficulty that democratic institutions and cultures are largely tied to nation-states.

Global democracy, then, simultaneously involves the problems of democratizing globalization and of globalizing democracy. This chapter addresses one piece of the resulting puzzle and it does so from just one perspective, namely, that which John Dewey most fully developed in his 1927 tract, *The Public and Its Problems.*[3] Following Dewey, I take it that like all democracy-related problems, this one comprises both institutional and political-cultural dimensions—and, also like Dewey, I focus on the latter, although at the end of the chapter, I endorse an unstartling institutional prescription.

Dewey recognized that constitutional rights, governmental institutions, and the vote are insufficient for a sustainable democracy without the public will and values to make democracy work. Broadly described, the traditional candidates for the required motivations are enlightened self-interest (the Hobbesist option modified to reject Hobbes's antidemocratic recommendation), nationalism or some analogous communitarian bond of citizen loyalty (Mill's view in his polemic with Lord Acton), and the civic republican option (for instance, Rousseau's) where commitment to civic virtue overrides particular interests.

Though Dewey's dense prose sometimes suggests sympathy with aspects of each of these options, the perspective I draw from his work, not caring for the purpose of the current discussion whether I've exactly captured his actual intent, departs from all three of them.

Dewey's Hegelian intellectual background counsels rejection of the neo-Hobbesist picture for taking the calculating individual as a social atom rather than as a moment within the interactions of preexisting groups. Communitarian alternatives fail to account for the fact that individuals are shaped by a multitude of overlapping and sometimes even conflicting group identifications. If the neo-Hobbesists expect too little of citizens in the way of common political values, the civic republicans ask for too much in demanding a single menu of overriding values in the face of the plurality of norms that both inform and compete with democratic political orientations. It is in reaction to these deficiencies that Dewey's notion of a "public" comes into play.

"The public," as he puts it, "consists of all those who are affected by the indirect consequences of transactions to such an extent that it is deemed necessary to have those consequences systematically cared for."[4] This characterization highlights two dimensions of publics—objective and subjective. Objectively, a public is made up of people beyond those who interact in face-to-face contact and whose interactions have ongoing and significant effects on one another. This might be called (departing from Deweyan terminology) a public *en soi* whose "publicness" admits of being so deemed by an independent observer. To be a full public—a public *pour soi*—it must also be understood as such by its members. The mark of a full public—sometimes called by Dewey a "great community" as opposed to the "great society," which constitutes its objective base—is that its members recognize a common interest in confronting problems they all face and see resolving these problems by means of collective action as a common good.[5]

Dewey's publics share characteristics with what Jean-Paul Sartre over three decades later called "groups," as opposed to "collectives."[6] In both analyzes, the sought-for political units are more than individuals who happen to have the same purposes and who engage in similar activities dictated by these purposes: Sartre's example of such a collective is people queued up to get on a bus. For a public, the consequences of ongoing interactions must be both known (Sartre: "intelligible as common actions insofar as they are common") and, in Dewey's phrase, "esteemed and sought for," again as joint projects to achieve common goals.[7]

As an engaged political philosopher, Dewey was not mainly proposing his view about publics as a social-scientific hypothesis; rather, also like Sartre with respect to "groups in fusion," he was asking about the conditions in which such publics could be encouraged as part of a democratic political project.

Neither he nor Sartre was concerned with transnational publics (though neither saw state boundaries as impermeable with respect to democratic formations either),[8] since each had local political projects in mind: Dewey to counter contemporary U.S. elitist critics of democracy (specifically in *The Public and Its Problems,* Walter Lipman) and Sartre to find a way of incorporating Marxist class analysis into socialist politics while avoiding anti-individualism. Nonetheless, I submit that the effort has both general political-theoretical significance and specific application to globalization.

From the point of view of political philosophy, a focus on publics throws into relief a precondition common to nearly all other approaches to democracy. The coexistence of acknowledged common purpose, on the one hand, and persisting conflicts within publics, on the other, provides a context for those who see rules of political interaction as products of a social contract. It solves a puzzle in this tradition about how, if people are entirely self-interested, they could enter into a contract in good faith, but if they can do this, a contract would not be necessary (if people are able to contract to contract, they need not contract at all). Dewey's focus also helps to explain the more recent incarnations of this puzzle in social choice theory of how coordination among self-interested voters is possible without appeal to brute irrationality and of how constitution building can ever get off the ground.[9] Publics in the Deweyan sense stand between fully cooperative or coordinated collectives on the one hand and warring or wholly uncoordinated individuals on the other.

Dewey is sometimes adduced as a forerunner of deliberative democracy whose advocates confront the problem that while deliberation is best conducted in local and face-to-face forums, the theory is meant to legitimize broad social policy. This problem is less intractable when it is taken into account that local deliberation is often undertaken on the part of people who see themselves as parts of broader publics that address problems cutting across local boundaries. Similarly, confrontation of persisting problems for liberal pluralism—toleration of the intolerant, setting boundaries to the public/private divide—is facilitated when these are regarded as problems encountered within frameworks of already existing publics rather than as intractable "liberal paradoxes."

Deweyan publics are different from "peoples" in the sense employed by radical-pluralist democratic theorists who analyze the ways that social agents aim to achieve political hegemony by representing themselves and their goals as embodiments of the people as such. This approach has the advantage of demystifying the category of "the people," which is most dramatically and opportunistically employed by populist demagogues. Publics are also subject to manipulation by populists when the latter propose themselves not just as representing the various particular aims of already politically engaged social agents, but also as the society's best or only hope of confronting common problems. That publics predate peoples and are thus "apolitical" on the radical pluralist view helps to explain how populists can appeal to ordinary, politically inactive or uncommitted citizens and the speed with which they fall out of favor when they fail to address the problems a public confronts.[10]

Of course, coordination is often lacking, voting sometimes has outcomes counter to majority will, constitutions do not get off the ground, local deliberation does not translate into respect-commanding policy, the pluralist paradoxes continue to plague liberal-democratic theory and practice, and populism sometimes exhibits staying power, even when it is ineffective at addressing persisting social problems. In a Deweyan view, these things are made possible partly because publics are not always or easily achieved or sustained, and a full democratic public is usually an ideal to be approximated rather than a fully attained state.[11] As a prototypical Pragmatist, Dewey's main intent was, with respect to those places where it is important for there to be self-conscious publics, to identify opportunities for and obstacles to achieving them. In the rest of my comments, I propose some hypotheses to this end regarding two global problems: threats to the world's environmental sustainability and persisting, enormous disparities in the economic resources required for sustenance and for meaningful lives, sometimes misleadingly described as the "North/South" divide.

That there already exists an objective global public there can be no doubt. The very term "globalization" connotes the interconnectedness of states of affair in any one part of the globe with those of the other parts. The examples of adverse human effects on the natural environment and global disparities in wealth are obvious cases in point. Moreover, one can see the beginnings of the formation of a global public as the consequences of environmental degradation and gross economic inequalities are being felt worldwide. Though besieged and flawed, the Kyoto Accord and UN initiatives to redress economic disparities are evidence of such awareness. The question is whether or to what extent reactions of these sorts derive from or might prefigure a public *pour soi*.

Extrapolating from Dewey's treatment, four conditions seem necessary for achieving and sustaining a full-blown public: common goals, peaceful reconciliation of conflict, self-awareness, and appropriate institutional structures.

For cosmopolitan civic republicans such as Jean Cohen, Richard Falk, and Michael Walzer, the analogue of a global public is a global civil society the members of which are bound together by certain shared values: endorsement of human rights, commitment to democracy, respect for the rule of law, an undertaking to pursue the public good, and other such civic virtues extended transnationally.[12] In my view, this condition is too strong. Even if citizens of all the countries of the European Union (the cosmopolitans' showcase example) can be said to share such civic virtues, it is evident that this cannot now be generalized to the entire world,[13] so a global civil society from this point of view would be a very demanding ideal.

On a Deweyan conception, however, publics are not places of homogenous values, but preconditions for addressing common problems among people who otherwise may have a variety of sometimes diverging values. To the extent that forging a common political culture based on civic-republican ideals is a possible or, indeed, a desirable goal,[14] publics would figure, again, as preconditions for such an undertaking rather than its outcome. A common problem conceived by the public, then, might be to forge such a culture.

At the same time, a global public must be conceived of more robustly than in terms of value-free mutual accommodation of self-interested parties. Because they face large-scale and ongoing common problems, members of a public must see themselves as part of it for the long haul and be prepared to make some individual sacrifices without certainty that these will be offset by future benefits. In the absence of any common normative values, defection or the fear of defection by others would make public commitment too fragile. One such value, a certain sort of pacifism, will shortly be taken up. In addition to this, members of a public must share some pretheoretical normative intuitions, where this means something other than commitment to a common foundational ethical theory or agreement upon the precise interpretations of the intuitions.

Regarding the example of global environmental problems, some may be inclined toward an anthrocentric others to a biocentric orientation, as these are articulated in the environmental-ethical literature, and many may be ignorant of or agnostic about these debates. But among the things that sustain public confrontation of global environmental degradation is an attitude of opprobrium toward individuals and institutions who knowingly contribute to this degradation for their own short-term gain.[15] Similarly, while members of a public may give different weights to egalitarian policies and have different views about their exact nature and limits, they must surely all share the intuition that there is something morally skewed about a world where the combined net worth of its 358 richest individuals is equal to that of 45 percent of its poorest—that is, 2.3 billion people![16]

The pacifistic condition is that members of a public rule out violence when there are conflicts among them in addressing common problems. This condition, of course, would be superfluous if there were no conflicts severe or persisting enough for violence to be a temptation. Many environmentalists have decried flaws in the Kyoto Accord, as for example in its provision for buying and selling pollution credits. The amount of wealth transfer from rich to poor regions is far below egalitarian standards, and principles for distributing what aid there is are contested. Whether or to what extent these shortcomings derive from general lack of will—hence calling into question the prospects for a gelling global public relative to problems of environmental crises and global poverty—is a crucial question. But even if the will were present, these or other flaws would likely persist in virtue of conflicts between nations and within them over priorities and methods.

One motive for a determination among otherwise conflicting members of a public to avoid violence would be moral commitment to pacifism in general. Perhaps some do sincerely endorse such an ethic, but it would be unrealistic and therefore risky to count exclusively on it as a general motivation. At the same time, it is also risky to count on calculating self-interest—I should avoid settling conflicts by force in case I lose—since those with this mind-set will be disposed to employ force when they think themselves protected or when they judge potential gains worth the risk. Rather, commitment to nonviolence among sometimes conflicting members of a public as envisioned by Dewey is motivated by factors that fall between or perhaps combine morality and self-interest.

Such a public is sparked by problems people face in common and is fully developed when they both recognize the problems as common and also understand that these must be jointly faced. Peaceful resolution of conflicts in such a context is recognized as a precondition for public confrontation of the common problems; thus, as long as a public exits, its members will see breaking ranks as destructive of it, and an ethic against doing so will be one of the things that holds the public together. Of course, some may still break ranks, but the disposition against doing this is stronger than case-by-case calculations. As with any collective action (to put this point another way), publics confront the danger of self-interested defection—that is, they are in a prisoner's dilemma. But contrary to those deployments of social choice theory that address this dilemma as equally intractable in any context, from a Deweyan perspective such problems are worthy of interest only in actual circumstances, where they will be more or less severe depending on features specific to them.

It should also be noted that because publics come into being to address discrete problems, the same body of people might form a public relative to some problems, but not others. Since these are the same individuals, the pacifistic commitment must cut across problem-relative publics. Therefore, this condition provides one basis for a generalized public. Another impetus in this direction obtains when different problems implicate one another. The cases of world poverty and environmental crises provide a good example. Degradation of environments is especially pronounced in the poorer parts of the world, thus creating a mandate for environmental justice.[17] Poverty prompts environmentally destructive activities such as deforestation out of sheer desperation.

Before turning to the next condition for a public, it is apt to flag an alternative view of the bonds that might hold a public together, namely, hostility to other publics. Russell Hardin maintains that current ethnonationalist hostilities should be seen as ways that groups solve internal problems of coordination: conflict within an ethnic or national group is muted by common hostility to other groups.[18] It would bode ill for the prospects of a global public if this were the sole basis for public bonds. However, I do not think that outgroup hostility is the only source of public coherence. Sartre's theory suggests an alternative when he addresses the role of conflict with "others" (*autres*) in his treatment of the transition from collectives to groups.

Challenging situations that confront people—"otherness" (*altérité*)—are instrumental for fusion of a collective into a group. In the collective made up of commuters waiting for a bus, each person recognizes only superficial similarities and differences of oneself and the others, for instance, as subject to the same transit schedule or as occupying a different place in the queue, and conflicts, if they exist at all, are trivial (jostling for position) and in no way defining of one's identity. By contrast, in the case of a group, people's conceptions of themselves are intimately tied up with recognition of themselves as confronting common problems.[19] Since Sartre was mainly interested in his *Critique* to explain the origins of a self-conscious working class, he did not pursue the question of whether conflicting classes can jointly form a single collective, but I see nothing in principle to prevent this. As between conflicting *autres* and challenging *altérité*, the latter is the main fusing motivation, of which persisting conflict with another group is common but not the only species. Global problems may themselves be viewed as another species of *altérité*. They are macro challenges calling for collective action to be confronted and which despite other conflicts among those challenged, spark the awareness and joint determination essential to a Sartrean group or a Deweyan public.

The third condition for a public is partially definitive of the notion of a public *en soi*. "The primary difficulty," Dewey writes, "is that of discovering the means by which a scattered, mobile and manifold public may so recognize itself as to define and express its interests."[20] A question posed by this formulation is how these means are discovered and by whom. One option is that experts educate a populace to an understanding of its publicness. This option smacks of antidemocratic social engineering and elitist paternalism. However, if it is publics themselves that engage in self-discovery, a chicken-and-egg dilemma is confronted.

The pragmatic orientation of Dewey helps to resolve this difficulty. Rather than viewing problems where the means to an end presuppose that elements of the end have already been achieved as an insurmountable dilemma, on this orientation problem solving is viewed as a self-building process where some, but not all, elements of a goal are among the means to its full realization: Pragmatists prefer "pulling one's self up by one's bootstrap" metaphors to "chicken-and-egg" ones. In the process in question, education figures prominently. The closing section of *The Public and Its Problems* is devoted to the vital role of education in the formation of publics, and in one of many essays on this topic Dewey extols the public school system for "bringing a certain integrity, cohesion, feeling of sympathy and unity among the elements of our population."[21]

Moreover, notwithstanding unfounded charges against Dewey's educational theories for being exclusively populist, he acknowledged the crucial role of experts and educators. In a project of helping to bring a public to self-recognition, the skills and knowledge of scholars, writers, and teachers (such as those, presumably, reading this book) can and should make important contributions. However, Dewey also held that professional intellectuals do not come from nowhere, but are products of their societies, and, like Karl Marx, he acknowledged as well that the educators need always themselves to be educated.[22] So the interaction between a populace and its expert intellectuals is part of the spiral in a public's quest for itself.

Although a champion of direct, participatory democracy on local levels, Dewey insisted that the scope of problems faced by a public calls for political representation that, in order to be accountable and hence democratic, requires that a public's self-recognition give it "weight in the selection of official representatives and in the definition of their responsibilities and rights."[23] The necessity for representation—the fourth condition for an ongoing public—is clear in the case of a global public due to its scale. This, of course, requires an institutional framework, the obvious candidate being a strengthened (and otherwise greatly fixed up) United Nations. This is the unstartling institutional recommendation alluded to at the beginning of this chapter.

Arguably, the formation of the UN, or at least marshaling of public support for it, required and reflected something like a global public exhibiting the characteristics described above. Addressing global poverty, as called for in the association's 2000 Millennium Declaration and coordinating world efforts to meet environmental crises (as in the "Bruntland" Report and the Kyoto Protocol), requires such a body. As to becoming more democratically responsible, the reforms recently proposed in the UN's self-study point in appropriate directions. In particular, they aim to move the organization away from its originating structure in order to avert warfare among major military powers by giving them veto power over each other and everyone else to a more inclusive association. It would also require simultaneously giving the organization more powers and, at the level of nation-states and perhaps also regions, providing for citizen participation in selecting delegates and setting agendas. Moreover, should the interaction of the organization with social movements of the sort that began in the Rio and Beijing conferences be expanded, this would open another avenue for public input.

Reforming and strengthening the UN is, of course, no small challenge. But this undertaking is made all the more difficult due to resistance on the part of its most powerful member, the United States, which under the Bush administration even went so far as to appoint to the UN an ambassador (John Bolton) who had been openly hostile to it. In my view, this situation is more than mere continued geopolitical jockeying for position, but is symptomatic of a most serious impediment to a global public.

A brief historical excursion into a recent (at least recent to me) episode in left-wing politics will be helpful both to explicate this impediment and to exemplify a complexity in any effort to foster or sustain a public. Traditional thinking about democracy and political morality on the Marxist left through the first two-thirds of the twentieth century was premised on there being two incommensurate and diametrically opposed normative political orientations: bourgeois and proletarian. As Lenin put it, "We cannot speak of 'pure democracy' as long as different classes exist; we can only speak of class democracy."[24] A similar idea is expressed in the pamphlet by Trotsky, *Their Morality and Ours*.[25] Beginning in the late 1960s the Eurocommunists (misleadingly so described because they included Communist party theorists and leaders from Japan and parts of South America as well as from Italy, France, Spain, and Great Britain) rejected this standpoint in favor of one that posited general democratic and political norms, potentially shared by them and by champions of capitalism within their respective nations.

Despite allegations by its left-wing distracters, this perspective did not reject the notion of there being structural class conflicts, but maintained that national projects to protect and extend democracy could be jointly conducted by representatives of otherwise conflicting class-based parts of a population. Such projects, they maintained, were both important for their own sakes and opened an avenue to a peaceful transition to socialism. Their complaint against the Leninists was that these aims were inhibited by disdain for democracy building as a societywide goal.[26] Put in the terms of this chapter, the Eurocommunists were looking to participate in national publics that cut across class and other lines. Due to the demise of Communism generally beginning in 1989, we shall not know how the Eurocommunist efforts would have fared, but given the relatively large bases of the European, South American, and Japanese Communist parties at the time, success in the efforts would certainly have been required for forging national and international publics around democracy-related problems.

The Eurocommunist project and the Leninist orientation it opposed exemplify two dimensions of a general inhibition to the formation of publics. In the Leninist viewpoint, society is fragmented into two hostile camps such that projects common to all members of the society are impossible. At the same time, this perspective promoted social homogenization, not just in reducing the varying identifications of working people to class identification, but even with respect to class differences themselves insofar as the working class was supposed to represent the long-term interests of all humanity. Eurocommunism resisted both sides of this orientation by seeking common democracy-building social projects and recognizing and respecting the variety of motivating identities—national, ethnic, professional, gendered, and so on—within a population. Though few, if any, of the Eurocommunist theorists could refrain from ranking the political importance of these motivations so as to put class-based ones first, they broke with the earlier habit of viewing extra-class identifications as harmful detractions from class struggle, and they were also prepared to respect those with procapitalist attitudes, including capitalists themselves, insofar as they were sincerely prepared to engage in joint democracy-enhancing projects.

The Eurocommunists thus (unwittingly) adopted Dewey's approach to the encouragement of publics, which was simultaneously to seek out and promote overarching unity while respecting differences. The two sides of a public-encouraging project are illustrated in Dewey's charge to the school system cited above, where he endorsed "the recognition that different people are going to have different ideals and beliefs but yet that in American public and national life . . . we have enough common work, common responsibilities and common interest and sympathy so that in spite of all these other distinctions we can go on working together."[27] The general point is that publics require a blend of nonhomogenizing unity and antifragmenting diversity, which, as Dewey recognized better than most, is no easy accomplishment.

I conclude this contribution by citing another example of the general point, now considering the political right. How contemporary it is depends on what political changes take place in the United States between the time these chapters are written and their actual publication. Readers who do not share the political views that will shortly become evident may take the example as an imaginary one to illustrate the general theoretical point; readers who share the views, especially if they reside in the United States, should also take it as support for a claim about the urgency of participating in public-building activities.

In his book on the prospects for a global civil society, whose government he calls a "cosmocracy," John Keane identifies as "the great if dangerous political issue of our times" whether the United States will "play the role of a catalyst of a more effective and democratic form of cosmocracy" or instead "seek world domination."[28] To my mind and with respect to the current political U.S. administration, this is, alas, not an open question. Nothing that I have seen coming from that administration and its main backers is conducive to either a global or a national public.

Now a Deweyan public comprising adherents of both egalitarian and neoliberal philosophies is possible, provided that neither camp is hypocritical in its professed commitment to solving common macro problems. However, the intimate ties the U.S. administration's highest-placed members have with private enterprises directly profiting from their policies tells against a picture of them as sincere adherents to neoliberal theoretical principles that they think, against their egalitarian critics, are best for the nation and the globe in the long run. In the language of Trotsky's pamphlet, and notwithstanding inflated democratic and Christian rhetoric, "their" morality seems to be no more than aggrandizing an already unconscionable concentration of wealth and political power in the hands of a small minority, which includes themselves. Globally, this manifests itself in the world domination project feared by Keane, part of which involves retreat from and attack against attempts to construct representative global institutions and sabotaging efforts to confront environmental threats and world poverty.

The resulting orientation on a global level is marked by homogenizing pressures toward conformity with a single world order marked by free-market capitalism and a democratic practice and culture modeled on U.S.-style electoral politics combined with fragmenting politics, especially with respect to Islamic parts of the world. The stance toward Islam and its relation to other world religions and cultures promoted by the current administration's advisors and publicists is informed by a "clash of civilizations" perspective, to use the term coined by Samuel Huntington,[29] picturing the world as divided between noble and ignoble populations described in inflammatory language. Supporters of al Qaeda and other terrorist sects are clear examples of those from Islamic societies who fuel this stance. Their rhetoric is echoed within religious fundamentalist sects in the United States, which, with citizen fear of terrorism, is played to by its current government to support reckless military actions with dubious motives. Confronting tensions in which world religions are implicated is itself a good candidate for a problem that calls for response by a global public, but formation of such a public is severely impeded to the extent that divisive, demonizing attitudes are promulgated.

The same administration pursues policies that are destructive to the achievement of the U.S. *national* public that so concerned Dewey nearly a century earlier. Nationalist rhetoric, increasingly infused with religious dimensions, paints a homogenizing picture of a "true American" at the same time that the country is sharply divided along party-political lines. Claw-backs of what public goods had earlier been secured, along with tax policies, deregulation, and selective government subsidies, work so glaringly to the exclusive benefit of the rich and the largest corporations that national projects cutting across class lines are increasingly unlikely. Add to this encouragement given to the fundamentalist religious right, and the task of forging a U.S. public—now seeing its own government as a problem collectively to be addressed—appears most challenging. Daunting as this task is, I conclude that its successful undertaking is essential if the global problems alluded to in this chapter can ever be addressed by a global public.

Notes

1. A draft of this chapter was presented at a conference on Democracy and Global Justice, Departments of Philosophy and Political Science, Washington and St. Louis Universities, April 2005. Thanks are due to participants at this conference and to Claudio Duran, Peter Fitting, and Stephen Scharper for useful comments.

2. Ulrich Beck uses the term "globality" to refer to globalization in this normatively neutral sense. Like other cosmopolitans, "globalization" is taken by him to be a positive challenge to national parochialism and constraint on regional governance. (He allows that sometimes globalization has antidemocratic and unjust consequences and reserves the term "globalism" as a pejorative description.) *What Is Globalization?* (Cambridge, UK: Polity Press, 2000), 9–10.

3. John Dewey, *The Public and Its Problems* (1927) in *John Dewey: The Later Works, 1925–1953*, vol. 2, 1925–1927, Jo Ann Boydston, ed. (Carbondale, IL: Southern Illinois Press, 1984), 235–371. [Also published by Alan Swallow, Denver, 1927.] References in square brackets throughout these endnotes are to the Swallow edition. I survey pragmatic as well as other approaches to globalization and democracy in *Democratic Theory: A Critical Introduction* (London: Routledge, 2002), chap. 9

4. Dewey, *Public,* 245–46 [15–16].

5. Dewey, *Public,* essay 5.

6. Jean-Paul Sartre, *Critique de la raison dialectique* (Paris: Éditions Gallimard, 1960), livre ID, livre IIA.

7. Sartre, *Critique de la raison dialectique,* 566–74, 598–650; Dewey, *Public,* 330 [151–52].

8. Although Dewey's main focus was on his native United States, he was more cosmopolitan than most of his contemporary political philosophers, both practically in his international advisory capacities, as in China and Turkey, and in his stance toward nationalism. While seeing a strong U.S. national identity as important to counteract parochialism, he was by no means a nationalist in a narrow sense, as is evidenced in the conclusion of an essay on "The Fruits of Nationalism" written in 1927: "Patriotism, National Honor, National Interests, and National Sovereignty are the four foundation stones upon which the structure of the National State is erected. It is no wonder that

the windows of such a building are closed to the light of heaven; that its inmates are fear, jealousy, suspicion, and that War issues regularly from its portals." In *John Dewey: The Later Works, 1925–1953*, vol. 3, 1927–1953, Jo Ann Boydston, ed. (Carbondale, IL: Southern Illinois Press, 1984), 152–57, at 157.

9. Gerald Strom notes the fact, for him puzzling, that the outcomes of legislative votes more closely approximate majority will than social choice theory predicts, *The Logic of Law Making* (Baltimore, MD: Johns Hopkins University Press, 1990), 73–75. Dennis Mueller addresses the problem of how constitution building is possible from within this perspective in his *Public Choice* (Cambridge, MA: Cambridge University Press, 1979), 268.

10. The application of radical-pluralist theory to the construction of "peoplehood" is developed by Ernesto Laclau in *On Populist Reason* (London: Verso, 2005), see 161–64 and *passim*. It should be noted that the notion of a public in Dewey's sense is also different from that of the "multitude" as this term is employed by Michael Hardt and Antonio Negri in their *Empire* (Cambridge, MA: Harvard University Press, 2000). For them, the multitude is "the set of all the exploited and the subjugated" (393) by a global capitalist empire, and as "the productive force" in that empire, this multitude has the potential to become "an absolute democratic power" against it (344). This category is meant by Hardt and Negri to replace the working class as understood in Marxist theory as a primary social agent of revolutionary social change. Publics, by contrast, cut across class lines and are not, except in a metaphorical sense, social agents. Whether or when the confrontation of problems partially constitutive of a public require or spark revolutionary change for their solutions is an open question.

11. Dewey, *Public*, 328–29 [148–49].

12. For example, Richard Falk, "Global Civil Society and the Democratic Project," in Barry Holden, ed., *Global Democracy: Key Debates* (London: Routledge, 2000), 162–78 at 171–74; also Martin Köhler, "From the National to the Cosmopolitan Public Sphere," in Daniele Archbugi, et al., eds., *Reimagining Political Community: Studies in Cosmopolitan Democracy* (Stanford, CA: Stanford University Press, 1998), 231–32, at 232.

John Keane classifies Dewey as a civic republican and nationalist in an essay critical of these perspectives, "Nations, Nationalism, and the European State," in a 1993 Centre for the Study of Democracy publication available at www.johnkeane.net/essays. Dewey's view quoted in note 8 above is one of several expressions of a critical stance toward nationalism. As to civic republicanism, Dewey certainly did encourage the nurturing of civic virtues, but he did not promote these as part of an overriding ethical system, the realism of which, especially on an international level, he doubted: see "Ethics and International Relations," (1923) *John Dewey: The Middle Works, 1889–1924*, vol. 15, 1923–1924, Jo Ann Boydston, ed. (Carbondale, IL: Southern Illinois Press, 1983), 53–64. As to civic republicanism, Dewey was more concerned that common civic values complement, preserve, and interact with those reflected in social differences than that they override them. This theme is addressed later in this chapter.

13. Shortly after the terrorist attack on the World Trade Center on September 11, 2001, Richard Falk gave a talk at my university where he discarded his previously prepared paper and, visibly shaken, reflected instead on this dramatic challenge to any claim that the world is moving toward a global civil society.

It is apt to note that the cornerstone of the cosmopolitan approach, the notion of a civil society itself, is far from clear. Contrast the characterizations by Michael Walzer and Jean Cohen in the collection edited by Walzer, *Toward a Global Civil Society* (Oxford: Berghahn Books, 1995): Walzer, "the space of uncoerced human associations and also the set of relational networks—formed for the sake of family, faith, interest and ideology—that fill that space," "The Concept of Civil Society," 7–27, at 7; Jean Cohen, "a sphere of social interactions distinct from economy and state, composed above all of associations (including the family) and publics," "Interpreting the Notion of Civil Society," 35–40, at 37. Walzer's characterization is much broader than Cohen's, most importantly not excluding economic "associations," and Cohen's definition is recursive or at least opaque on the crucial point by its addition of "publics" to the list. Like Walzer, Richard Falk includes the notion of civil society being voluntary ("the field of action and thought occupied by individual and collective citizen initiatives of a voluntary, nonprofit character"), but it is geared to social movement associations ("these initiatives proceed from a global orientation and are responses in part at least to certain globalizing tendencies that are perceived to be partially or totally adverse") in Holden, ed., *op. cit.* in note 12, 163.

14. For a criticism of the desirability of the global civil-societal project, see Danilo Zolo's contribution to the Holden collection, "The Lords of Peace," 73–86.

15. Dewey himself likely endorsed an environmental ethic compatible with his view about public problems that was independent of the foundational disputes and that recognized value pluralism in this domain, or at least this is the view of "environmental pragmatists" such as Andrew Light and Eric Katz. See their collection, *Environmental Pragmatism* (London: Routledge, 1996), which includes a pertinent essay by Larry Hickman on Dewey, "Nature as Culture: John Dewey's Pragmatic Naturalism," 50–72.

16. David Coburn, "Globalization, Neoliberalism, and Health," in Richard Sandbrook, ed., *Civilizing Globalization: A Survival Guide* (Albany: SUNY Press, 2003), 27–38, at 31. Although I have not attempted to update statistics on the disparity Coburn reports, I would be surprised to learn that it is anything but wider today.

17. Peter Wenz's *Environmental Justice* (Albany: SUNY Press, 1988) makes the case for the direct implication of environmental degradation in global injustices.

18. Russell Hardin, *One for All: The Logic of Group Conflict* (Princeton, NJ: Princeton University Press, 1995). I criticize Hardin's approach in an extended review, *Canadian Journal of Philosophy* 27/4 (December 1997): 571–94.

19. Sartre, *Critique*, livre I, D, see pages 410–11. It happens that I experienced something approaching the small-scale transformation of a collection of commuters into a group (though on a subway, rather than waiting for a bus) when, returning from work one afternoon with a host of other anonymous commuters in New York City, there was a city power shortage that trapped us underground. As it appeared the blackout was going to be of indefinite duration and that action on the part of passengers was required, I saw the collective beginning to fuse in the direction of a group in Sartre's sense.

20. Dewey, *Public*, 327 [146].

21. "The School as a Means of Developing a Social Consciousness and Social Ideals in Children" (1923), in *John Dewey: The Middle Works, 1889–1924,* vol. 15, 1923–1924, Jo Ann Boydston, ed. (Carbondale, IL: Southern Illinois Press, 1983), 150–57, at 151.

22. The reference is to Marx's 3rd Thesis on Feuerbach (1845), in *Karl Marx and Frederick Engels Collected Works* (New York: International Publishers, 1974), vol. 5, 3–5.

23. Dewey, *Public,* 283 [77].

24. V. I. Lenin, *The Proletarian Revolution and the Renegade Kautsky* (1918), in *V. I. Lenin Collected Works* (Moscow: Progress Publishers, 1963–1980), vol. 28, 226–325, at 242.

25. Leon Trotsky, *Their Morality and Ours* (1938) (New York: Pathfinder Press, 1973).

26. Joint statements made at meetings of European and Japanese Communist Party leaders in the mid-1970s outline the general principles of Eurocommunism. They are collected in *Recherches Internationnales,* nos. 88–89 (1976).

27. Dewey, "The School as a Means of Developing a Social Consciousness and Social Ideals in Children," in Boydston, ed., 1983, at 154.

28. John Keane, *A Global Civil Society?* (Cambridge, UK: Cambridge University Press, 2003), 121.

29. Samuel Huntington, *The Clash of Civilizations and the Remaking of the World Order* (New York: Simon and Shuster, 1977).

Index

Contributors

Deen K. Chatterjee teaches philosophy at the University of Utah and is the editor-in-chief of the forthcoming multivolume *Encyclopedia of Global Justice* and the series editor of *Studies in Global Justice*. His publications include, most recently, *The Ethics of Assistance: Morality and the Distant Needy* (2004).

David A. Crocker is senior research scholar at the Institute for Philosophy and Public Policy and the Maryland School of Public Policy at the University of Maryland. He held the UNESCO chair in the philosophy department at the University of Valencia, Spain, and has been a visiting professor at the University of Munich and twice a Fulbright Scholar at the University of Costa Rica. Among his publications are *Praxis and Democratic Socialism* (1983); editor (with Toby Linden) *Ethics of Consumption: The Good Life, Justice, and Global Stewardship* (1998); *Florecimiento humano y desarrollo internacional: La nueva ética de capacidades humanas* (1998); editor (with Jesus Conill) *Republicanismo y educación cívica: Más allá del liberalismo?* (2003). His new book, *Ethics of Global Development: Agency, Capability, and Deliberative Democracy*, will be published by Cambridge University Press.

Frank Cunningham is professor of philosophy and political science at the University of Toronto, where he teaches social and political philosophy. He is a former chair of the philosophy department and principal of Innis College at the University of Toronto, a fellow of the Royal Society of Canada, and has served as the president of the Canadian Philosophical Association. His most recent book is *Theories of Democracy: A Critical Introduction* (2002).

Carol C. Gould is professor of philosophy and political science at Temple University, editor of the *Journal of Social Philosophy*, executive director of the Society for Philosophy and Public Affairs, and vice president/president elect of the American section of the International Society for Philosophy of Law and Social Philosophy. She is the author of *Marx's Social Ontology* (1978), *Rethinking Democracy* (1988), and *Globalizing Democracy and Human Rights* (2004), editor of seven books including *Women and Philosophy*, *Beyond Domination*, *The Information Web*, *Cultural Identity and the Nation-State*, and *Gender*, and has published over fifty articles in social and political philosophy, feminist theory, and applied ethics.

William L. McBride is Arthur G. Hansen Distinguished Professor of Philosophy at Purdue University, immediate past president of the North American Society for Social Philosophy, and secretary general of the International Federation of Philosophical Societies. His publications include books on social and political philosophy in general, Marx, Sartre, Eastern Europe, and former Yugoslavia.

James W. Nickel is professor of law at the Sandra Day O'Connor College of Law, Arizona State University, where he teaches and writes in jurisprudence, constitutional law, political philosophy, and human rights law and theory. His book, *Making Sense of Human Rights* (2d ed.), was published by Blackwell in 2006.

Martha C. Nussbaum is Ernst Freund Distinguished Service Professor of Law and Ethics at the University of Chicago, appointed in the philosophy department, law school, and divinity school. She is an associate member of the departments of classics and political science, a member of the Committee on Southern Asian Studies, and a board member of the Human Rights Program. Her most recent books are *Frontiers of Justice* (2006) and *The Clash Within: Democracy, Religious Violence, and India's Future* (2007).

Andrew Oldenquist is professor emeritus of philosophy at The Ohio State University. He taught and wrote about ethical theory (e.g., "Loyalties," *Journal of Philosophy*, 1982) and Wittgenstein and more recently on social and political philosophy, beginning with *The Non-Suicidal Society* (1986). He taught these subjects, especially questions of nationalism and ethnicity, at Moscow State University and Leipzig University, and most recently has begun writing about the evolution of human nature and its relations to morals.

David Reidy is an associate professor of philosophy at the University of Tennessee. A lawyer as well as a philosopher by training, he has published widely on the work of John Rawls as well as the philosophy of law. His most recent book is *On the Philosophy of Law* (2006).

Kok-Chor Tan is associate professor of philosophy at the University of Pennsylvania. He is the author of *Toleration, Diversity, and Global Justice* (2000) and *Justice without Borders* (2004), in addition to articles on political philosophy and global justice. He is currently working on a book dealing with global justice under nonideal conditions.